FOUNDATIONS OF COMMUNITY JOURNALISM

FOUNDATIONS OF COMMUNITY JOURNALISM

EDITED BY

BILL READER
Ohio University

JOHN A. HATCHER
University of Minnesota Duluth

Los Angeles | London | New Delhi
Singapore | Washington DC

Los Angeles | London | New Delhi
Singapore | Washington DC

FOR INFORMATION:

SAGE Publications, Inc.
2455 Teller Road
Thousand Oaks, California 91320
E-mail: order@sagepub.com

SAGE Publications Ltd.
1 Oliver's Yard
55 City Road
London, EC1Y 1SP
United Kingdom

SAGE Publications India Pvt. Ltd.
B 1/I 1 Mohan Cooperative Industrial Area
Mathura Road, New Delhi 110 044
India

SAGE Publications Asia-Pacific Pte. Ltd.
33 Pekin Street #02-01
Far East Square
Singapore 048763

Acquisitions Editor: Matthew Byrnie
Editorial Assistant: Nathan Davidson
Production Editor: Karen Wiley
Copy Editor: Rachel Keith
Typesetter: Hurix
Proofreader: Jennifer Gritt
Indexer: Molly Hall
Cover Designer: Jennifer Crisp
Marketing Manager: Liz Thornton
Permissions Editor: Adele Hutchison

Printed in the United States of America

Library of Congress Cataloging-in-Publication Data

Foundations of community journalism/edited by Bill Reader, John A. Hatcher.

  p. cm.
Includes bibliographical references and index.

ISBN 978-1-4129-7466-0(pbk.)

1. Community newspapers. 2. Journalism, Regional. 3. Local mass media. I. Reader, Bill, 1970- II. Hatcher, John A.

PN4784.C73F78
2012 070.5'722—dc23

            2011022425

This book is printed on acid-free paper.

11 12 13 14 15 10 9 8 7 6 5 4 3 2 1

Contents

Foreword

Jock Lauterer

When I asked Jerry Brown to write the introduction to the third edition of *Community Journalism: Relentlessly Local* back in 2005, the then Montana J-school dean responded by describing how his Alabama hometown newspaper had endeared itself to many outhouse readers for its utilitarian use as an end product, so to speak.

Hardly the vaunted endorsement of community newspapers that I had imagined. But then the wily Dean Brown had his reasons: in his own vernacular way he was telling us that community journalism, with all its many variants, survives because of its universal, earthy, boots-on-the-ground connection to its reader/viewer/user.

My own interest in this particular branch of journalism stems from my college days at the University of North Carolina and the tutelage of professor Ken Byerly, whose 1961 textbook gave a formal name to this particular subfield of the profession: *Community Journalism*. Byerly suggested that the practice was akin to a "friendly neighbor" approach to journalism, which is not always a good thing. I make this clear in my own book:

> At best, our thresholds for accuracy and responsible reporting are greater because we are a part of the community we cover, not outside it. But there is a danger here as well. Does this community connection make us too timid to do the difficult stories? Too familiar to recognize the emerging trend? This is the real front line of community journalism: sorting out the degree, for example, to which we function as community boosters, or community watchdogs.[1]

---

[1] From page 7 in Lauterer, J. (2003). *Community journalism: The personal approach* (2nd ed.). Ames: Iowa State University Press.

Lately I have begun to think of community journalism under a slightly different concept—that of "roots journalism." Like roots music, roots journalism reflects the indigenous culture through storytelling. When the great bassist Christian McBride was asked what guided his music, he replied that he tried to keep his repertoire "rooted in the groove." It is that commitment to "rootedness" that has been community journalism's credo from the start, and which has propelled community newspapers and many other community journalism efforts through "the Great Recession" and beyond.

Likewise community journalism research.

I am able to commend to the reader this inaugural volume on community journalism research because Bill Reader, John Hatcher, and I go way back—and I can testify unequivocally that their "street cred" as in-the-trenches community journalists *and* academics also is rooted in the groove. That's a rare pedigree.

I first met Bill Reader at Penn State in the fall of 1991 when I was a freshman professor and Bill a senior journalism major and the new editor of a revived J-school lab newspaper (to which I'd be assigned as the faculty adviser). Not only did we put out some fine lab newspapers, but also Bill, while he was still only an undergrad, helped me realize the need for an updated textbook and handbook on community journalism (as Byerly's book was by then several decades old). Hence the first edition of my book, *Community Journalism*, published in 1995. Upon graduation from Penn State, Bill worked at various Pennsylvania community newspapers before returning to Penn State to earn his master's degree and then eventually moving on to teach at Ohio University, where he has distinguished himself as an inspiring teacher and relentless researcher.

John Hatcher, now at the University of Minnesota Duluth, burst upon my radar in the mid-1990s when he was performing innovative work in outreach education at SUNY Oswego's Center for Community Journalism. I suspect that CCJ's founders were, like me, inspired by the groundbreaking work done at the Huck Boyd National Center for Community Media at Kansas State, which for years had been the sole place community journalism research was gathered and shared. When it came my chance in 2001 to launch the Carolina Community Media Project at the University of North Carolina at Chapel Hill, I took my cue from Kansas State's Huck Boyd Center and Hatcher's work for the CCJ, building on their successes and learning from the speed bumps they had encountered along the journey.

In spite of such successful state-focused programs, I grew increasingly aware that community journalism research was going unrecognized and unvalidated on the national level. When in 2004 we launched the Community Journalism Interest Group at the Association for Education in Journalism and Mass Communication (AEJMC), not surprisingly, Reader and Hatcher were right there helping to lead the charge. That recognition—that community journalism research is valid and vital—brought a whole community of scholars in out of the academic cold. And I would argue that the research showcased by the Community Journalism Interest Group since then has been as profoundly rigorous, far-reaching, and significant as any. I credit that largely to Reader, the first research chair of the group, and Hatcher, who has contributed considerably to that research mission, including serving as research chair for the group in 2011. Several of the contributors to this book also were instrumental in building the research arm of the Community Journalism Interest Group.

While I am gratified that my book, *Community Journalism: Relentlessly Local*, has become "a classic" for how-to classes, as some have referred to it, my best effort—like that of Byerly before me in 1961—has its limitations. When serious students of community journalism finish my book, they invariably ask, "Now what?" And I have had nowhere to send them.

No longer. In this comprehensive and thorough text, we finally have a foundational road map for serious research in community journalism.

Here is the "nut graf" from Reader and Hatcher's preface:

A great deal of effort has been spent trying to define what is and what isn't community journalism, and, while definitions are important, they can also distract from the real power of this book—to help explain how a long tradition of research involving communities and journalism has constructed a rich foundation on which to build future study of community journalism.

Credit Reader and Hatcher for recruiting a blue ribbon community of scholars, whose chapters and essays in *Foundations of Community*

Journalism help take this discipline to the next level. It is my firm conviction that, in your hands, you hold a new classic.

Jock Lauterer *is director of the Carolina Community Media Project and a faculty member at the School of Journalism and Mass Communication at the University of North Carolina at Chapel Hill.*

Preface

For this book project, we thought about trying to find a firm, simple definition for *community journalism*, and in the end decided that doing so essentially misses the point. A great deal of effort has been spent trying to define what is and what isn't community journalism, and, while definitions are important, they can also distract from the real power of this book—to help explain how a long tradition of research involving communities and journalism has constructed a rich foundation on which to build future study of community journalism. Community journalism does have as its key components the work of journalism within the context of "community," and broadly defined it is journalism at the community level. Beyond that, attempting to define the term is akin to putting the cart before the horse—the concept should be more intricately defined by the research, and not vice versa.

Still, the concept of community journalism does have a well-established foundation, and outlining that foundation is the primary purpose of this book. From the start, our goal was to pull together into one volume a body of knowledge that would take months, perhaps years, of independent effort by individual graduate students and researchers. We can't count the number of times over the past three years that we've mentioned this book project to colleagues and have been asked, "How soon will it be ready? I have a graduate student who . . ." The typical lament is that it's difficult to find published research related to community journalism. In compiling this book, we realized that although such research may be difficult to find, it is by no means scarce. The concept has been studied, directly or indirectly, for decades; it just hasn't been categorized as such in the research databases.

This book is intended for graduate courses and advanced undergraduate courses in the journalism and mass communication discipline. It could be a primary text for courses devoted to the study of community journalism or a supplemental text for broader media-research courses. We hope it will find a spot on the bookshelves of those who teach journalism research courses as well as those who conduct journalism research themselves. The book is organized loosely along the lines of a typical research project: it starts by explicating the term and reviewing available literature, then outlines methodological considerations, and concludes with some suggestions for future research. Along the way, short essays from well-respected scholars provide additional insights and encouragements.

Beyond helping researchers quickly get up to speed on the concept of community journalism, another goal of this book is to reframe the concept for a new century. Although clearly derived from the 20th-century study of small-town newspapers, community journalism today must of course be viewed in much broader terms, as it cuts across media forms and serves all manner of communities. Whether a community is based on geographic ties, shared ethnicity, professional or ideological interests, or a common cause, most communities have at least some rudimentary journalistic effort (a newsletter, a blog, or a low-power radio broadcast, for example). The small-town newspaper may be the archetype of community journalism, but it is hardly the standard.

More importantly, those who study community journalism begin with an appreciation that journalism is not solely the purview of major national and international media outlets. In fact, the vast majority of journalism is done at the community level. For every big-city newspaper, for example, consider how many smaller journalistic enterprises operate in the ethnic enclaves, distinct suburbs, and cultural niches of that same city. Community journalism is thus very much like the bottom of an iceberg: it forms the greatest bulk of journalism produced in the world, but it goes largely unnoticed by the masses compared to the ubiquitous big-media names readily recognized in society at large (*The New York Times*, the BBC, *National Geographic*, Salon.com, etc.). Community media also are often overlooked by journalism scholars who may not initially see the value of in-depth study in this realm. Certainly, many scholars conduct studies on the news media nearby, and college-town newspapers may very well be the largest class of community media studied by graduate students and tenure-track professors. But too often, the local media are studied simply as exemplars of their bigger, more respected kin. The assumption is that community journalism is just journalism at a smaller scale.

The contributors to this book all suggest, in their own ways, that the distinction between community journalism and journalism itself is much more profound than matters of size, scale, and reach. Community journalism is integral to all aspects of community culture: history, economics, community identity, community values, policy debates and public opinion, and so on. Certainly, size and reach will profoundly affect how the *International Herald Tribune* operates compared to the weekly *Carthaginian* of Carthage, Mississippi. But community journalism encompasses more than just process and audience—it is concerned with the social fabric of community. The *International Herald Tribune* has an audience, but no discernible community; the *Carthaginian*'s audience is its community, including some local residents who don't subscribe to or even read the newspaper.

This book is a collection of some things borrowed and some things new. It's a marriage between renewed interest in the study of community journalism and a tradition of scholarly inquiry that has for decades looked at the role of news media in community life. From Alexis de Tocqueville's observations about community newspapers in *Democracy in America* (published in 1835), to a variety of popular memoirs by some notable "country editors" in the early and mid 20th century, to the sophisticated study of community-media relationships from the 1970s through today, there is no question that the concept of community journalism is built on a foundation of important earlier works. Moreover, scholarly interest in community journalism is being recognized as a formal subdiscipline, represented by numerous professional organizations as well as several scholarly organizations (see Appendix for a listing of those groups).

Above all, however, this book is meant not just to look back at what has already been learned about community journalism, but to prepare the next generation of scholars for a media environment in which community journalism no longer operates in the shadow of "big J" journalism. Established community media keep chugging along, and new community-focused journalism projects are cropping up all the time. Perhaps it's time that the largest portion of the journalism industry becomes the dominant focus of journalism scholarship as well.

Acknowledgments

This book project began a long time ago, and it was inspired mostly by those who were actively involved in developing the research mission of the Community Journalism Interest Group (COMJIG) of the Association for Education in Journalism and Mass Communication. We especially want to thank COMJIG founders Jock Lauterer (University of North Carolina at Chapel Hill) and Peggy Kuhr (University of Montana), whose leadership has drawn together a strong community of scholars.

The scholars who contributed chapters to this book also have our deepest gratitude. They graciously accepted feedback, patiently tolerated long delays, dutifully turned around revisions, and remained supportive of the project from the beginning. In order of appearance, they are Jack Rosenberry (St. John Fisher College), Eileen Gilligan (State University of New York at Oswego), Janice Hume (University of Georgia), Wilson Lowrey (University of Alabama), Diana Knott Martinelli (West Virginia University), George Daniels (University of Alabama), and, from Ohio University, Cary Roberts Frith and Hans Meyer.

We are also deeply grateful to the accomplished scholars who provided the short essays that add insights to this book. These scholars come from across the globe and broaden our view of the community-journalism relationship: Linda Steiner (University of Maryland), Gloria Freeland (Kansas State University), G. Michael Killenberg (University of South Florida), Sigurd Høst (Volda University College, Norway), Crispin C. Maslog (Asian Institute of Journalism and Communication, the Philippines), Lewis Friedland (University of Wisconsin–Madison), Stephen Lacy (Michigan State University), Guy Berger (Rhodes University, South Africa), Nicholas W. Jankowski (Virtual Knowledge Studio for the Humanities and Social Sciences, the

Netherlands), Carolyn Kitch (Temple University), and Chad Stebbins (Missouri Southern State University).

Two of those named above, Kuhr and Rosenberry, pulled extra duty as reviewers for various chapters of this book. Other reviewers included Douglas Fisher (University of South Carolina), Clyde H. Bentley (University of Missouri), Ken Smith (University of Wyoming), Tommy Thomason (Texas Christian University), Victor Pickard (New York University), Ralph E. Hanson (University of Nebraska Kearney), Thomas C. Terry (Idaho State University, Pocatello) and Janice Marie Collins (Eastern Illinois University). Their feedback was thoughtful and thorough, and this book is a much better work thanks to their important contribution. John Hatcher would also like to thank all the students of the fall 2010 class Community and Journalism, who were the brave test pilots of an early draft of this book and offered many useful ideas for revision and improvement.

Bill Reader wants to thank his colleagues at the E. W. Scripps School of Journalism who were especially supportive of this book, most notably distinguished professor emeritus Guido Stempel, III, associate professor Mary Rogus, and professor Eddith Dashiell; also, he is most grateful to his former colleague at Ohio, Daniel Riffe, who is now Richard Cole Eminent Professor at the University of North Carolina at Chapel Hill. He also thanks his "Kentucky colleagues," Elizabeth Hansen at Eastern Kentucky University and Al Cross at the Institute for Rural Journalism and Community Issues at the University of Kentucky, for years of lively conversation and excellent mentorship. And of course Reader is indebted to his former publisher, Lou Heldman; his former executive editor, John Winn Miller; and his former managing editor, Becky Bennett, who together at the *Centre Daily Times* showed how community journalism can reach its highest potential (I suppose we should all acknowledge former U.S. Representative Bud Shuster for giving us so much juicy corruption to write about in our "little paper.").

John Hatcher wants to thank his colleagues at the University of Minnesota Duluth for their encouragement and support of his research, including former dean of the College of Liberal Arts, Linda Krug; Writing Studies department chair Jill Jenson; and all his colleagues in the Department of Writing Studies. He also thanks his former editor at the *Daily Messenger*, Robert Matson, who inspired his passion in community journalism, and Mary Glick, founder of the

Center for Community Journalism at SUNY Oswego, whose vision launched his career as a teacher and scholar of community journalism. He thanks his wife, Michele Hatcher, who supports and endures him in too many ways to mention.

We want to thank those who provided us with the intellectual support to tackle such a project. From SAGE, of course, we are grateful to the original acquisitions editor we worked with, Todd Armstrong; to editorial assistant Nathan Davidson, who kept this project on the tracks and pushed it to completion; and to Rachel Keith, for her very good copyediting.

Finally, we thank the countless community journalists we have met over the years, who have left us humbled by their passion for quality journalism and tireless dedication to their communities.

—Bill Reader and John A. Hatcher

PART I

Background and Explication

1

Community Journalism

A Concept of Connectedness

Bill Reader

The concept of *community journalism* long has been regarded as a specific practice of gathering, packaging, and distributing news in predominantly small, distinct geographic markets, with an emphasis on local news and information about community life. For many decades in the 20th century, "community journalism" was used as a synonym for "small-town newspapers." Yet in the first decade of the 21st century, renewed interest in the cultural roles of journalism in community life has broadened the concept to something that reaches well beyond newspapers in small towns and includes various media in many different types of communities—special-interest magazines, online-only newsletters for professional communities, local independent radio, "hyperlocal" websites, and so on. Some of that interest has been assumed to represent a *stunde null* in the study of community journalism, with some scholars suggesting that the concept of community journalism is new and emerging. In fact, contemplation of community journalism as a distinct concept can be traced back to at least the middle of the 20th century, and perhaps even to the formative days of journalism studies decades before that. Those early works were mostly essays or textbooks focused on professional practice; that is, most were primarily how-to texts rather than "why" texts, and most were written for students and professionals, not scholars looking to research the topic under any kind of theoretical framework. There are a few exceptions, of course. For example, Anderson, Dardenne, and Killenberg suggested in the mid 1990s that "news organizations, especially local newspapers, should occupy a prominent place in a community's life and conversation. Viewing community as a place of inquiry asks journalists to consider what messages and dialogues are necessary to increase the perception of commonalities" (1994, p. 101). Those attempts at theory building have been instrumental in the maturation of community journalism as a distinct subdiscipline, and that focus has in turn attracted a small but dedicated collective of scholars and inspired several university-based initiatives.

The goal of this chapter is to analyze the original texts that focused specifically on *community journalism* as a distinct term. Later chapters will focus on the scholarly research that followed the development of the concept.

❖ ORIGINS

The term *community journalism* appears to have been coined in the 1950s by the late Kenneth R. Byerly, a newspaper publisher turned professor at the University of North Carolina at Chapel Hill. After joining the UNC faculty in 1957, Byerly was assigned to teach a course called "Country Weekly Newspaper Production," but it seems he didn't care for the course title. In a personal letter to Jock Lauterer (one of Byerly's students in the 1960s, and now a leading scholar in the community journalism discipline), Byerly said his dispute with the course title was that not all community newspapers were in the countryside, and not all of them were weeklies (Lauterer, 2006, p. xviii). The course was renamed "Community Journalism." Byerly then used the term as the title of his 1961 textbook, a collection of observations and essays by him and scores of other community journalists. That book's utility today is mostly as a historic document, as it is dated and was devoted exclusively to newspapers in the U.S. Yet there is much in Byerly's book that transcends time, geography, and media forms.

Community Journalism was a comprehensive, mid-20th-century guide to newspaper publishing in small towns, suburbs, and distinct neighborhoods in large cities. It addressed practical matters: approaches to covering various types of local news (accidents, schools, obituaries, etc.), editing opinion pages (editorials, letters from the community, public service work), and managing the business aspects of a for-profit newspaper (public relations, advertising and circulation management, financial management, even strategies for starting or purchasing a newspaper). It was also a 400-page articulation of the distinctions between community journalism and marquee news media of the time—specifically, the large-circulation daily newspapers in major cities that were considered the paragons of the news industry. Those differences were most often framed in terms of the relationships between journalists and members of their audiences. In his preface, Byerly explained the concept of community journalism as such:

> Community newspapers today are burgeoning in big city and suburban areas and have new strength in small cities and towns. They offer much in employment, satisfaction, income, service, and ownership. A reason for the success of these . . . newspapers is their "friendly neighbor" relationship with readers. This affinity also creates problems for community newspapers which differ from those of the metropolitan press. (1961, p. v)

Byerly's proposal that community journalism differs from metropolitan journalism was further explained throughout the book, but one passage provides a poignant summary: "Community newspapers have something that city dailies lack—a nearness to people. This is a great strength, and a great problem" (1961, p. 25). For all of us community journalism scholars, that notion of "a nearness to people" provides a common theoretical anchor.

From a research perspective, the study of community journalism is largely the study of the relationship dynamics between journalists and the communities they serve: it is concerned with the degree and implications of "connectivity" between journalism and communities. That connectivity has been tested in some research, such as one study that found that audiences have more regard for their local newspapers than for newspapers in general (Lavrakas & Holley, 1989) and another demonstrating that editors of some small newspapers viewed ethics more in terms of responsibility to their communities than did some editors of large newspapers, who tended to view ethics more in terms of the professional reputation of the newspaper itself (Reader, 2006). That "nearness to people" can, Byerly argued, increase the community's accessibility to the journalists (often described in terms of "bumping into them on the street"), which in turn can increase journalists' sense of accountability for their behaviors within a community. It also can cause the journalist to be much less forthcoming with information that could be embarrassing or harmful to individual community members or to the community as a whole (a concept explored in some detail in the oft-cited University of Minnesota studies of Tichenor, Donohue, & Olien, 1980). As an example of that community-focused restraint, Byerly included in his book this explanation from the editor of a small Wisconsin weekly:

> No weekly newspaper can live in close harmony with its readers and properly serve its community if it hears all and tells all. A daily reporter can record and report all of the personal exchanges in a council meeting, for example. The weekly reporter should use his own good judgment when mere personal conflicts arise—and he should print only that which is constructive.
>
> This is not being dishonest with readers. It does not mean that the paper must cover up anything. It simply means that the whole truth should be the constructive truth—not petty palaver. (1961, p. 26)

Another example of the idea of "good judgment" appears in Byerly's chapter on covering "Courts and Crime," in which he addressed the pros and cons of publishing the name of a drunken driver who asked that his name not be printed (1961, pp. 83–87). On the one hand, Byerly argued, printing the names of offenders adds to the legal punishment in the form of public embarrassment, which could be harmful to the individual and (more importantly) his innocent family members. But Byerly also found that many editors argued in favor of publishing such names, and for various reasons: to deter crime, to ensure the accused gets a fair trial in the public eye, to alert the public to the misdeeds of their neighbors, to set the record straight rather than to allow the rumor mill to spread the news, and to demonstrate that the newspaper will not play favorites just because an offender makes a personal plea to "keep it out of the paper." It is that kind of routine, interpersonal dilemma, Byerly suggested, that journalists in large media outlets rarely must (or are willing to) consider. He argued that journalists working for larger media might, for example, simply fall back on legal arguments (the public's *right to know*, rather than the community's *need to know*), but smaller, local media also had to weigh the best interests of the community against the best interests of the individual members of that community. The broader standards of detached journalism could not simply be applied as a matter of course in such a close-knit situation.

❖ THINKING BEYOND "COUNTRY EDITORS"

Byerly may have coined the term *community journalism*, but the idea that journalism at the community level is different from regional/ national/global journalism was hardly a new idea in the mid 20th century. The importance of local, community-focused media was celebrated by democracy's early champions, not least among them Alexis de Tocqueville, who wrote in his *Democracy in America*:

> A newspaper is an adviser one need not seek out because it appears voluntarily every day to comment briefly upon community business without deflecting your attention from your own. . . . So as men become more equal and individualism more of a menace, newspapers are more necessary. The belief that they just guarantee freedom would diminish their importance; they sustain civilization. (1835/2004, pp. 600–601)

Well into the middle of the 20th century, the work of the community press was similarly heralded as the backbone of democracy, as celebrated in occasional profiles of the "country editors" working in idyllic small towns. Those often romanticized accounts appeared in national magazines such as *The Saturday Evening Post* (Byers, 1937; "The Country Newspaper," 1946) and *The Nation* (Conason, 1975). That romanticism also was captured in the memoirs of some renowned "country editors," such as:

- William Allen White of *The Emporia Gazette* in Kansas. White's editorial, "What's the Matter With Kansas?" earned him national attention, and his editorials against the Ku Klux Klan won him both deep admiration and seething scorn. His autobiography won a posthumous Pulitzer Prize in 1947.

- Henry Beetle Hough of the *Vineyard Gazette* on Martha's Vineyard, whose 1940 memoir *Country Editor* won critical acclaim across the nation. *The Atlantic Monthly* gushed, "This is an oasis book, the oasis exasperated journalists, editors, and printers dream of when their jobs begin to bind" (Hough, 1974, back cover).

- John Henry Cutler of the *Duxbury Clipper* on Cape Cod, whose first memoir, *Put It on the Front Page, Please!* (Cutler, 1960), was described by a *New York Times* critic as "one of the gayest weekly mirrors of New England small town life. . . . If you are planning to start a paper, by all means read Mr. Cutler's book. . . . In any event, you will find here a stimulating view of country life in America" (Cutler, 1965, back cover).

The romantic ideal of the country editor was tempered, of course, by anecdotes that were not at all flattering to the community press. Early critics of community journalism focused on the "friendly neighbor relationship" as something that threatened journalistic independence, arguing that it could lead to timidity and laziness lest journalists offend their "neighbors" with aggressive reporting of community conflicts. To many critics in the upper echelons of the profession, community journalism became a euphemism for the old-style "booster press" common in the 18th and 19th centuries.

Much of that criticism was, again, a result of assumptions by the elites of the profession that they were the ones who set the standards that all should follow. In his second memoir, *Cancel My Subscription, Please!*, Cutler (1965) recalled a letter he received from the editor of a national journalism trade magazine, scolding the small-town editor for not publishing the names of local residents arrested for drunken driving. Cutler's response was:

Why add to the penalty meted out by law? In a small town, who is punished more in this case, the offender, or his wife and children? If a town is small enough to support a friendly, neighborly paper, isn't it big enough to omit a name that would make publicity the worst part of the punishment? (Cutler, 1965, p. 136)

Framed as an ethical debate, the passage demonstrated that Cutler's concern in that situation was more for the effects of his journalistic choices on an individual member of the community than on the routines and standard practices of the broader journalism profession.

Comparisons within the community media provided more meaningful criticisms, many of which have been supported by anecdotal evidence of local journalists reporting on serious local problems. For example, the community media in and near Libby, Montana, did little to report on the asbestos poisoning in the community by a large vermiculite mine nearby, and the problem wasn't reported to any depth until Andrew Schneider of the *Seattle Post-Intelligencer* broke the story in 1999 (Moss & Appel, 2001). There are also many newspapers and newspaper companies that invest very little in their newsrooms, and as such live up to the stereotype of what Lauterer (2006) calls "the bottom-feeders of community journalism" (p. 56). Lauterer, a strong advocate of community journalism in general and community newspapers especially, frankly acknowledges that "many small-town papers seem to attract and harbor the washed-out derelicts of our business; community papers at their worst become sort of a stale backwater for the flotsam and jetsam of journalism" (Lauterer, 2006, p. 44).

A noteworthy early excoriation of the "lazy community newspaper" stereotype came in 1964, when media critic Ben Bagdikian wrote a scathing rebuke of the "lazy editor" in *Harper's Magazine*. Although Bagdikian's scorn was primarily aimed at the publicity services that produced the ready-made propaganda that could be published as news copy, he did not spare the small-town newspaper editor who, facing a deadline and staring at an empty hole on a page, would go "fishing through the purple mats and yellow mimeographed canned editorials in his lower drawer, feeling for one exactly nine column-inches long" (p. 103). In the opening paragraphs of that essay, Bagdikian challenged the heroic mythos of the "country editor":

> The unperishing myth of American journalism is the ideal of the small-town newspaper as the grass-roots opinion-maker of the nation, the last bastion of personal journalism, the final arena where a single human being can mold a community with his convictions and fearless iconoclasm. Needless to say, there are some small papers like this and they are marvels to behold. But the fact is that most small

dailies and weeklies are the backyard of the trade, repositories for any piece of journalistic junk tossed over the fence, run as often by print-shop proprietors as by editors. Mostly they serve as useful bulletin boards of births, deaths, and marriages (providing this news comes in by its own initiative); only in exceptional cases do they raise and resolve important local issues. When it comes to transmitting signals from the outside world, a remarkable number of these papers convey pure—that is, unadulterated—press agentry. Its subject matter, which is printed both as "news" and as editorial comment, ranges from mouthwash to politics—usually right wing. (p. 102)

Bagdikian's suggestion was to become a new unperishing myth of the profession—the belief that small-town journalism was somehow substandard to the big leagues, rather than just different. Yet even Bagdikian was careful to not use a broad brush to condemn all community newspapers, writing:

To imply that a small circulation automatically means surrender to boilerplate is unfair to a number of small dailies and weeklies which, whatever their politics, are plainly the product of diligent personal editorship, and precisely in those places where this takes courage because the editor does literally have to face his readers on the street. (p. 110)

Those "diligent" community journalists are not hard to find. State and regional journalism organizations give hundreds of awards each year to community media (newspapers, TV stations, online-only publications) that do noteworthy journalism at the community level.

The academy and the profession tend to feed that stereotype of the "lazy paper" with their own brand of hero worship for the big-league players of journalism and their international acclaim. That, too, is an old story. In 1909, for example, James E. Rogers wrote in *The American Newspaper*:

Obviously it is absurd to assert that a small four-paged country journal . . . in any way compares with the huge twenty-four paged daily of a large city . . . we find both as regards size and influence, that "the power of the press" rests absolutely with our cities and not with the country. (cited in Riley, 1938, p. 39)

Consider also this more recent example: In the months of hand-wringing in America over the 2007 sale of Dow Jones & Co. and its flag-ship *The Wall Street Journal* to global media baron Rupert Murdoch and his News Corp., nearly all of the commentary and analysis focused on whether Murdoch would meddle with the respected independence of *The Wall Street Journal*. Only a handful of the hundreds of such articles and essays even mentioned the two dozen–plus community newspa-pers also owned by Dow Jones via its Ottaway Newspapers subsidiary. Many of the Ottaway newspapers were respected community papers that had earned strong market penetration in their communities and fre-quent awards from state press associations. They also were immensely successful businesses. According to an article in *The Boston Globe*,

> the Ottaway community publications posted operating profits of $48.2 million last year on $252.2 million in sales, outstripping the $33.9 million in profits on revenue of $1.1 billion for the Dow Jones operating group that includes the *Journal* and *Barron's* magazine. (Weisman, 2007, p. D1)

That is a 19% return from the Ottaway newspapers, compared to about 3.4% return from the company's flagships. Dismissing the community newspapers as "those silly little Ottaway papers" (Weisman, 2007), Murdoch vowed to sell off the community newspapers almost imme-diately after purchasing Dow Jones; his eyes were fixed on *The Wall Street Journal*. But one of the business owners in a New England com-munity served by an Ottaway newspaper said to the *Globe*:

> Certainly we're all talking about it, and we're all concerned about it. . . . The Ottaway papers tend to be local papers. They're not centralized. If any of these papers were to lose that local flavor, the readership would plunge. And that would create a void for the local advertisers. (Weisman, 2007, p. D1)

Coverage of the sale of Dow Jones can serve as an exemplar for the current schism between mainstream journalism and community journalism. It's a case in which the famous and powerful media mogul expressed more concern for prestige than for profitability, and the local business owner expressed more concern about the "local flavor" of a community newspaper than about who owned it.

❖   BUSINESS AS A HOLISTIC ASPECT OF
      COMMUNITY JOURNALISM

The concerns of the local business owner about the flavor of a small-town newspaper illustrate another important criticism of community journalism—the close connections between the business side of the operation and the news side. Community journalism is usually much less rigid in regard to the "wall" between newsroom operations and business operations typically found at larger news organizations (An & Bergen, 2007). It is certainly far less adversarial, viewing advertisers not just as sources of revenue, but also as legitimate members of the community. Some community editors consider advertising to be editorial copy and will accept only ads that are appropriate for their readers, preferring advertisements from businesses within the community.

In his memoir, Hough suggested that approaches to advertising provided another example of how community journalism differed from the journalism of the major newspapers of his day:

> On the face of it, the cost of reaching a million readers through country weeklies was greater than the cost of reaching a million readers through city dailies; and there were plenty of city dailies which claimed to cover not only entire states but regions of states.
>
> It was a curious anomaly which found the *Gazette*, for instance, too costly a medium to be used by the nation's largest and wealthiest corporations, yet a practical and economical medium for a small grocery store with an advertising budget of a hundred dollars a year. The truth was, of course, that there was no absolute advantage or disadvantage in respect to cost; there was simply a difference in the point of view. . . .
>
> [O]ur advertisers were known to our readers as human beings, as individuals, and I think this tendency to personalize them—a tendency inherent in the treatment of news in a country weekly—was of more value than countless columns of disingenuous promotion copy could have been. (1974, pp. 265–271)

Aside from that advertiser-as-neighbor philosophy, organizational structure of community news operations also has played a role in the more accommodating attitudes community journalists may have toward their advertisers. Community media tend to have small and undifferentiated staffs. Many community newspapers are run by only one or two people (in many cases, the owners). In such situations, the business aspects of community journalism benefit from being both flexible and personal, and the community journalist is faced with wearing many different hats. If there is a "wall" in many community media, it is a wall within the journalist herself. In his 1974 textbook *Community Journalism: A Way of Life*, small-town editor/publisher Bruce M. Kennedy described the business side of community journalism this way:

> A community newspaper editor's day is not strictly newspapering, for he is also a small-town businessman. . . .
> [N]o newspaper can continue to publish the news, pictures, and advertising of a small community unless that newspaper also shows a profit. The editor brings his talents for journalism, his creative abilities, to the weekly newspaper; the businessman's side of his nature, instinctive or acquired, brings the profit. It is a tribute to this distinguished profession that the weekly newsman can play both roles, striking this difficult balance of making a business profitable and a newspaper excellent and not have the two interfere with each other. (p. 195)

It is important to note that three generations of textbooks about community journalism—Byerly's foundational text of 1961, Kennedy's text of 1974, and Lauterer's contemporary text first published in 1995—include chapters about the business concerns of a community news product. So do the community-editor memoirs mentioned earlier. Like the chapters discussing how best to cover local government, how best to include content reflecting on community life, and how to use the editorial page to spark public debate on all manner of issues, the chapters about managing the business aspects of community media focused largely on the connections between media and their communities. Hough alluded to that very point in his memoir, recalling when a larger daily newspaper tried to compete with the *Vineyard Gazette*:

> The acute and direct competition came into our field when a neighboring daily decided that it would "cover like a friendly blanket" our towns and many others in order to offer some thousands of "rural and suburban circulation" for a price in the slave

market of mass advertising. . . . This daily believed that a familiar formula could be applied, that it was only necessary to print names, names, names, in order to enjoy circulation and the respect of readers. . . . The truth was that the traditional formula was idle and silly. The thing which makes people in small towns read their papers is news, and they have no interest whatever in names—even their own—which do not mean something at the time and in the context of town life. . . .

In the long run the daily's personal items were so padded and its general news so garbled that we had little to fear from the competition. No desk man ever troubled to learn the place names in our county, and the geography attributed to us was remarkable. (1974, pp. 267–268)

An important subtext of Hough's recollection is the issue of scale. Byerly, Lauterer, and many others have suggested that scale is a primary delineation of what is community journalism and what is not. In particular, the word "small" is ubiquitous in the literature: "small-town," "small circulation," "small staffs," "small radio stations," "small newspapers." The allusion is that community journalism cannot exist in larger media, and certainly not in national and international media. Attitudes toward the myth of the small (Is it of little consequence? Is it perhaps more "authentic," to evoke Walter Benjamin [1969]?) should be the focus of more intense scholarly consideration.

❖ BEYOND "BIG" VERSUS "SMALL"

Past and continued research into differences between "large" and "small" news media has been and will continue to be important, but such studies are not necessarily concerned with community journalism. The truth is that a reporter on the lead TV news team in a sprawling city could be much more connected to the community than a member of a three-person weekly newspaper operation in a town of a few thousand people. It may be more difficult for journalists serving large, pluralistic audiences to have strong connections to their communities, and it may be quite easy for such connections to be established by a reporter serving a small, homogeneous audience, but neither that difficulty nor that ease will alone dictate the strength of the connection.

Consider this hypothetical situation: When the graduate of a journalism school takes her first reporting job at a hyperlocal news website in a suburb where she has no personal ties, and then leaves the job after eight months having neither liked the community nor cared about its people, it would be difficult to say that she had strong connections to the community. Likewise, who can really argue that a journalist who has lived and worked his whole life in a single large metropolis cannot practice community journalism because he works for the most popular TV news station in that city?

For scholars in the social-scientific paradigm, such scenarios raise an interesting question: What is the operationalization of community journalism? Is it the size of the outlet, the size of the community, the attitudes of individual members of the community toward the journalist (and vice versa)? Is the fact that a national-politics blogger has only a few hundred readers all the evidence necessary to say that he is a community journalist? Organizational and audience size may be a useful metric in the study of community journalism, but it cannot be the only one.

Perhaps a more useful metric than size is content, specifically content classified as "community focused." Traditionally, that has meant "local news," but the concept of "local" is too confining in an age when many communities transcend physical proximity of the members. There are many examples of community journalism that serves such scattered collectives. Consider the *Small Farmer's Journal*, a quarterly magazine published in rural Oregon and reaching like-minded readers around the globe, and at this writing entering its fourth decade of publishing; or the *Shambhala Sun*, a bimonthly magazine for devotees of Western style "engaged Buddhism." An analysis of letters to the editor published in those two magazines revealed strong rhetoric of community, as if the magazines themselves served as the nexus of community, and all attached to it—writers, editors, advertisers, and subscribers—as members of those distinct communities (Reader & Moist, 2009). Obviously, such publications have no "local" to serve, but their content is focused entirely on their communities.

In communities of place, local information has been at the core of community media, regardless of whether that information is serious news or trivial gossip, courageous editorials or banal lists of property transfers. But it is the presence (perhaps the dominance) of the trivial and the routine that provide observable clues of community connections; such information is rarely found, and certainly never with any frequency, in the pages or broadcasts of major news media. Gibbs (1995) suggested that local news is "people-oriented, location-specific news about such things as who won ribbons at the county fair, or when the city's going to fix that big chuckhole on Main Street" (p. 33). Morton contended that community journalists are "chroniclers of local minutiae and the concerns of everyday life" (1990, p. 57). To be sure, serious news—coverage of local government and local courts, of conflicts between the powerful and the vulnerable, of crime and tragedy, of scandal and triumph—is also part of the mix. But in community media, even the serious has a decidedly local focus. Some analysts have noted that the coverage of news often thought mundane by big-league journalism standards (zoning board hearings, homecoming parades, comprehensive listings of even the most trivial police reports) is just as important, if not more so, to community life than large-scale, award-winning service projects aimed at revealing unusually large statewide and national problems (Morton, 1990; Sheppard, 1996).

How that community-focused information is gathered and processed is another distinguishing characteristic of community journalism. In community journalism, the audience is often quite involved in the procedure, with much content being suggested, requested, or even submitted by people in the community. Hence the typical publication in community media of check-passing photos, group shots of kindergarteners, reader-submitted essays and opinions, and galleries of pictures of family reunions or deer hunters with their trophies. In that regard, community journalism has long been a forum for so-called "citizen journalism" and interactive in a very real sense, even before the Internet came to be. Online communication has expanded and improved that interactivity, for certain, but it did not create it.

From a pragmatic standpoint, the small staffs of community media rely on citizen submissions to supplement what the staff could produce itself. But in many ways, such deference to what the community sees as newsworthy is at the core of the concept: community journalism typically places less value on the norms of the profession at large (as codified in most trade publications, college textbooks, and journalism school classrooms) than it does on the norms of the individual communities they serve. Bruce Kennedy, the small-town newspaper editor, put it this way:

It's rewarding to be part of nearly everything involving your community, the printable as well as the unprintable. It's flattering to have your opinions asked for, your counsel sought, whether you're really as wise as all that or not. You build many monuments in [the] newspaper business. Your newspaper and energy leave a wake of new buildings, successful projects, guidance, and direction. Helping others, boosting the community, the area, or "the cause" will become, like the Thursday paper days, endless. . . . Small-town newspapering is belonging. (1974, pp. 7–8)

❖ CONCLUSION

As a new generation of scholars refocuses on community journalism as a distinct part of the broader mass communication discipline, it is important to not only gather past research into a cohesive collection of studies, but to take that inquiry in new directions that study "connections" using a variety of methods and theoretical frameworks.

As with most things involving community journalism, however, that lament also is hardly new. In 1938, John Winchell Riley, Jr., of Rutgers University wrote in the *American Sociological Review*:

The typical country weekly, in addition to its personal journalism, its boiler plate fillers, its articles on extraordinary or exciting local events, is a series of chatty confidences about the town's everyday living. Its few pages are packed with columns headed "Local Items" or "Personals" or "People We Know." These columns contain all the miscellany of the community's ordinary and expected events: its births, marriages, and deaths; its comings and goings; its family and club changes; above all, the non-economic, leisure activities of its members. . . . Yet, the country newspaper, consistent and detailed register though it may be, has been given very little consideration as a possible source for sociological research.

Its desirability as a source is indubitable. Obviously such a paper has two advantages over most other sources available for the various kinds of community studies: In the first place, it provides material for the intensive study of trends from an historical standpoint; and this material is so consistent and repetitive in nature that, with the employment of proper precautions, it lends itself in a number of ways to quantification. In the second place, the weekly offers the sociological investigator the possibility of avoiding any marked bias in his selection of material. Convenient as this source may be, however, its importance may be more questionable. This depends upon the accuracy of its data, and the degree to which they actually are consistent over time. Thus any estimate of its importance must rest upon a broader knowledge of the nature of the country weekly itself. (pp. 39-40)

Despite the contributions of several important and helpful studies over the past decades, the field of community journalism remains largely unexplored, and the depths uncharted. Scholars who are intensely interested in the role of journalism in communities should attempt to take up Riley's challenge, albeit 70-plus years after the fact, and against many entrenched institutional biases against the "silly little papers" that dominate the journalism world.

❖ REFERENCES

An, S., & Bergen, L. (2007). Advertiser pressure on daily newspapers. *Journal of Advertising, 36*(2), 111–121.

Anderson, R., Dardenne, R., & Killenberg, G. M. (1994). *The conversation of journalism: Conversation, community, and news.* Westport, CT: Praeger.

Bagdikian, B. H. (1964, December). Behold the grass-roots press, alas! *Harper's Magazine,* 102–110.

Benjamin, W. (1969). The work of art in the age of mechanical reproduction. In *Illuminations: Essays and reflections* (pp. 217–251). New York: Schocken Books.

Byerly, K. R. (1961). *Community journalism.* Philadelphia: Chilton.

Byers, M. R. (1937, May 29). I want to see the editor. *The Saturday Evening Post,* 100–105.

Conason, J. (1975, November 8). A press for the people. *The Nation,* 467–468.

The country newspaper: Symbol of democracy. (1946). *The Saturday Evening Post, 218*(47), 160.

Cutler, J. H. (1960). *Put it on the front page, please!* New York: Ives Washburn.

Cutler, J. H. (1965). *Cancel my subscription, please!* New York: Ives Washburn.

Gibbs, C. (1995). Big help for small papers. *Quill, 83*(2), 32–35.

Hough, H. B. (1974). *Country editor.* Riverside, CT: Chatham.

Kennedy, B. M. (1974). *Community journalism: A way of life.* Ames, IA: Iowa State University Press.

Lauterer, J. (2006). *Community journalism: Relentlessly local* (3rd ed.). Chapel Hill: University of North Carolina Press.

Lavrakas, P. J., & Holley, J. K. (1989). Images of daily newspapers in their local markets. *Newspaper Research Journal, 10*(3), 51–56.

Morton, J. (1990). Newspapers seeking a sense of community. *Washington Journalism Review, 12*(8), 57.

Moss, M., & Appel, A. (2001, July 9). Protecting the product: A special report: Company's silence countered safety fears about asbestos. *The New York Times*, p. A1.

Reader, B. (2006). Distinctions that matter: Ethical differences at large and small newspapers. *Journalism and Mass Communication Quarterly, 83*(4), 851–864.

Reader, B., & Moist, K. (2009). Letters as indicators of community values: Two case studies of alternative magazines. *Journalism and Mass Communication Quarterly, 85*(4), 823–840.

Riley, J. W., Jr. (1938). The country weekly as a sociological source. *American Sociological Review, 3*(1), 39–46.

Sheppard, J. (1996). The strength of weeklies. *American Journalism Review, 18*(6), 32–37.

Tichenor, P., Donohue, G., & Olien, C. (1980). *Community conflict and the press.* Beverly Hills, CA: Sage.

Tocqueville, A. de. (2004). *Democracy in America* (A. Goldhammer, Trans.). New York: Penguin. (Original work published 1835)

Weisman, R. (2007, July 26). Ottaway readers, advertisers cast wary eye on Dow Jones talks. *The Boston Globe*, p. D1. Retrieved April 19, 2011, from http://www.boston.com/ae/media/articles/2007/07/26/ottaway_readers_advertisers_cast_wary_eye_on_dow_jones_talks/

Community Journalism
Must Tackle Tough Local Issues ●

Linda Steiner

Community journalism is credited with representing, reinforcing, and even constructing community. The form speaks to, from, and about community, presumably bringing people together with an understanding of their shared frame of reference, and their responsibility for upholding it. Definitions of small-town/weekly/community (those terms are typically treated as equivalent) news media imply several common features, including relentlessly local content, limited orientation in size and geography, and local, independent ownership. Howard Ziff's (1986) distinction between "provincial" and "cosmopolitan" newspapers still holds: the former are grounded in local values, to be criticized only on behalf of other, deeply held communal beliefs. The latter insist on objectivity and stand above local values.

Nevertheless, both kinds of news organs share an inherent responsibility to gather and report stories of vital interest to citizens, including external threats and challenges as well as internal conflicts and tensions. Moreover, glowing praise of independent community weeklies often ignores that community newspapers increasingly are units of chains, edited by careerists without local roots, and written by people who don't know one another and rarely meet up at regional offices. They regularly produce special editions celebrating the "anniversaries" of the locality or newspaper, but often are unable to put contemporary problems into historical context. No less driven by bottom-line considerations than are urban dailies, owners of weeklies rarely spend money, or risk advertising revenue, to probe local tensions and deep-seated problems. Morris Janowitz's 1952 findings are perhaps all too relevant a half century later: community media foreground social and personal news, local volunteer associations, municipal services, and community involvement; they avoid or ignore controversy. Astute readers may resent all of that. Or perhaps, with their remote-controlled garage openers and far-flung social networks, readers neither care nor feel part of the community.

Community journalism too often exploits how "community" is a "warmly persuasive word . . . never to be used unfavourably," as

Raymond Williams put it (1983, p. 76). That said, taking community or community newspapers seriously requires critical examination of both concepts, specifically by questioning the prevailing notions of community undergirding local journalism. Even the "common" roots linking "communion," "community," and "communication," as James Carey famously emphasized (1989, p. 18), do not make homogeneity the goal of community or democratic processes. That is, community spirit, to the extent it is desired, does not depend on denying interconnections to issues of the "outside" world, ignoring internal conflict, or excusing unpleasant realities such as religious bigotry or racism as part of local culture. If condescension toward community journalism is unwarranted, so is complacency from within community journalism.

Even small towns do and should include diverse people with different understandings and experiences. People committed to fellowship must appreciate diversity and make room for pluralism and argument. Vigorous intercourse among different people enriches community. Communities thus need local news institutions (whether printed, Web-based, or broadcast/cablecast) that engage citizens in animated, provocative discussions of their heterogeneity and diversity.

This is no brief advocating scurrilous personal attacks, unethical half-truths, or exaggerated contentiousness. But community journalists, if they are willing, can inspire critique and even investigation of local problems. Community journalists can engage people in civic processes and enlarge their political presence so they can actively respond to Carey's stipulation that community institutions nurture citizens' moral, political, and intellectual capacities.

❖ REFERENCES

Carey, J. W. (1989). *Communication as culture.* New York: Routledge.
Janowitz, M. (1952). *The community press in an urban setting.* Chicago: University of Chicago Press.
Williams, R. (1983). *Keywords: A vocabulary of culture and society.* New York: Oxford University Press.
Ziff, H. M. (1986). Practicing responsible journalism: Cosmopolitan versus provincial models. In D. Elliott (Ed.), *Responsible journalism* (pp. 151–166). Beverly Hills, CA: Sage.

Linda Steiner *is a professor and director of research and doctoral studies at the University of Maryland's Philip Merrill College of Journalism. She studies how and when gender matters in news and newsrooms and how feminist groups use media. Other research areas include media ethics, journalism history, and public journalism. Steiner is editor of* Critical Studies in Media Communication *and serves on six editorial boards. Her most recent book is* Key Concepts in Critical Cultural Studies *(University of Illinois Press, 2010), coedited with Clifford Christians of the University of Illinois at Urbana–Champaign.*

2

Key Works

*Some Connections Between Journalism
and Community*

Jack Rosenberry

The literature of journalism and community is broad and deep, with
roots in pioneering sociological investigations of how media institutions relate to the world around them. Two themes that run throughout that literature are (a) that the defining characteristic of community
journalism is the intimacy that the organizations and the people who
practice it share with the institutions and individuals they cover, especially as reflected in content selections, and (b) the interaction of community journalism organizations with the institutions and imperatives
of the local community structure. Those themes pervade the historical
key works reviewed in this chapter, which largely focused on community newspapers in their local geographic areas, as well as more
contemporary investigations that include various forms of media and
address community in ways that go beyond sheer geography.

Research into the nexus of community and journalism covers a wide range of styles and formats. Descriptions of the nuts and bolts of putting out a community newspaper that are frequently used to establish principles of the practice are textbooks such as those by Byerly (1961), Kennedy (1974), and Lauterer (2006). A common thread running through those how-to manuals is that the level of personal detail in community news stories sets them apart from other styles of journalism, and the notion that coverage decisions extend from the newspaper's being a community stakeholder. (Those distinctions are explored more fully in Chapter 1.)

The body of scholarly research about community journalism includes several methodological approaches, including case studies and qualitative interviews of community journalists that closely examine professional practices. Detailed social-scientific investigations with sophisticated statistical analyses illuminate fine-grained distinctions among variables such as media content, audience behavior, community characteristics, and measures of community attachment. Most of that research focuses on newspapers, describing and investigating small-town rural papers as well as those covering suburbs, city neighborhoods, and cultural communities defined by race, ethnicity, or interest.

But a growing body of work looks at electronic and online media, such as an investigation of how online hyperlocal news sites reflect some of the same community integration functions as weekly newspapers (Rosenberry, 2010b) and another looking at the importance of "locality" in radio broadcasting (Torosyan & Munro, 2010). This chapter will review a mix of approaches involving research that has community media as the focus of analysis, as well as historical works that are important milestones in building theories of how journalism and community relate to each other.

❖   EARLY SOCIOLOGICAL STUDIES

One characteristic of great research is its heuristic value—its ability to inspire further work that builds on its findings (Littlejohn, 1999). Perhaps nothing in the literature of community journalism has been used as a springboard for further study more frequently than Morris Janowitz's early 1950s research into neighborhood community newspapers in

Chicago. Janowitz's work, which first appeared in a 1951 article in *Public Opinion Quarterly*—and a year later in book form—established a view of the community press as both an indicator of and an impetus for social change. A second edition of the book, with a new preface and a new epilogue, was published in 1967, helping to spawn the extensive "community ties" research discussed later in this chapter.

Janowitz inherited the University of Chicago's grand tradition of using the city as a "natural laboratory for sociological investigation" (Rogers, 1994). The school had long focused on investigating communication and society, generating research such as the famous Payne Fund Studies of the 1920s (*Motion Pictures and Youth*, 1933) about the impact of movie viewership on audiences. Another noted Chicago researcher was Robert Park, a newspaper reporter turned academic whose contributions include studies of the immigrant press. Janowitz's work was a multi-methodological study of newspapers in some of Chicago's 75 recognized neighborhoods circa 1950. He analyzed neighborhood demographics, analyzed the content of three newspapers, surveyed readers, and conducted in-depth interviews with the papers' managers and residents of the neighborhoods they served. Janowitz used the urban community press as a vantage point for assessing one of the key lines of sociological inquiry of the mid 20th century: research into the impact that local institutions had within larger urban areas as the cities grew, referred to as "specialization within generalization" (1967, p. 5). The urban community press was "one of the social mechanisms through which the individual is integrated into the urban social structure" (p. 9).

Janowitz studied and wrote about—albeit in a more formal, academic style—the same relationship between newspaper and community described by Byerly, Kennedy, and Lauterer: how the contents and function of the community press are linked to the social requirements of the community. Two of the four hypotheses in Janowitz's work addressed that idea directly: (a) "The community press acts as a mechanism which seeks *to maintain local consensus through the emphasis on common values* rather than on the solution of conflicting values" (1967, p. 11, emphasis added) and (b) "At every point in the operation of the local community newspaper, its mass communication effects are *inextricably interrelated with the personal communications and social contacts which link the newspaper's personnel, the community leaders and the readership clientele*" (p. 13, emphasis added). The other two hypotheses addressed how community newspapers developed along with satellite business districts within cities that provided advertising support, and how the community papers helped to both shape and reflect the social and political structure of a neighborhood.

Janowitz documented how local newspapers helped individuals find their way in a complicated world of organizations, institutions, and activities at the neighborhood level as they navigated the larger metropolis. The community press did that by emphasizing coverage of controversies within the local community versus larger citywide institutions. A newspaper's content maintained consensus and emphasized local values through coverage of social, religious, youth, and cultural organizations. Those findings parallel Lauterer's ideas about covering news in an "us versus them" fashion, and Byerly's and Kennedy's observations regarding the promotion of local clubs and social events. Similarly, Janowitz concluded that intimacy of coverage was key to the paper's success as a local institution: "The community newspaper's emphasis on community routines, low controversy and social ritual are the very characteristics that account for its readership" (1967, p. 130).

❖ COMMUNITY TIES

Janowitz's work led directly and indirectly to a vast body of research exploring how media use, community characteristics, and an individual's sense of community connectedness relate to one another. That came to be known as the community ties research agenda. That broad and deep agenda included demographic and psychographic research, single studies, and collected bodies of work. For example, Edelstein and Larsen (1960) used Janowitz to illustrate that people with a strong "newspaper orientation" were more likely to be longtime residents of their community, to have a positive view of it, and to engage in more social participation. A set of descriptive (nontheoretical) studies conducted by academics at the behest of a newspaper trade group, along with study of how community demographics affected newspaper readership, laid much of the groundwork.

Many of those projects were successful in showing a positive correlation between use of newspapers and individuals' ties to the community. But they were less successful in answering another important question: Which variable—community ties or newspaper use—was dependent, and which was independent? Did greater newspaper use cause people to become more connected to their communities, or were those who had stronger community attachments (for whatever reasons) more likely to read newspapers because of those attachments? Could the relationship be iterative, and, if so, could a newspaper encourage a feedback loop by engaging in certain activities that would improve the community's general sense of itself, building stronger community attachments that could then translate into more newspaper usage?

❖ ANPA NEWS RESEARCH CENTER REPORTS

Research into the relationship between community characteristics and newspaper usage was a popular topic of study in the mid to late 1970s. Both the academy and the newspaper industry were interested in declining readership and the dwindling of multi-newspaper markets. A common subject of investigations at the time was whether structural variables such as community demographics could predict or explain the forces behind those declines. (Looking back with three decades of hindsight, it's clear that what those efforts documented were the first cracks in a dam that now has burst, in the form of plunging readership and circulation among large daily newspapers in the first decade of the 21st century.)

That body of work included a number of studies conducted under the auspices of the American Newspaper Publishers Association, through the ANPA News Research Center. That center supported administrative research designed to help editors and publishers understand their communities and markets better in the hope of building readership and circulation. Many studies were focused on metropolitan markets, but some explored the nature of small-town community newspapers.

Shaw (1978), for example, did a study based on personal interviews with 700 residents of four small towns in Tennessee and concluded that the degree to which they enjoyed their paper and how much utility it had for them helped to distinguish regular readers from occasional readers. Stephens (1978) used a telephone survey to compare reading habits with "community attachment," which he measured with a scale based on Janowitz's work. Stephens concluded that "a strong sense of attachment to the community in which one lives is a more important determinant of reading more than one newspaper than age, years of residence in the community, socioeconomic status, family income or education" (p. 2). In a report a year later, also based on a telephone survey, Stevenson (1979) concluded that "the heart of the newspaper audience continues to be people with strong and permanent ties to the community who look for information and guidance to use in maintaining civic links" (p. 2).

In a report done for ANPA based on a meta-analysis of 50 previous academic studies, Stone (1978) evaluated the community characteristics that might predict readership and concluded that home ownership was the key variable. Around that time, Stone also investigated circulation determinants based on community demographics and content characteristics, and found, among other things, that local content was the main distinction between smaller-circulation community newspapers and larger-circulation dailies (Stone & Morrison, 1976).

❖ THEORY BUILDING OF STAMM AND ASSOCIATES

Documenting the relationship between newspaper usage and community structural variables (such as home ownership and length of residence) and psychographic ones (such as "attachment") was an area of investigation that grew from previous studies of community characteristics. As that research agenda unfolded, other researchers began asking questions about what those connections really meant in the life of the community and of the individual readers. They also began to raise the question of causal direction more explicitly. Notable among the scholars pursuing that was Keith Stamm of the University of Washington, who, along with various associates on different projects, sought to look even deeper into the concept of community ties.

The general focus of Stamm's agenda was that newspaper usage and community ties/attachments should be seen as multifaceted constructs. In his view, research needed to get beyond studying the very broad comparisons of reading or subscribing, as a dependent variable, to "attachment" or demographics, as an independent variable. The earliest appearance of that work was in an ANPA report in which Stamm and an associate broke down "community involvement" into five components, relating each of them to different aspects of subscribing to newspapers. They concluded that the simplest form of involvement—a desire to keep up with community happenings—was the best single predictor of whether someone subscribed to more than one newspaper and how much time was spent reading those papers (Stamm & Fortini-Campbell, 1981).

A central theme of Stamm's work was that individuals' ties to their communities had various components and that those ties changed over time, making it incorrect to measure the construct as a static, unitary variable, as so many research projects attempted to do. A monograph published by Stamm and Fortini-Campbell (1983), building on their work from their 1981 ANPA report, introduced the idea that community, which traditionally had been rooted in a physical locale, should be construed on multiple dimensions of not only place but also structure (community institutions) and process (shared interests). They maintained that residents developed ties to each of those three dimensions differently, depending on how long they had lived in the community and whether they planned to stay there.

In a few journal articles (e.g., Stamm & Weis, 1982; Weis & Stamm, 1982) and a later book (Stamm, 1985), those ideas were expanded to include a notion of dynamic ties and newspaper readership behavior, meaning that both the community ties individuals had and their reading behavior could change over time. For example, an occasional newspaper reader could become a subscriber who still mostly skimmed the paper, and then later a devoted consumer of nearly everything in it. Likewise, a community newcomer eventually might become a long-time resident. In a later essay that served as a postscript to that work, Stamm (1988) returned to discussing the reciprocal nature of the relationship. He argued that certain types of ties might be the antecedents of newspaper usage and others might be the result.

❖ EXTENSIONS OF THE COMMUNITY-TIES HYPOTHESES

Other scholars have used Stamm's ideas as a starting point for even more detailed investigations of the relationship between community and media usage. Jackson (1982) used Stamm's distinctions of place, process, and structure to examine how suburban newspaper readers were more attached to the lifestyle of suburbia as a key tie than to a particular geographic community. Viswanath, Finnegan, Rooney, and

Potter (1990) used Stamm and Fortini-Campbell's four-part resident typology as a basis for investigating different forms of community ties developed through newspaper versus cable television use. Torosyan and Munro (2010) drew on Park and Stamm for the theoretical underpinning of a study of listener satisfaction for local stations given recent industry ownership consolidation.

Jeffres and Dobos (1983) used the division devised by Stamm and Fortini-Campbell for a study that also built on Janowitz's work by investigating content interests of readers of neighborhood newspapers in Cleveland. Paek, Yoon, and Shah tested seven hypotheses rooted in a mix of what Stamm identified as "place" variables and "process" variables in relation to media use and community participation. They concluded that "socially active, connected individuals become more likely to participate in public life when they live in communities with a strong local print culture" (2005, p. 597).

❖ COMMUNITY COVERAGE BY ETHNIC MEDIA

Another type of community that transcends simple geography is one rooted in ethnicity, race, or cultural heritage. The study of media serving those communities is a burgeoning field whose roots also can be traced back to the University of Chicago. Park examined the immigrant press in Chicago, primarily serving Polish and other eastern-European groups, and concluded that its popularity was rooted in various causes, including the sense of intellectual and social liberation that immigrants gained from reading native-language newspapers and the value those papers had in helping readers become oriented to their new communities (Janowitz, 1967).

In a more contemporary frame, Lauterer (2006) devotes a chapter to Spanish-language media, with six case studies of how small English-speaking newspapers sought to address the influx of Hispanic residents to their communities and one case study of a Spanish language newspaper. Coverage of the explosive growth of Latino media also can be found readily in trade publication articles (e.g., Bailon, 2005; Chepesiuk, 2007; Fitzgerald, 2002).

Research into ethnic media does have some gaps, however. Absent from Janowitz's study, for example, is any analysis of the African-American press in Chicago. That is notable because it was a vigorous part of the city's life, as documented by scholars who have examined the operation of newspapers such as *The Chicago Defender* (e.g., Ross & McKerns, 2004; Stroman, 1981). In the preface to the second edition of his book, Janowitz (1967) notes that analysis of those papers was purposely excluded because the goal of his research was to examine community press coverage at the neighborhood level, whereas "the Negro press sought to appeal to the Negro community as a whole" (p. xii). Conceiving of community in ways that went beyond geography was not a part of the scholarly mind-set at that time.

A substantial body of research does exist on the history of the ethnic press. That work covers the African-American press (e.g., Dann, 1971; DeSantis, 1998; LaBrie, 1977; Simmons, 1998; Suggs, 1996; Thornton, 2006), as well as the Native American press (LaCourse, 1979; Littlefield & Parins, 1984; Murphy & Murphy, 1981; Riley, 1976) and the Latino press (Gutierrez, 1977; Melendez, 2005). Going beyond histories, some research in the form of content analyses, case studies, surveys, and interviews can be found about contemporary media that serve those racial and ethnic communities. Although that work has not reached the breadth and coherence of the agenda that developed around more general theories of community ties, much of it does center on construction of cultural identity. Ojo (2006), for example, completed a case study of a newspaper covering the black community in Montreal, Canada, as a way of evaluating how the ethnic media constructed cultural identity differently from the mainstream media. In a similar vein, Mayer (2001) examined how Latino media in San Antonio contributed to the development of cultural identity.

Divergent news coverage by ethnic media is another area scholars have explored. Rivas-Rodriguez (2003) examined coverage differences between online and print Latino media in San Diego, based on both a content analysis and interviews with editors. A comparison of content in native-Alaskan newspapers to content in nonnative publications found that although similar topics were addressed in both, the level of attention differed dramatically. The researchers called the level of coverage of native topics in the nonnative press "amazingly low" (Murphy & Avery, 1983, p. 320) because it amounted to about 2% of coverage even though natives comprised about 20% of the readership. Daniels (2006) analyzed how four Native American media outlets covered the shootings of 10 students in Red Lake, Minnesota, and reported that they set themselves apart from mainstream media by providing news by and for Native Americans. Loew and Mella (2005) used a content analysis of four Native American newspapers in Wisconsin, combined with interviews and focus groups, to illustrate the impact of the papers' coverage on conceptions of tribal sovereignty. They concluded that "tribal newspapers contribute to and reflect their readers' heightened sense of tribal identity and nationhood" (p. 102). The thread running through those investigations is the contribution media make to community identity and integration, a theme that can be traced back as far as Park and Janowitz.

As powerful and significant as the many investigations of the connections between media use and community ties have been, they are not the only lenses through which scholars have sought to study journalism and community. Other research has involved application of general topics from media studies specifically to the work of community journalists, especially ethical behavior and standards of community journalists.

❖   THE JOURNALIST IN THE COMMUNITY

Although Byerly, Kennedy, and Lauterer often applauded the close relationships of community journalists with the individuals and institutions they cover, they also found those relationships have a built-in potential for ethical problems regarding conflicts of interest—a topic that has drawn some scholarly interest. As Lauterer put it in a chapter about journalistic ethics,

> the work of the great community newspaper is made more complex by its difficult multiple and conflicting roles as fair and balanced reporter of the news while also serving as advocate for all that it finds good and worthwhile in the community. (2006, p. 261)

One line of that work focuses on attitudes and behaviors of editors and publishers, a topic to which even Janowitz (1967) devoted an entire chapter, is called "The Social Role of the Community Publisher." Another project addressing the same theme is a case study by Northington (1992), who explored an editor's role in helping to establish a college in a small Kentucky town. Tezon (2003) also reviewed how publishers see their roles in their communities. Akhavan-Majid (1995) found that publishers from smaller newspapers were more likely to be active in local business and professional organizations; those who became involved in civic affairs were more likely to perceive themselves as part of the policymaking process and less likely to see their role as community "watchdogs." Reader (2006) did in-depth interviews with editors of newspapers large and small, and found that the level of accountability to the community did affect decision making. "At larger newspapers, the emphasis seems to be to preserve the reputation of the institution of the newspaper, whereas at smaller newspapers the starting point seems to be to manage journalists' individual connections with their communities" (p. 861).

Coble-Krings (2005) conducted interviews with staff at three Kansas weeklies to examine what happens when conflicts of interest arise. She specifically explored what happens when staff members serve in community positions (including an instance in which an editor also was mayor of a town in his newspaper's coverage area) and how community journalists deal with friends and relatives as sources. Bunton (1998) used in-depth content analysis and ethical imperatives derived from social responsibility theory to study how community newspapers in two neighboring towns covered the same community controversy.

"Community" and Other Areas of Journalism Studies

A deep body of literature exists in areas such as media law, media economics, implications of new technology for media and journalism, and broadcast journalism as a practice distinct from print. Numerous texts and journals are devoted to each of those areas, and within them a few investigations focused on community journalism can be found. Community journalism–based investigations are not prominent or numerous in any of those arenas, but a few that can be cited by way of example follow.

Broadcasting

Within the broadcasting arena, the emphasis of community studies has been on radio and its ties to the community. That makes intuitive sense, given the development of radio as a niche medium once television came on the scene. Television was dominated by nationwide networks, and even local television

(Continued)

(*Continued*)

was limited to expansive regions around large cities. Radio, on the other hand, continued to serve small towns, and a large metro area that might have only a few TV stations often would be served by a dozen or more radio stations, some of them serving specialized communities—for example, ethnic ones. As Torosyan and Munro put it, for the radio industry "the concept of 'localism' has traditionally been held to be both a bedrock value and a competitive necessary" (2010, p. 33).

Recent studies tend to pursue the issues of radio localism from an economic/regulatory standpoint, especially deregulation of market structures by the U.S. Federal Communications Commission and the resultant concentration in station ownership (Hilliard & Keith, 2005). Reed and Hanson's (2006) case study of Allegheny Mountain Radio in West Virginia sought to illustrate that radio produced by and for members of a community was a viable alternative to conglomerate-owned commercial stations. In another case study, Hood (2007) examined the impacts of news produced outside the local market when radio stations are part of large ownership groups. Hubbard (2010) used an experiment and found slight preferences for local origination and a marginal preference for local ownership.

Law and Economic Issues

Radio is not the only area in which economic theory and legal issues lay at the root of investigation of community journalism. Coulson, Lacy, and Wilson (2000) examined a number of ownership and market characteristics of weekly newspapers in what they called a baseline study of the industry, documenting variation in type of ownership, type of circulation, geographic location, and day of publication, along with the impact of those variations on advertising rates, advertising cost per thousand, and circulation. Lacy and Dalmia (1993) compared penetration data for metropolitan dailies, community dailies, and weeklies in Michigan at two different points during the 1980s. They found that penetration declined similarly for weeklies and community dailies operating under the umbrella of larger metro newspapers, which they interpreted as the audience's seeing them as acceptable substitutes.

On the legal side, Hansen and Moore used a mailed survey of editors at weekly and small daily newspapers in Kentucky to see whether fear of libel created a chilling effect in what they published. Their work found that "respondents who had been threatened just once had a significantly higher chilling effect score than those who had never been threatened" (1990, p. 94).

Technology

Like law and economics, the role of new technology in community journalism is an area that scholars are starting to explore, with particular attention to the technology used by small-circulation newspapers. Niebauer, Abbott, Corbin, and Neibergall (2000) used the theory of diffusion of innovations (Rogers, 1983) to investigate adoption of computers for tasks across the operation at Iowa newspapers (newsroom, advertising, administrative, etc.). They found that daily papers large and small were well along in adopting new communication technology, but weeklies lagged behind. In another diffusion study, Ketterer (2003) surveyed small dailies and weeklies in Oklahoma regarding use of the Internet as a reporting tool and concluded that it had diffused to the majority of newspapers that had Internet access at that time. (It should be noted that since 2003, high-speed Internet access has increased in rural areas, making a follow-up study of particular interest.) Adams (2007) used an e-mail survey of editors to establish some of the characteristics of weekly newspapers' use of the Web for news presentation. Online editions were seen as complementary to the printed newspaper by the editors in her survey.

❖ CONCLUSION

Perhaps the key trend that stands out in reviewing more than a half century of investigation into community journalism research is the steady evolution of "community" as a concept that encompasses more than local geography. Janowitz's analysis focused on neighborhoods composed of only a few city blocks. Byerly favored the term "community" journalism over "country" journalism but still focused mostly on newspapers covering small towns and the rural countryside around them.

But over time, as Sim (1969) documented, greater mobility has loosened individuals' ties to narrow geographic locales. Individuals today commonly identify with communities that have nothing to do with their place of residence. Thus, a logical evolution of key themes from past research would investigate how those concepts of identity-building and intimacy of media and audience are articulated as the nature and definition of community evolve away from its geographic roots. An early example of that can be seen in Jackson's 1982 study that conceived of suburban community as more a "place of mind" than of locality. The idea that virtual communities can exist and reinforce the community ties of the offline world is another relevant area for research in the modern era (see, for example, Blanchard & Horan, 2000; Kling, 1996; Nip, 2004; Prell, 2003; Rosenberry, 2010a).

In this effort, Stamm's fine-grained analyses offer a theoretical basis for defining variables, especially the level of attachment (type and intensity of the "tie"), and creating definitions of community that transcend geography through "process" (shared interests) and "structure" (institutions). Although Stamm and his associates sought to hone certain concepts to new levels, at its core their research agenda sought to explain the connection between two basic variables: attachment to the local geographic community and usage of the corresponding local newspaper. The tools they created can now be applied to new ways of looking at community and social integration that go beyond that basic relationship, especially because many "communities of interest" exist and communicate online rather than through printed products.

Community media by definition serve narrow interests, first defined by geography and now by other criteria. Thus, a corollary avenue of investigation might relate to dangers inherent in narrowly focused media that inhibit community building by allowing like-minded individuals to merely reinforce one another's views without considering how their tightly knit group fits into broader communities—the process Janowitz called "specialization within generalization." As media become more fragmented, especially in the electronic and online arena, that concept seems especially ripe for deeper investigation.

❖ REFERENCES

Adams, J. W. (2007). U.S. weekly newspapers embrace Web sites. *Newspaper Research Journal, 28*(4), 36–50.

Akhavan-Majid, R. (1995). How community involvement affects editor's role. *Newspaper Research Journal, 16*(4), 29–41.

Bailon, G. (2005). Speaking Spanish. *American Editor, 843*, 5.

Blanchard, A., & Horan, T. (2000). Virtual communities and social capital. In G. D. Garson (Ed.), *Social dimensions of information technology: Issues for the new millennium* (pp. 5–20). Hershey, PA: Idea Group.

Bunton, K. (1998). Social responsibility in covering community: A narrative case analysis. *Journal of Mass Media Ethics, 13*(4), 232–246.

Byerly, K. R. (1961). *Community journalism.* Philadelphia: Chilton.

Chepesiuk, R. (2007). The thriving Spanish-language media: Challenges and opportunities. *Quill, 95*(1), 14–16.

Coble-Krings, L. (2005, September). *Weekly dilemmas: A study of ethics and community journalism in small towns.* Paper presented at the Huck Boyd Symposium, Milwaukee, WI.

Coulson, D. C., Lacy, S., & Wilson, J. (2000, August). *Weekly newspaper industry: A baseline study.* Paper presented at the annual conference of the Association for Education in Journalism and Mass Communication, Phoenix, AZ.

Daniels, G. L. (2006). The role of Native American print and online media in the "era of big stories": A comparative case study of Native American outlets' coverage of the Red Lake shootings. *Journalism, 7*(3), 321–342.

Dann, M. E. (1971). *The black press, 1827–1890: The quest for national identity.* New York: Putnam.

DeSantis, A. D. (1998). Selling the American dream myth to black southerners: *The Chicago Defender* and the great migration of 1915–1919. *Western Journal of Communication, 62*(4), 474–511.

Edelstein, A. S., & Larsen, O. N. (1960). The weekly press' contribution to a sense of urban community. *Journalism Quarterly, 37*, 489–498.

Fitzgerald, M. (2002). Latino papers grow like kudzu. *Editor and Publisher, 135*(1), 6.

Gutierrez, F. (1977). Spanish-language media in America: Background, resources, history. *Journalism History, 4*, 34–31, 65–67.

Hansen, E. K., & Moore, R. L. (1990). Chilling the messenger: Impact of libel on community newspapers. *Newspaper Research Journal, 11*(2), 86–99.

Hilliard, R., & Keith, M. (2005). *The quieted voice: The rise and demise of localism in American radio.* Carbondale: Southern Illinois University Press.

Hood, L. (2007). Radio reverb: The impact of "local" news reimported to its own community. *Journal of Broadcasting and Electronic Media, 51*(1), 1–19.

Hubbard, G. T. (2010). Putting radio localism to the test: An experimental study of listener responses to locality of origination and ownership. *Journal of Broadcasting and Electronic Media, 54*(3), 407–424.

Jackson, K. M. (1982). Local community orientations of suburban newspaper subscribers. *Newspaper Research Journal, 3*(3), 52–59.

Janowitz, M. (1951). The imagery of the urban community press. *Public Opinion Quarterly, 15*(3), 519–531.

Janowitz, M. (1967). *The community press in an urban setting: The social elements of urbanism* (2nd ed.). Chicago: University of Chicago Press.

Jeffres, L. W., & Dobos, J. (1983). Neighborhood newspaper audiences. *Newspaper Research Journal, 4*(2), 31–42.

Kennedy, B. M. (1974). *Community journalism: A way of life.* Ames: Iowa State University Press.

Ketterer, S. (2003). Oklahoma small dailies, weeklies use Internet as reporting tool. *Newspaper Research Journal, 24*(2), 107–113.

Kling, R. L. (1996). Synergies and competition between life in cyberspace and face-to-face communities. *Social Science Computer Review, 14,* 50–54.

LaBrie, H., II. (1977). Black newspapers: The roots are 150 years deep. *Journalism History, 4,* 111–113.

LaCourse, R. (1979). Native American journalism: An overview. *Journalism History, 6,* 34–38.

Lacy, S., & Dalmia, S. (1993). Daily and weekly penetration in non-metropolitan areas of Michigan. *Newspaper Research Journal, 14*(3–4), 20–33.

Lauterer, J. (2006). *Community journalism: Relentlessly local* (3rd ed.). Chapel Hill: University of North Carolina Press.

Littlefield, D. F., & Parins, J. W. (1984). *American Indian and Alaska Native newspapers and periodicals, 1826–1924.* Westport, CT: Greenwood Press.

Littlejohn, S. (1999). *Theories of human communication.* Belmont, CA: Wadsworth.

Loew, P., & Mella, K. (2005). Black ink and the new red power: Native American newspapers and tribal sovereignty. *Journalism and Communication Monographs, 7*(3), 99–142.

Mayer, V. (2001). From segmented to fragmented: Latino media in San Antonio, Texas. *Journalism and Mass Communication Quarterly, 78*(2), 291–306.

Melendez, A. G. (2005). *Spanish-language newspapers in New Mexico, 1834–1958.* Tucson: University of Arizona Press.

Motion pictures and youth. (1933). New York: Macmillan.

Murphy, J. E., & Avery, D. R. (1983). A comparison of Alaskan native and non-native newspaper content. *Journalism Quarterly, 60,* 316–322.

Murphy, J. E., & Murphy, S. M. (1981). *Let my people know: American Indian journalism 1828–1978.* Norman: University of Oklahoma Press.

Niebauer, W. E., Jr., Abbott, E., Corbin, L., & Neibergall, J. (2000). Computer adoption levels of Iowa dailies and weeklies. *Newspaper Research Journal, 21*(2), 84–94.

Nip, J. Y. M. (2004, May). The relationship between online and offline communities: The case of the Queer Sisters. *Media, Culture and Society, 26*(3), 409–428.

Northington, K. B. (1992). Split allegiance: Small-town newspaper community involvement. *Journal of Mass Media Ethics, 7*(4), 220–232.

Ojo, T. (2006). Ethnic print media in the multicultural nation of Canada: A case study of the black newspaper in Montreal. *Journalism, 7*(3), 343–361.

Paek, H.-J., Yoon, S.-H., & Shah, D. V. (2005). Local news, social integration and community participation: Hierarchical linear modeling of contextual and cross-level effects. *Journalism and Mass Communication Quarterly, 82*(3), 587–606.

Prell, C. (2003). Community networking and social capital: Early investigations. *Journal of Computer Mediated Communication, 8*(3). Retrieved April 19, 2001, from http://jcmc.indiana.edu/vol8/issue3/prell.html

Reader, B. (2006). Distinctions that matter: Ethical differences at large and small newspapers. *Journalism and Mass Communication Quarterly, 83*(4), 851–864.

Reed, M., & Hanson, R. (2006). Back to the future: Allegheny Mountain Radio and localism in West Virginia community radio. *Journal of Radio Studies, 13*(2), 214–231.

Riley, S. G. (1976). The Cherokee Phoenix: The short, unhappy life of the first American Indian newspaper. *Journalism Quarterly, 53*(4), 666–671.

Rivas-Rodriguez, M. (2003). *Brown eyes on the Web: Unique perspectives of an alternative online publication.* New York: Routledge.

Rogers, E. M. (1983). *Diffusion of innovations.* New York: Free Press.

Rogers, E. M. (1994). *A history of communication study: A biographical approach.* New York: Free Press.

Rosenberry, J. (2010b, October 10–12). *Online hyper-local news sites fulfill classic functions of community journalism.* Paper presented at the ninth annual Conference on Media Convergence, Columbia, SC.

Rosenberry, J. (2010a). Virtual community support for offline communities through online newspaper message forums. *Journalism and Mass Communication Quarterly, 87*(1), 154–169.

Ross, F. G. J., & McKerns, J. P. (2004). Depression in "the promised land": The *Chicago Defender* discourages migration, 1929–1940. *American Journalism, 21*(1), 55–73.

Shaw, E. F. (1978). *Newspaper reading in small towns* (ANPA News Research Report 12). Washington, DC: American Newspaper Publishers Association.

Sim, J. C. (1969). *The grass roots press: America's community newspapers.* Ames: Iowa State University Press.

Simmons, C. A. (1998). *The African American press: A history of news coverage during national crisis with special reference to four black newspapers, 1927–1965.* Jefferson, NC: McFarland.

Stamm, K. R. (1985). *Newspaper use and community ties.* Norwood, NJ: Ablex.

Stamm, K. R. (1988). Community ties and media use. *Critical Studies in Mass Communication, 5*(4), 357–361.

Stamm, K. R., & Fortini-Campbell, L. (1981). *ANPA News Research Report 33.* Washington, DC: American Newspaper Publishers Association.

Stamm, K. R., & Fortini-Campbell, L. (1983). The relationship of community ties to newspaper use. *Journalism Monographs, 84.*

Stamm, K. R., & Weis, R. (1982). Toward a dynamic theory of newspaper subscribing. *Journalism and Mass Communication Quarterly, 59,* 382–389.

Stephens, L. (1978). *The influence of community attachment on newspaper reading habits* (ANPA News Research Report 17). Washington, DC: American Newspaper Publishers Association.

Stevenson, R. (1979). *Newspaper readership and community ties* (ANPA News Research Report 18). Washington, DC: American Newspaper Publishers Association.

Stone, G. C. (1978). *Using community characteristics to predict newspaper circulation.* (ANPA News Research Report 14). Washington, DC: American Newspaper Publishers Association.

Stone, G. C., & Morrison, J. (1976). Content as a key to the purpose of community newspapers. *Journalism Quarterly, 53,* 494–498.

Stroman, C. A. (1981). *The Chicago Defender* and mass migration of blacks, 1916–1918. *Journal of Popular Culture, 15*(2), 62–67.

Suggs, H. L. (Ed.). (1996). *The Black press in the Middle West, 1865–1985.* Westport, CT: Greenwood Press.

Tezon, A. L. (2003). *Cheerleaders, watchdogs and community builders: How rural weekly newspaper publishers in the Midwest view their roles.* Paper presented at the Newspapers and Community-Building Symposium at the annual convention of the National Newspaper Association, Kansas City, MO.

Thornton, B. (2006). Pleading their own cause: Letters to the editor and editorials in ten African-American newspapers, 1929–30. *Journalism History, 32*(3), 168–178.

Torosyan, G., & Munro, C. (2010). EARwitness testimony: Applying listener perspectives to developing a working concept of "localism" in broadcast radio. *Journal of Radio and Audio Media, 17*(1), 33–47.

Viswanath, K., Finnegan, J. R., Jr., Rooney, B., & Potter, J. (1990). Community ties in a rural Midwest community and use of newspapers and cable television. *Journalism Quarterly, 67*(4), 899–911.

Weis, R. J., & Stamm, K. R. (1982). How specific news interests are related to stages of settling in a community. *Newspaper Research Journal, 3*(3), 60–68.

Bringing Scholars and Professionals Together ●

Gloria Freeland

Making the connection between journalism research and journalism practice is not always easy, and that is particularly true in community journalism. There are relatively few scholars conducting meaningful research of community news media, and even fewer working community journalists who have the time or interest to listen to what scholars in the "ivory tower" have to say about the practices of journalism.

There are, however, some efforts to bring academics and the profession together. One such effort is the annual Newspapers and Community-Building Symposium, cosponsored by the Huck Boyd National Center for Community Media at Kansas State University and the National Newspaper Association (NNA) Foundation. Since the 1990s, the symposium, which celebrated its 16th anniversary in the fall of 2010, has provided a unique opportunity for journalism educators and newspaper publishers and editors to share ideas and research relevant to community newspapers.

In the beginning, the symposium was scheduled as an add-on to the NNA's regular annual convention. After several years, however, attendees recommended that the symposium become an integral part of the convention so that more people might attend. Now symposium sessions are scheduled throughout the two-day NNA convention.

For the first few years of the symposium, completed research papers were printed and distributed to those attending the NNA convention. Now they are put into PDF format and distributed on CDs for NNA members, and they also are made available on the Huck Boyd Center and NNAF websites. Many of the papers have been reworked for publication in scholarly and professional journals.

Regardless of the distribution method, research topics covered in the symposia always have been varied and useful for community journalists. Over the years, topics have included ethical dilemmas in community-building; newspaper market studies; research of community newspaper redesign; Internet business models; building community involvement through religion reporting; computer-assisted reporting skills; bringing the obituary back to life; how to make a small newspaper look bigger online; the role of newspapers in communities when populations become more diverse; how weekly newspaper editors view their roles in their communities; the "ad rep" as business coach; training strategies; covering the military; ethics in photojournalism at community media; establishing a community history beat; academic-journalism partnerships; the importance of strong editorial pages; and many more.

All of those topics are important, but some that bear repeating are those dealing with how community media can reach young people, how community journalists can better cover the diverse interests of their communities, and how community news media can make the most of new technology.

Although community media haven't been immune to the "Great Recession" of the late 2000s, most have been able to weather the storm more easily than their bigger counterparts. As long as those community media continue to cover their communities well, they will, by all indications, survive and thrive. Journalism scholars could learn a lot from the resilience of community media, and community journalists also could learn a lot from scholars who carefully and seriously study all aspects of the journalism profession. The Newspapers and Community-Building Symposium and similar forums will continue to bring those two sides of journalism together and remain useful opportunities for scholars to showcase their research and to develop new research ideas.

Gloria Freeland is director of the Huck Boyd National Center for Community Media at Kansas State University and coordinator of the annual Newspapers and Community-Building Symposium held in conjunction with the National Newspaper Association conventions. Before beginning her career at Kansas State in 1983, she worked on several Kansas newspapers; was a Peace Corps volunteer in Ecuador; worked as a reporter, then comanager, of The San Jose News in Costa Rica; and was the communications coordinator for the International Trade Institute at Kansas State.

3

The Minnesota Team

Key Studies of Institutional Power and Community Media

Eileen Gilligan

National and metropolitan newspapers and broadcast media in the 21st century are making efforts to increase interactivity between their audiences and the producers of news. Three decades ago, the "Minnesota team"—Phillip J. Tichenor, George A. Donohue, and Clarice N. Olien—conducted a series of studies that showed how such interactivity already was taking place between community newspapers and their local audiences. Those long-standing, less formal procedures of give and take among smaller communities and their local newspapers may be what larger news organizations are today trying to develop and codify in an effort to hold on to their diminishing audiences. Internet-based communication aside, the media-audience interactivity that is becoming a bigger presence among mass media today has long been central to, a problem for, and sustained by the workings of community media. The theories and findings of the Minnesota team

form a foundation from which to examine not just community journalism in general, but more specifically the workings and effects of
Internet-based journalism and its interactivity with the many different
types of communities found in modern society.

Tichenor, Donohue, and Olien spent 30 years doing research
together at the University of Minnesota, where they focused on community journalism issues and, in doing so, provided some of the most
important works upon which modern community journalism research
can be built. Their sense of teamwork was explicit: they rotated lead
author position with each publication and insisted that colleagues and
students cite them in full as opposed to "first author et al." Although
their research endeavors spanned many media-related topics, their
major contributions can be grouped into three areas. First, their quantitative approach led to important theoretical development for the
overall field of mass communication research with the Knowledge
Gap Hypothesis (1970) and its revision in 1975 (Donohue, Tichenor, &
Olien, 1975). The trio also provided extensive research into community
newspapers and their audiences, which was typically the community
where each news organization was based; as such, the Minnesota Team
provided key research into the connections between newspaper readers and their community and the interactive nature of that relationship.
Calling it the "structural pluralism model," they demonstrated that
media actions vary depending on the type of community structure
in which they work. Finally, applying that research to the function
of news organizations or newspapers in all communities from small
to metropolitan, Donohue, Tichenor, and Olien (1995) proposed that
journalists do not act as much as watchdogs on government as they do
guard dogs, or protectors, of the community.

Their studies contributed broadly to theory building in the growing
field of mass communication, according to Tankard (1990). Although
still referred to as the Knowledge Gap Hypothesis, their proposal—
even in the initial paper of 1970—laid a clear foundation for developing
a theory of information flow and use in a community. That conceptual
framework continues to inspire insights and new studies as new media
debut and usage patterns change. Although grounded in community
newspapers as their research medium, their theories have been applied
across media forms, including forms that came to be long after their theories were first developed. Their succinct, direct, clearly written articles
make their work accessible to students, faculty, and professionals alike,
and perhaps reflect Tichenor's early training as a newspaper journalist.

❖ THE KNOWLEDGE GAP HYPOTHESIS

In 1970, when hopes were still strong for the media's growing ability to keep the public informed by distributing information more easily than ever before, Tichenor, Donohue, and Olien dispelled the myth of those promises. After more than five years of working together, they published their landmark study, "Mass Media Flow and Differential Growth in Knowledge," in *Public Opinion Quarterly* (1970). The "Knowledge Gap Hypothesis," as they termed it, proposed that people with more education and interest in public affairs and science would gain more knowledge from news media than would people with less education and less interest in public affairs. Although increased exposure to news media might lead to greater knowledge and interest in public affairs for those with less interest and education—or "status," as the researchers defined it—the increased exposure also meant an even greater acquisition of information and interest for those who already had a jump start. Instead of finding a reduction in the knowledge differential thanks to modern mass media, they found the infusion of information from the media had actually increased the differential, a phenomenon they named the "knowledge gap." That revelation, based on a combination of research including "news diffusion studies, time trends, a newspaper strike, and a field experiment" (p. 159), seemed to crack the notion that media could be the great informational equalizers between the educated and less educated. The researchers offered one possibility for closing the knowledge gap, however: sustained high-intensity media publicity that would lead more highly informed audience members to reach a ceiling of information while less-informed audience members caught up in knowledge. Corresponding to the times in which that research was conducted, the article concentrated on public-affairs knowledge and news about scientific gains, such as the space exploration programs of the era. Four decades later, the evolution of "new media"—such as smartphones, social networking, and iPads—calls for new studies along those lines to examine whether the gaps are decreasing or increasing in the new-media landscape.

In their groundbreaking 1970 article, Tichenor, Donohue, and Olien suggested "several contributory reasons why the predicted knowledge gap should appear and widen with increasing levels of media input" (pp. 161–162). Those five factors are (a) communication skills, (b) stored information (or existing knowledge), (c) relevant social contacts, (d) selective exposure (acceptance and retention of information), and (e) the mass media system itself. From the start, the researchers recognized the implications for knowledge-gap research in developing nations, both between and within countries' populations. Their findings also helped scholars study media other than news. For example, the knowledge gap is cited frequently for the successes and failures of the long-running Public Broadcasting Service TV show *Sesame Street*. The program was designed initially to increase the educational foundation for inner-city, low-income children, and although that did occur, researchers also found that children from families of higher socioeconomic status gained even more knowledge than the target audience, ultimately raising information levels but widening the gap between the "haves" and the "have nots" (Cook et al., 1975).

Tichenor, Donohue, and Olien revisited that hypothesis a few years later with an article published in 1975 (Donohue, Tichenor, & Olien, 1975). Although based in community newspapers, their work started a major stream of research that continues today. The Knowledge Gap Hypothesis spawned hundreds of studies around the world, and by the end of 2010, according to a Google Scholar search, it had been cited in 728 articles. Many of those studies have examined limited conditions and/or applied that theoretical approach to a number of different community issues, including health-related topics (Alcalay & Bell, 1996), rural planning (McDonald, 2008), environmental concerns (Griffin, 1990), political knowledge (Liu & Eveland, 2005), and international perspectives, such as political learning in South Korea (Sei-Hill, 2008). As the diffusion of computer technology has become more widespread, many scholars have applied the Knowledge Gap Hypothesis to what they called the new "digital divide" (McDonald, 2008), which represents the gap in access to computers and networks between the "haves" and the "have nots" (Van Dijk & Hacker, 2003). Although the Knowledge Gap Hypothesis initially was applied at a macro level of analysis, later studies that examined the influence of information processing (Grabe, Yegiyan, & Kamhawi, 2008), personal interest (Chew & Palmer, 1994), and motivation (Viswanath & Kahn, 1993) took the hypothesis to an individual level of analysis as well.

Tichenor, Donohue, and Olien (1970) pointed out that print media lacked "constant repetition which facilitates learning and familiarity among lower-status persons" (p. 162). That suggestion has particular utility in the study of community journalism in the Internet age. Perhaps an individual's use of the Internet may allow increased repetition that can more easily lead to greater knowledge and a shrinking knowledge gap on certain community topics and issues. Other technology, such as texting and email, also allows community members to quickly and directly receive information pertaining to topics of their choosing, particularly with regard to mobilizing information about local events or breaking news. Certainly the Internet allows for greater access to topics of particular interest to users who are motivated to seek that information, including information that may be absent or under-covered in community media. In addition, access to the Internet means access to a heterogeneous offering of information regardless of the homogeneity of the community in which the user lives. Those newer variables in the spectrum of media use give today's researchers a wide open field for new inquiry along the lines started by the Minnesota Team.

Despite the Knowledge Gap Hypothesis's enduring contribution to mass communication research, many do not regard that theory as the most important contribution to the field by Tichenor, Donohue, and Olien. Instead, many view it as a "bell ringer" that "might bring attention to their main contribution—the application of a structural approach to the study of mass communication," according to Tankard (1990), who wrote about the team and used comments they sent him in a letter in 1987.

❖ EDITORS AND THEIR COMMUNITIES:
   THE STRUCTURAL APPROACH

Unlike many mass communication researchers, Donohue, Olien, and Tichenor did not rely on *The New York Times* or other metropolitan newspapers as their focus of inquiry. Rather, they turned to the smaller, rural communities in which they lived and had grown up, many of which still host vital and viable community newspapers in the early 21st century. If the Knowledge Gap Hypothesis was the trio's big splash in media research and theory development, their ongoing work considering media use in smaller communities, often contrasting it with media use in metropolitan areas, became their mainstay. Those studies offer a lasting look at how people do and do not get their news. The Minnesota Team made it clear that small-town news media should not be overlooked as a source of data that can be applied and at times generalized to journalism and mass communication as a whole. The statistical differences they found between media in small communities and those in larger, more diverse (usually metropolitan) areas also support conceptualizing community journalism as a separate dimension from metropolitan and national journalism.

With two rural sociologists on the team (Olien and Donohue; Tichenor was the journalist among the three), the trio analyzed the influence of how communities are organized and how community structure relates to the distribution and use of media among citizens (Donohue, Olien, & Tichenor, 1980; Tichenor, Donohue, & Olien, 1973). They proposed a "structural model" that Cho and McCleod (2007) said

> provides a theoretical rationale behind relationships between community characteristics, knowledge, and participation. They [Tichenor, Donohue, and Olien] identify "structural pluralism" as an important community characteristic. High-pluralism (heterogeneous) communities are characterized by high population density, education levels, and per capita incomes. They also have highly differentiated economic infrastructures and exhibit more conflicts among diverse groups contending for power. Conflict tends to increase knowledge and participation levels. Moreover, individuals in these communities tend to have greater access to a wider variety of news and information, further elevating knowledge and participation levels. By contrast, homogeneous communities have low population density, education levels, and per capita incomes, with less differentiated economies. These consensus-oriented communities tend to be less accepting of social conflict. When combined with lower levels of information flows, these factors tend to lead to lower levels of knowledge and participation. (p. 208)

The structural pluralism model for how information flows in a community and how information is used allowed the team once again to provide a starting point for much subsequent research. Their structural model noted the importance of conflict as a news topic, as it tended to draw more attention from all community members than other topics.

Although Olien, Tichenor, and Donohue's research remained squarely at the macro level of analysis, future research along those lines by other scholars turned to the individual level (e.g., D. M. McLeod, personal communication, 2009). For example, in a 2006 study, Armstrong suggested expanding the structural pluralism model to a dual-flow concept. She argued that the community pluralism model should be revised to include a dimension of ethnic leaders within communities in addition to the traditional structural indicators the trio relied on. In a study of 31 U.S. communities where leaders were identified as white or non-white, Armstrong found greater statistical support for the two-dimensional model in "capturing the dissemination of power within a community" (p. 287). She also noted that isolating "the role of power distribution within a community and its influence on news content" reinforced "the relationship between community pluralism and its influence on news content" (pp. 297–298), in support of earlier findings by the Minnesota Team. Armstrong attempted, in essence, to combine the structural approach with a social-psychological approach Tichenor, Donohue, and Olien did not incorporate. Researchers who are interested in that line of research can look at the structure of a community and then go a step further to see who leads the important institutions of modern communities, including the institutions of communities not based on proximity (that is, so-called "virtual communities").

Twenty years ago, Tankard (1990) predicted a long future for studies using the structural approach. When he summed up that contribution by Donohue, Olien, and Tichenor, he wrote, "After all, the structural approach is dealing with the relationships between the mass media, knowledge, conflict, power, social class, and social inequality—some of the most important concepts in human society" (p. 267). D. P. Demers (personal communication, June 4, 2009), however, noted that many of the researchers who used that approach—and had studied with the Minnesota Team—had moved on to other areas of interest or even begun retiring, leaving that line of inquiry lying fallow. Given the drastic changes in media over the last decade, even more research questions wait to be answered. With Internet use at more than 75% in the U.S. population (Internet World Stats, n.d.), cable and satellite television available to nearly all households (National Cable &Telecommunications Association, 2008, p. 10), and texting being adopted as a dominant communication tool by "everyone" from teens to grandparents, how do those usages shift the relationships among media, knowledge, and power concentration in communities? How do those factors affect our perceptions of what communities are, and what role do those media play in the formation of new communities? The structural pluralism model provides an excellent starting point for addressing such important questions.

❖ THE GUARD DOG: PERSPECTIVES ON THE ROLE OF JOURNALISTS

In 1995, after three decades of studying journalism inside and out, Donohue, Tichenor, and Olien—all professors emeriti at the time— published "A Guard Dog Perspective on the Role of Media." That theoretical essay turned the myth of the watchdog journalist on its head. Instead of watching for errors, fraud, and other misdeeds among government officials and other leaders in a community, community journalists of the 1990s produced much more content that appeared to protect those officials, leaders, and the systems they worked in, according to the researchers. That perspective grew out of their studies using the structural approach to describe media roles in a community. They argued that in smaller communities, which tended to be more homogenous and consensus oriented, local media tended to be more supportive of local government and other key institutions in the community. In larger communities, which tended to be more heterogeneous and therefore more conflict savvy, the journalists or local media tended to perform more of the traditional adversarial role of watchdog, or at least did so more often than their small-town peers.

Donohue, Tichenor, and Olien (1995) argued that "the guard dog metaphor suggests that media perform as a sentry not for the community as a whole, but for those particular groups who have the power and influence to create and control their own security systems" (p. 116). In contrast, they argued, in smaller, homogenous communities with a "consensus atmosphere, the media are sleeping guard dogs" (p. 116). Where conflict or controversy is covered, it usually concerns an outside threat, such as a new requirement by the federal government. "Where different local groups have conflicting interests, the media are more likely to reflect the views of the more powerful groups" (p. 116). The researchers offered as an example the phenomenon of national discount retailers moving into rural areas: while community leaders might be concerned about losing locally owned downtown business, consumers might look forward to the benefits of having big-box stores in their communities, and in those situations, the media coverage was more likely to focus on community leaders' opinions while the opinions of less powerful citizens received less coverage. That follows traditional patterns of news coverage in which "regular" citizens receive less space in news stories than official sources (Sigal, 1973).

The guard dog metaphor certainly can be extended to larger media in larger communities, especially regarding coverage of U.S. foreign affairs by U.S. media. "The tendency is to present crises in a framework that is consistent with U.S. foreign policy toward the country in question," the trio noted (Donohue, Tichenor, & Olien, 1995, p. 117), citing Chang (1989) and other scholars (e.g., Hallin, 1989) who have documented the U.S. media's pro-U.S. bias in reporting world affairs.

Like most of the Minnesota Team's contributions, the guard dog metaphor is not limited to the study of community journalism. Their focus on community media, however, makes their studies especially important for community-focused research by others. For example, scholars could study whether Internet use by journalists and audience members allows more opportunities to gather information from a variety of points of view, including international viewpoints that previously have been essentially absent from community level discourse. Does that change the approach of the mainstream media in the U.S. to include more "outside" perspectives in international news coverage? Does that expand the reach and influence of community media when decidedly local issues (such as local tragedies and high-profile scandals) achieve national or global interest?

The guard dog perspective exemplifies the Minnesota Team's best scholarly ability, as suggested by Demers (2009): they took the pieces they liked best from a variety of theoretical approaches to develop their own approach. In their "guard dog" essay, Donohue, Tichenor, and Olien (1995) drew upon mainstream mass communication researchers, such as Minnesota colleague T. K. Chang, in addition to Herman and Chomsky's (2002) critical book alleging biased U.S. media coverage, especially with regard to the U.S.'s dealings in El Salvador. The Minnesota Team also pitted the guard dog metaphor against two other possible roles: "lapdog" and "oligarchy member." "Lapdog" media were viewed as completely submissive to community authorities and framed "all issues according to the perspectives of the highest powers in the system" (Donohue, Tichenor, & Olien, 1995, p. 120). The difference was that "the guard dog conception is based on deference to authority" as opposed to total submission, as guard dog media do report conflict depending on the situation and relative power of the groups involved, whereas "lapdog" media either ignore or gloss over such conflict (p. 120). Many critical scholars, on the other hand, have viewed community media as full-fledged members of a ruling oligarchy in society. Donohue, Tichenor, and Olien disagreed: "The guard dog perspective holds that media are not a separate or equal power, but that they provide *a means* by which the power oligarchy is maintained" (p. 122, emphasis added). Although that role may be easier to document or find among small community newspapers, certainly the scholarship of hegemony (e.g., Gitlin, 1980) draws similar conclusions regarding the mainstream media's acting to protect the status quo.

Positioning the guard dog metaphor for future research, the Minnesota Team (Donohue, Tichenor, & Olien, 1995) suggested several approaches for analyzing conflict and uncertainty: reporting on individuals versus power structures; intensity of guard dog reporting; evaluating media coverage by "outgroups"; and acceptance of the guard dog role in pluralistic communities. Some studies have attempted to follow up on the guard dog metaphor, but that perspective on the role of media and the research group's hypotheses remain ripe for future research, especially considering the increased level of public scrutiny and participation in communication via the Internet, handheld devices, and other communication technology.

❖ FUTURE CONTRIBUTIONS

The benefit and beauty of good theory is that it provides an enduring framework for understanding how an aspect of the universe works. Tichenor, Donohue, and Olien offered at least three important frameworks for analyzing the relationship between media and audiences and their interactivity. Although their research was based largely on community newspapers, others quickly applied their findings to the use of larger media, from national newspapers to television news. Applying their theories to the study of digital media and audience effects was not far behind, and will continue as the media and audience use of them continue to evolve.

Certainly the effects of differences in knowledge within communities will continue to be explored, especially as audiences for print news media move to online media as major sources of their news. Although most knowledge-gap studies look at information retrieved at one point in time, perhaps future studies will consider following news consumers as they switch their sources of news and then track the existence or size of the knowledge gap. As more community newspapers go online and as they incorporate multimedia storytelling, more opportunities will unfold for scholars to trace knowledge gaps on a variety of topics among particular communities.

The role of the media is changing more than ever as citizen journalists join the more traditional reporting ranks and as independent bloggers peddle their ideas to online audiences. In the new media landscape, it may become as difficult to define a "journalist" as it is to decide which type of "dog" that journalist appears to be. Ideally, having more journalists (amateur and professional), especially in smaller communities, may result in more watchfulness over government and other leading players in communities. Perhaps the notion of the journalist as watchdog will make a renewed appearance in that evolving milieu, or the watchdog role will shift to members of communities who are better equipped to gather and report criticisms of government, corporations, special-interest groups, and cultural institutions—including community media themselves. Scholars would do well to examine just how new-styled citizen journalists are carrying out those watchdog roles and whether and how professional journalists are changing their roles, too. Also, as scholars examine the decline of large metropolitan daily newspapers and the perception of a "failing" newspaper industry grows, it's important to remember the conceptual and real-world difference between metropolitan newspapers and community newspapers. The effects of Internet competition and a lagging economy on one dimension (metropolitan daily newspapers) are not necessarily the same on community newspapers, most notably printed weeklies.

Perhaps the area most in need of study is the influence of the audience via interactive communication with editors and other gatekeepers (as broached by Shoemaker, 1991). Tichenor, Donohue, and Olien placed much of the community's interests on the shoulders of the community newspaper editor. If interactivity truly is a goal of news consumers, then we ought to see that influence in the final products. For example, some news organizations have tried asking readers to vote online for the story ideas they think should be the top story in the next day's newspaper, or vote on which topics should receive the most in-depth treatment or coverage. Could such interactivity lead to news products that will be more reflective of community interests (and, by extension, keep those media in business)?

Tichenor, Donohue, and Olien (1970) pointed out in their original "knowledge gap" article that print media lacked "constant repetition which facilitates learning and familiarity among lower-status persons" (p. 162). Perhaps an individual's use of the Internet may allow increased repetition that can more easily lead to greater knowledge and a shrinking knowledge gap regarding certain topics and issues. Certainly the Internet allows greater access to topics of particular interest to users who are motivated to seek that information. In addition, access to the Internet means access to a heterogeneous offering of information regardless of the type of community in which the user lives. Concern about access to computers and the Internet seems to have waned in many places, with increasing integration of computers into public spaces such as schools, workplaces, libraries, and even Internet cafés (not to mention expansion of home Internet access). The Internet and related technologies open a new array of conditions for examining the knowledge gap, structural pluralism in communities, and the changing roles of journalists in the communities they cover, whether those communities are small or large, and whether those communities have members who live in close proximity or are scattered around the globe.

❖ REFERENCES

Alcalay, R., & Bell, R. A. (1996). Ethnicity and health knowledge gaps: Impact of the California wellness guide on poor African American, Hispanic, and non-Hispanic White women. *Health Communication, 8*(4), 303–329.

Armstrong, C. (2006). Revisiting structural pluralism: A two-dimensional conception of community power. *Mass Communication and Society, 9*(3), 287–300.

Chang, T. K. (1989). Access to the news and U.S. foreign policy: The case of China, 1950–1984. *Newspaper Research Journal, 10*(4), 33–44.

Chew, F., & Palmer, S. (1994). Interest, the knowledge gap, and television programming. *Journal of Broadcasting and Electronic Media, 38*(3), 271–287.

Cho, J., & McLeod, D. M. (2007). Antecedents to knowledge and participation. *Journal of Communication, 57*, 205–228.

Cook, T. D., Appleton, H., Conner, R. F., Shaffer, A., Tamkin, G., & Weber, S. (1975). *Sesame Street revisited*. New York: Russell Sage.

Donohue, G. A., Olien, C. N., & Tichenor, P. J. (1980). Leader and editor views of role of press in community development. *Journalism Quarterly, 62*(2), 367–372.

Donohue, G. A., Tichenor, P. J., & Olien, C. N. (1975). Mass media and the knowledge gap: A hypothesis reconsidered. *Communication Research, 2*(1), 3–23.

Donohue, G. A., Tichenor, P. J., & Olien, C. N. (1995). A guard dog perspective on the role of media. *Journal of Communication, 45*(2), 115–132.

Gitlin, T. (1980). *The whole world is watching.* Berkeley: University of California Press.

Grabe, M., Yegiyan, N., & Kamhawi, R. (2008). Experimental evidence of the knowledge gap: Message arousal, motivation, and time delay. *Human Communication Research, 34*(4), 550–571.

Griffin, R. J. (1990). Energy in the eighties: Education, communication, and the knowledge gap. *Journalism Quarterly, 67*(3), 554–566.

Hallin, D. (1989). *The "uncensored war": The media and Vietnam.* Berkeley: University of California Press.

Herman, E. S., & Chomsky, N. (2002). *Manufacturing consent: The political economy of the mass media.* New York: Pantheon Books.

Internet World Stats: Usage and Population Statistics. (n.d.). *Internet usage and population in North America.* Retrieved April 20, 2011, from http://www.internetworldstats.com/stats14.htm

Liu, Y., & Eveland, W.P. (2005). Education, need for cognition and campaign interest as moderators of news effects on political knowledge: An analysis of the knowledge gap. *Journalism and Mass Communication Quarterly, 82*(4), 910–929.

McDonald, D. G. (2008). Knowledge gap. In P. J. Lavrakas (Ed.), *Encyclopedia of survey research methods* (pp. 409–411). Thousand Oaks, CA: Sage.

National Cable & Telecommunications Association. (2008). *2008 industry overview.* Retrieved April 21, 2011, from http://i.ncta.com/ncta_com/PDFs/NCTA_Annual_Report_05.16.08.pdf

Sei-Hill, K. (2008). Testing the knowledge gap hypothesis in South Korea: Traditional news media, the Internet, and political learning. *International Journal of Public Opinion Research, 20*(2), 193–210.

Shoemaker, P. (1991). *Gatekeeping.* Thousand Oaks, CA: Sage.

Sigal, L. (1973). *Reporters and officials.* Lexington, MA: D. C. Heath.

Tankard, J. W. (1990). Donohue, Olien and Tichenor and the structural approach. In W. D. Sloan (Ed.), *Makers of the media mind: Journalism educators and their ideas* (pp. 258–267). Hillsdale, NJ: Lawrence Erlbaum.

Tichenor, P. J., Donohue, G. A., & Olien, C. N. (1970). Mass media flow and differential growth in knowledge. *Public Opinion Quarterly, 34*(2), 159–170.

Tichenor, P. J., Donohue, G. A., & Olien, C. N. (1973). Mass communication research: Evolution of a structural model. *Journalism Quarterly, 50*(3), 419–425.

Van Dijk, J., & Hacker, K. (2003). The digital divide as a complex and dynamic phenomenon. *The Information Society, 19*(4), 315–326.

Viswanath, K., & Kahn, E. (1993). Motivation and the knowledge gap. *Communication Research, 20*(4), 546–563.

❖ FURTHER READING

Donohue, G. A., Olien, C. N., & Tichenor, P. J. (1985). Reporting conflict by pluralism, newspaper type and ownership. *Journalism Quarterly, 62*(3), 489–507.

Donohue, G. A., Olien, C. N., & Tichenor, P. J. (1986). Metro daily pullback and knowledge gaps: Within and between communities. *Communication Research, 13*(3), 453–471.

Donohue, G. A., Olien, C. N., & Tichenor, P. J. (1989). Structure and constraints on community newspaper gatekeepers. *Journalism Quarterly, 66*(4), 807–845.

Donohue, G. A., Tichenor, P. J., & Olien, C. N. (1973). Mass media functions, knowledge and social control. *Journalism Quarterly, 50*(4), 652–659.

Donohue, G. A., Tichenor, P. J., & Olien, C. N. (1978). Community structure and media use. *Journalism Quarterly, 55*(3), 445–455.

Olien, C. N., Tichenor, P. C., & Donohue, G. A. (1988). Relation between corporate and editor attitudes about business. *Journalism Quarterly, 65*(2), 259–266.

Olien, C. N., Tichenor, P. J., Donohue, G. A., Sandstrom, K. L., & McLeod, D. M. (1990). Community structure and editor opinions about planning. *Journalism Quarterly, 67*(1), 119–127.

Tichenor, P. J., Donohue, G. A., & Olien, C. N. (1977). Community research and evaluating community relations. *Public Relations Review, 3*(4), 96–109.

Tichenor, P. J., Donohue, G. A., & Olien, C. N. (1980). *Community, conflict & the press.* Beverly Hills, CA: Sage.

Tichenor, P. J., Nnaemeka, A. I., Olien, C. N., & Donohue, G. A. (1977). Community pluralism and perceptions of television content. *Journalism Quarterly, 54*(2), 254–261.

Tichenor, P. J., Olien, C. N., & Donohue, G. A. (1976). Community control and care of scientific information. *Communication Research, 3*(4), 403–424.

Tichenor, P. J., Olien, C. N., & Donohue, G. A. (1987). Effect of use of metro dailies on knowledge gap in small towns. *Journalism Quarterly, 64*(2), 329–336.

Tichenor, P. J., Olien, C. N., Harrison, A., & Donohue, G. A. (1970). Mass communication systems and communication accuracy in science news reporting. *Journalism Quarterly, 47*(4), 673–683.

The Human Background to Research ●

Eileen Gilligan

There is an important life to research—behind what gets published in journals—that stems from numerous factors, from the researcher's childhood experiences to her choice of graduate school. While faculty researchers study questions about how the world works, graduate students study how that research gets carried out. Scholars' legacies extend beyond the printed page to the students they worked with, who soon grow into scholars in their own right. Phil Tichenor, George Donohue, and Clarice Olien trained many researchers as they followed their own scholarly agenda. In addition to teaching courses about public opinion, science writing, and media and social change, media scholar Tichenor joined rural sociologists Donohue and Olien as they worked through the agricultural extension program at the University of Minnesota to research small communities and their use of mediated knowledge. The duration of their collaboration is unprecedented in social science research, according to Guido H. Stempel in his 2003 book, *Media and Politics in America: A Reference Handbook*. The team members specialized with Olien as the methodologist, Donohue as the theoretician, and Tichenor as the writer, according to David W. Demers (personal communication, June 4, 2009), who received his Ph.D. at the University of Minnesota with Tichenor as his advisor. In 1994, the team received the Paul J. Deutschmann Award for outstanding contributions to research from the Association for Education in Journalism and Mass Communication. But true to tradition, only Tichenor showed up to accept the award; the three scholars rarely attended the same conferences at the same time (D. P. Demers, personal communication, June 4, 2009; S. Dunwoody, personal communication, May 9, 2009; D. M. McLeod, personal communication, June 12, 2009).

Although the three researchers spent their careers studying through the rural sociology center at a metropolitan university, their upbringing also was grounded in rural life. Tichenor grew up in Sparta, Wisconsin, and received his bachelor's and master's degrees in agricultural journalism from the University of Wisconsin–Madison by 1956. Donohue was born in the Long Island town of Great Neck, New York, in 1924, but earned his degrees from Washington State University in Pullman. Olien was born and raised in Clarkfield,

Minnesota, a town that 2000 census figures show had fewer than 1,000 people. She earned her bachelor's degree in secondary education from the University of Minnesota in 1955 and her master's degree in sociology with a minor in anthropology from there in 1962. Their paths crossed in the early 1960s at the Center for Rural Sociology, housed on the St. Paul campus of the University of Minnesota, when Tichenor took a job there as a writer for the agricultural extension service.

Preferring the title "Professor" to "Doctor," which he believed highlighted a "contrived social status difference between professional and Ph.D. faculty" (Demers, in press), Tichenor had the ability to appreciate perspectives other than his own. "One of his greatest strengths was his anti-dogmatic kind of thinking when it came to research," said Demers, now a professor at Washington State University (personal communication, June 4, 2009). After critical scholars Stuart Hall and Noam Chomsky spoke at Minnesota, Demers recalled Tichenor noting the similarities in their views and the structural approach of his work. Hall and Chomsky "saw the media as institutions of social control which was how Phil found it," Demers said (personal communication, June 4, 2009). Tichenor "basically brackets different perspectives and says 'What's the value in this?' . . . And he pulls it out of there without becoming judgmental," according to Demers. "Structure can't explain everything," he recalled Tichenor saying. At a time when other mass communication researchers were taking more social-psychological approaches, the Minnesota Team introduced the concept of conflict (especially over issues) into a community's variables.

Olien and Donohue worked with other sociologists at the center in St. Paul while Tichenor maintained an office there and in the School of Journalism and Mass Communication on the university's main campus in nearby Minneapolis. Doug McLeod, who worked at the center as a research assistant for three years, described Donohue as "insightful, charismatic and analytical. That, in combination with his physical stature, reminded you of a football coach" (personal communication, June 12, 2009). McLeod, now a professor at the University of Wisconsin–Madison, added, "He was someone you would want to follow into battle." The team's research interests grew out of Tichenor's "interest in journalism and [Donohue's] in community structure," explained McLeod, another Tichenor Ph.D. advisee (personal communication, June 12, 2009). They wanted "to see the role that media play in social conflict and high pluralistic versus low pluralistic communities." With regular grant funding, they worked with several graduate assistants and undergraduate assistants in a center with few distractions other than the library next door, McLeod recalled. "It was a great place to work."

❖ REFERENCES

Demers, D. P. (in press). *The ivory tower of Babel: Why the social sciences have failed to live up to their promises.* New York: Algora.
Stempel, G. H. (2003). *Media and politics in America: A reference handbook.* Santa Barbara, CA: ABC-CLIO.

Eileen Gilligan is a professor of journalism at the State University of New York in Oswego. She covered state government in Delaware as a newspaper reporter and earned a Ph.D. in journalism and mass communication research from the University of Wisconsin–Madison.

PART II

Theories and Methods

4

Community Journalism and Community History

Janice Hume

The history of America is written in the stories of its communities, and media have told communities' stories almost from the start. From centuries-old warnings of yellow fever and smallpox epidemics to modern accounts of community reactions to natural disasters, media have recorded the struggles and triumphs of their villages, towns, and neighborhoods. "America began in the quest for community," noted historian David Nord (2001), who suggested that our associations have been "built, maintained, and wrecked in communication" (p. 2). He wrote, "At the vortex of many collective efforts to build community or to undermine it has been formal, public, printed communication, including journalism" (p. 2). Alexis de Tocqueville (1840/1904) observed in 1832 the healthy appetite early Americans had for newspapers, and the importance of that reading habit for the health of the democracy: "The newspaper brought [Americans] together, and the newspaper is still necessary to keep them united" (p. 599). He explained:

> The laws of the country . . . compel every American to co-operate
> every day of his life with some of his fellow-citizens for a common
> purpose, and each one of them requires a newspaper to inform
> him what all the others are doing. (p. 600)

Indeed, newspapers have connected readers politically, economically, and culturally, not just in the U.S., but as Benedict Anderson (1991) argued, in nations around the world, from Latin America to Indochina. Newspapers followed people to the frontier and to the suburbs, changing with the times and evolving technologies, and adapting to new economic realities. They have been an integral part of the fabric of national life, and they remain rich repositories of community history, yet many of *their* stories have yet to be told.

This chapter surveys the histories of community journalism, and calls for more complete and varied research into the relationship between local news and the construction and maintenance of communities. There is much work to be done. The stories of small and small-town newspapers, local radio and television broadcasting, and now social networks and hyperlocal interactive journalism made possible by digital technologies are important historically in part because they help us understand ourselves. Sociologist Michael Schudson (1991), writing about the storytelling function of newspapers, suggested that

> the stories we tell ourselves and circulate among ourselves serve
> as reminders of who we are and what we're about. . . . [T]hese sto-
> ries, this culture, as a system of reminders make a very big differ-
> ence in what we do with and in our lives. (p. 427)

Today, mediated storytelling is changing thanks to interactive technologies that allow online discussion forums and citizen-generated photos, video, and commentary. The online obituary page provides a good example, as its traditional presentation in print has expanded to include visuals, music, and community conversation. The "'cyber-obit' now allows the bereaved to help frame the death stories and build the memorials, liberated from the linear, non-interactive formats of the past" (Hume & Bressers, 2009–2010).

But why is history important? Wouldn't scholars be better served spending their intellectual resources studying, for example, the modern economic state of community journalism, or its role in civic affairs?

Those are important and immediate concerns. Why should we look backward as well as to the future? In a famous 1931 address to the American Historical Association, Carl Becker admitted that history can "be understood only tentatively, since it is by definition something still in the making, something as yet unfinished" (1932/1985, p. 36). Yet we seek the past purposefully, according to Robert Jones Shafer (1974), because history enables us to "understand better than any other discipline the public events, affairs and trends of [our] own time" (p. 15). Historians seek to reconstruct the past "with fullness and truth," to "capture the thoughts and feelings" of a different era, and to comprehend history in its "fullness of meaning," according to James D. Startt and William David Sloan (2003), who write, "At the very least knowledge of what others have done before helps [us] to understand what it is possible to do" (p. 20). So why study *journalism* history? Schudson (1997) offers a challenge and a warning:

> Students of journalism or "the media" in general are often attracted to the subject because they believe journalism to be important. Fair enough. But the importance of journalism, relative to other factors in human affairs, is to be demonstrated, not assumed. (p. 46)

Unfortunately, the historical importance of community journalism, although acknowledged anecdotally, has not been fully demonstrated. Media scholars have made some extraordinary contributions, such as David Nord's (2001) *Communities of Journalism: A History of American Newspapers and Their Readers*; Sally Foreman Griffith's (1989) *Home Town News: William Allen White and* The Emporia Gazette; Christine Pawley's (2001) *Reading on the Middle Border: The Culture of Print in Late-Nineteenth-Century Osage, Iowa*; Gerald J. Baldasty's (1992) *The Commercialization of News in the Nineteenth Century*; David Dary's (1998) *Red Blood and Black Ink: Journalism in the Old West*; and David Copeland's (1997) *Colonial American Newspapers: Character and Content*. But to date we have no comprehensive scholarly history of community journalism. And although there have been numerous worthy smaller case studies focusing on a particular editor, an individual newspaper or broadcast station, a geographic region, or a particularly memorable event, together they provide a scattered record—a few promising glimpses but no clear vision of the past.

Perhaps that gap in the historical record can be explained in part because "community journalism" has been such a difficult concept to define. Some would consider it to be weekly—or at least non-daily—newspaper journalism, as did Robert F. Karolevitz, who wrote *From Quill to Computer: The Story of America's Community Newspapers* to commemorate the centennial of the National Newspaper Association in 1985. He noted the "semantic problem" of distinguishing big-city neighborhood newspapers from metropolitan papers, and editors from publishers, in setting the parameters for his work (p. 4). Writing in broad strokes, and in a celebratory style, Karolevitz considered the contributions of journalists from the colonial era to the computer era, and included not only a section about "Front Pages of the Past" but also mini-profiles of the origins of weekly journalism in all 50 U.S. states. David J. Russo (1980) tackled the history of the "country press" of the mid 19th century, exploring the origins and substance of local news reporting. He explained:

> Most American newspapers in the nineteenth century were published in towns and villages, that is, in communities whose small size meant that local news could naturally and easily be passed on orally. And yet, the so-called "country press" displayed the same tendency to feature regular accounts of local news as the city journals—and at the same time. . . . Why should editors of small circulation weeklies bother to write about matters that their readers already knew about? (p. 4)

Russo (1980) offered no clear-cut explanation for why community, or "country," newspapers began including local news, but he did find that in the mid 19th century, "newspapers in America—rural and urban—became, in effect, 'community journals,' that is, papers whose contents bore a significant relationship to the communities where they were printed" (p. 35). Those community journals provide a treasure trove of resources for the historian because, unlike long-lost radio and television broadcasts of the 20th century and early online publications, many have been preserved and archived.

❖   FINDING "COMMUNITY" IN JOURNALISM

So, can "community" be defined only as a small town, and "community journalism" the published, or broadcast, or digitized stories for and about that town? In her thoughtful *Home Town News*, Griffith (1989) sought to define community journalism in terms of its qualities, both attractive and otherwise, via the philosophies of William Allen White, the famous early-20th-century editor of *The Emporia Gazette* in Kansas. Small-town newspapers in White's world embodied "appreciation for the simple pleasures of life, celebration of the common man and woman . . . by redefining 'news' in terms of equality, familiarity, and continuity," she wrote (p. 159). But they also "reinforced the authority of economic elites . . . discouraged open discussion of controversies . . . countenanced the public shaming of individuals in the interest of enforcing moral norms" (p. 160). Griffith found that community journalism embraced the ideals of progressivism and boosterism:

> White had developed a new understanding of the purpose of the small-town newspaper, one that remains at the heart of community journalism today. In the *Gazette* he simultaneously celebrated and fostered a feeling of community that was based on the assumption that all its members shared his booster beliefs. In pursuing this vision he honored Emporians and their daily lives; he placed them at the center of a universe of concentric circles emanating outward from "Emporia, U.S.A." If this vision was provincial and often unequally applied, it nonetheless affirmed for many of its readers that their lives were significant and meaningful. (p. 184)

As those diverse studies illustrate, to begin to build a proper history of community journalism is to grapple with the very definitions of *journalism* and *community*.

Robert V. Hine (1980) has written about the features and values of the "ideal community," including not only a sense of place and definable space, but also shared perspectives—be they religious, psychological, economic, or cultural—and historical memory. Russo (1974) struggled to describe community and reviewed several sociological, historical, and theological attempts to do so. He wrote, "As to definition, one is tempted to urge that students of community allow the people whom they study to say what a community is. The people who live in them have always had some perception of what communities are" (pp. 11–12). Pawley (2001) asked, "At what point is a community too big to be considered local?" She wrote of nations and towns as "geographically bounded spaces symbolically endowed with the collective

memories of their inhabitants who attach to their neighbors, the countryside, and the urban landscape, enough emotional power to generate a
sense of community" (p. 4). Russo (1974) contended that states, regions,
and nations are communities, just as towns and cities are. "All communities are social and ecological—that is, they involve relationships
between human beings living in association with each other and within
their physical environment" (pp. 11–12). Daniel J. Monti, Jr. (1999), in his
social and cultural history *The American City*, writes simply that places
have stories:

> The secret of who we are as a people, why we mattered at all and
> the difference we made, is locked up in the civic diary we call
> newspapers and in the everyday routines that we left behind for
> others to follow or amend as they saw fit. It is not just the best and
> worst of who we were that we pass on, but the story of all our glo-
> rious near hits and misses as well, all the occasions when we came
> together and how we made sense of those moments. (p. 5)

Many scholars of communities note the existence and credit
the influence of local newspapers. Pawley (2001) noted that in the
19th century, few towns existed in which newspapers, magazines, and
low-priced novels weren't available. Local newspapers helped define
their communities, with the power to both unite and divide, she wrote,
by "drawing a boundary around those whom they imagined to be their
readers." She suggested that newspapers have "occupied a central
place in the cultural construction of American communities" (p. 169).
Historian Merle Curti's groundbreaking *The Making of an American
Community* (1959) noted the importance of the newspaper as a premier
"educational agency" in 19th-century Wisconsin. Scholars from the
time of Tocqueville have connected the idea of community—of intellectual and cultural associations—with democracy. "Social capital,"
including social trust, has fascinated recent media researchers who
have linked newspaper reading with community health, including
civic participation (Jeffres, Lee, Neuendorf, & Atkin, 2007).

❖   COMMUNITY JOURNALISM IN COLONIAL TIMES

The earliest newspapers in the colonial era did not serve such a noble civic
function. Richard Brown (1989), who studied the diffusion of information

in America from 1700 to 1865, noted that newspapers were nonessential, minor commercial ventures that did not match the well-developed familial and commercial networks for exchanging important information face to face or by letters. *The Boston News-Letter*, Anglo-America's first long-lasting newspaper, "rarely sold more than 300 copies per issue even fifteen years after [founder John Campbell] had started, and more often, especially in the early years, the figure was closer to 200" (p. 37). Hardly a news gatherer or news breaker in the modern sense, the *News-Letter* was more a reference source for political texts, a place for facts about the arrival of ships and the deaths of prominent citizens, and a record of extraordinary events. Copeland (2000), who has written extensively about colonial newspapers, noted a growth spurt in the mid 1700s due to the French and Indian War, and the public's need for information about it. News was becoming more important, and by 1775, 40 newspapers existed in America, including at least one in every American colony. He wrote,

> Newspapers depended on letters, people arriving in town by land or sea, other newspapers, official government announcements, and correspondents for news. The correspondent, a person who lived somewhere in or near a town, wrote to the printer telling him about local occurrences. The idea of a reporter who went out and gathered the news did not exist. (p. xi)

However, local newspapers did facilitate public debate of issues, Copeland wrote, including press freedom, inoculation, relations with native populations, women's rights, and education and religion, to name but a few.

Eventually, the biggest debate in colonial-era newspapers involved the question of independence. Standard media history textbooks such as *The Press and America* by Michael Emery, Edwin Emery, and Nancy L. Roberts (2000) and William David Sloan's *The Media in America* (2002) note the American Revolution as a time of great press influence. Rodger Streitmatter (2008) wrote,

> Such redefinition of human history doesn't erupt overnight, as forces had been working long before the fifty-six rebels signed their names to the Declaration of Independence. Among those forces were the words of determined men who possessed both the talent and the intellectual insight to craft passionate prose that demanded freedom from an oppressive government. (p. 7)

❖ THE PRESS AND FRONTIER COMMUNITIES

Although this chapter focuses primarily on the United States, community media the world over provide historical information and cultural cohesion, particularly from the frontiers of civilization in all eras. For example, Chris Atton and James F. Hamilton (2008) pointed to 14 radio stations founded in 2002 in Columbia, "owned and operated by indigenous peoples, enabling them to produce programmes that challenge the dominant representations of their communities" (p. 105). Kevin Howley (2005) pointed to community media around the world as asserting and protecting local identities against the encroachment of globalization (p. 40). The study of news media in frontier regions can provide a richer history of the expansion and retraction of communities over time. During the American National Period and beyond, newspapers moved west, helping to establish and define new communities as Native American publications sought to protect older ones. Indeed, western migration can be traced by the dates newspapers appeared in new communities in the territories. That "frontier press" has been the topic of much scholarly work about both individual newspapers and editors as well as about larger trends. Dary (1998), for example, sought "to capture the social memory of newspaper journalism in the West during the nineteenth and early twentieth centuries" and to "capture and affirm the flavor, emotion, and color of newspaper journalism" (p. xiii). He explored the writing and reporting styles of frontier journalists, their politics, their mixing of news and opinion, their boosterism, their business practices, their sometimes violent tendencies, and their technological challenges.

Some frontier press histories have focused on a particular state or region, such as Wanda Garner Cash and Ed Sterling's (2005) *The News in Texas*, an edited collection of essays written to commemorate the 125th anniversary of the Texas Press Association:

> ... newspapermen and newspaperwomen essentially became family with their counterparts from cattle ranches and grasslands, cotton country, the oil patch, mineral troves, farmlands, citrus groves and wilderness areas.... This fraternity has been a catalyst in the progress and development of Texas ever since. (p. xi)

Mark W. Hall (1980) wrote about journalism in California and noted that the earliest newspapers in that state resembled their colonial-era forebears. Other histories home in on specific towns, such as Fredric Brewer's (1991) "Against All Adversities: The Pioneer Printers of Brookville, Indiana," and James E. Cebula's (1979) "The New City and the New Journalism: The Case of Dayton, Ohio." Some authors have preferred to focus on influential editors, such as B. B. Tilley (1975), who wrote "A Voice in the Wilderness" about "Francis S. Latham and the *Randolph Recorder*" of western Tennessee; Lee Nash (1976), who wrote "Scott of *The Oregonian*: Literary Frontiersman" about Harvey W. Scott, an editor and literary leader in late-19th-century Oregon; and Lewis O. Saum (1970), whose "Colonel Donan and the Image of Dakota" is about a journalistic "boomer" who "convinced the potential settler that Dakota was Paradise rather than desert" (p. 271).

Some community journalism histories have looked to publications serving alternative communities that may or may not have been geographically bound. For example, Matthew Lindaman (2004) examined the ethnic newspaper *Ostfriesische Nachrichten* (or "East Frisian News"), which targeted a specific German immigrant population in Iowa in the late 1800s. He found that "by linking the isolated communities and inviting the East Frisian immigrants to participate in an open discourse, the paper allowed readers to reify old traditions while negotiating the new American culture" (p. 78). Gerald J. Baldasty and Mark E. LaPointe (2002–2003) considered the role of *The Northwest Enterprise*, a newspaper that "attempted to inform, unify, and advance African Americans in the Pacific Northwest. It acted as a force against white racism and as a voice of solidarity in Seattle and the surrounding region" (p. 14). Not so successful were mimeographed newspapers published in a California migrant labor camp in the 1930s; James Hamilton (1999) found that those workers failed to find "a cultural means by which [they] could collectively see their situation, organize, and work to change it" (p. 79). Another example was the Italian-language press in Pennsylvania, which, for a variety of reasons, including "short-sighted opportunism," failed to achieve any kind of political influence within the ethnic communities it served, according to Stefano Luconi (1999).

❖ RISE OF THE URBAN COMMUNITY

When rural Americans flocked to the cities during the Industrial Revolution, newspapers began to serve new types of communities. Griffith (1989) wrote,

The network of communities painfully created in the nineteenth century was progressively dismantled during the turn to the 20th [century.] [A]s the frontier closed, the cities that now dominated the culture swelled through immigration from abroad and domestic movement from farm to town and from South to North. (p. 27)

Industrialization and urbanization heralded a new era for journalism. The number of towns and cities with 8,000 or more people doubled between 1880 and 1900, and by the turn of the century, 33% of Americans were city dwellers. Daily journalism exploded, but weeklies, too, thrived, and tripled in number. John Cameron Sim (1969) noted that the decade 1910 to 1920 was a high point for weekly newspapers, with 16,850 publishing in the U.S. in 1910. Monti (1999) wrote of the role of "ethnic enclaves in contemporary cities." Though spread throughout a city, people of different ethnicities

> were able to remain in touch and were drawn back to their old neighborhoods by the shops, organizations, and acquaintances that stayed there. . . . [T]hese "unbounded communities" certainly were vital to the social well being of the persons who were tied to them. (p. 97)

Media historians have grappled with the changes in journalism during that tumultuous time. Nord (1985), for example, has written about the urbanization of journalism in Chicago, specifically focusing on *The Chicago Daily News*. He distinguished it, and newspapers like it, from the "big-city press." He wrote,

> I have called the urban vision of the *Daily News* a vision of public community—public because it was non-traditional, nonface-to-face, nongeographical, built on government, formal organization, and mass communication; community because it was rooted in shared private interests, common experience and sympathy, and a deep sense of independence. (p. 438)

Following World War II, Americans moved in droves to the suburbs, creating still more kinds of news-consuming communities and soon a vibrant suburban press to serve them. Hal Lister (1975) argued that the "suburban press" was an important "third force in newspaper journalism," different from metropolitan dailies and small weeklies.

Chroniclers of weekly newspapers during the mid 20th century worried that the community press would decline, but others predicted the community newspaper would survive and flourish. And in the 1970s and 1980s, interest in community newspapers "intensified and they, improbably, [became] the most lucrative newspaper properties in the country," according to Aurora Wallace (2005). With small staffs and high advertising-to-news ratios, they made money, and lots of it. Thus they became attractive to investors, and about 40% of weeklies were sold in the 1990s, many more than once, Wallace noted. Such ownership turmoil had an impact on local coverage and on the community connections upon which the community newspaper had been built.

Newspapers also had competition for local audiences and advertising revenue from other community-focused media—radio and television broadcasting. Robert L. Hilliard and Michael C. Keith (2005) wrote that

radio began as a local phenomenon, bringing information, then education, music and the arts, culture and entertainment to the communities in which radio stations were located. . . . Less than a decade after the first radio station with a regular schedule went on the air in 1920, regional and ultimately national networks expanded radio into a national phenomenon. (p. 1)

Unfortunately, wrote Hilliard and Keith, modern consolidation has resulted "in the demise of local radio services to individual communities, concomitantly resulting in the not-so-long-term possible demise of radio itself" (p. xiii). Charles Fairchild (2001) considered modern community radio to be different from mainstream commercial broadcasting, and wrote that "community radio stations in North America are structurally, operationally, and ideologically marginal institutions" (p. 4). In other parts of the world, however, community radio is an important form of grassroots communication. In Columbia, community radio "is used to hand down tradition, language, music and local wisdom and memory" (Atton & Hamilton, p. 106). Bush Radio in Cape Town, South Africa, has been used as an instrument of protest, according to Tanja E. Bosch (2006). In many cases, Fairchild wrote, the development of community radio was "due in large part to the strong reactions by many people to the aggressive expansion of specifically American media worldwide" (p. 279). In addition, local television programming efforts have existed since the 1970s, yet there has been "a schism between the promise of that access and its actual implementation and reception," according to Linda K. Fuller (1994, p. 1). The role of broadcasting in fostering communities needs to be explored historically and in depth. (The role of community journalism in broadcasting is investigated more deeply in Chapter 9.)

In recent years, Jock Lauterer (2006) has written eloquently about the role of community journalism in contemporary times:

> At their best, community newspapers satisfy a basic human craving that the big dailies can't do, no matter how large their budgets—and that is the affirmation of the sense of community, a positive and intimate reflection of the sense of place, a stroke for our us-ness, our extended family-ness and our profound and interlocking connectedness. (p. 14)

If community journalism has indeed served those functions historically, then it is the duty of the historian to demonstrate it, as Schudson charged. But where should that task begin?

The first thing to understand about history is that any study, no matter how comprehensive, will provide only a piece of the puzzle, because of the peculiar limitations of the past. "Empirical history is merely the application of system and rigor to the study of the past," wrote Maryann Yodelis Smith (1989, p. 317). "Of the events in an era, only some are remembered, fewer are recorded, and only a small portion of those recorded will ever survive to be studied systematically by researchers." Yet those surviving artifacts of the past—the primary sources— are critical to the historian's work, which "always consists of a reasoned, systematic examination of surviving recorded happenings, written in a spirit of inquiry seeking the whole truth" (p. 317).

❖ "DOING" HISTORIES OF COMMUNITY JOURNALISM

The value of community media archives as historical records cannot be ignored, but a study of community journalism need not rely solely on such archives as primary sources. According to Startt and Sloan (2003), "primary sources are the raw materials of history. They are contemporaneous records, or records in close proximity to some past occurrence. Or they might be the original documents" (p. 158). Yet the historian must have some intellectual basis for analyzing those raw materials. Secondary sources are later interpretations that help us understand the past. "Historical understanding," Startt and Sloan wrote, is critical:

> One must develop an awareness of "time" regarding circumstances now vanished. . . . Historians often speak of the need to avoid "present-mindedness"—that is, viewing the past in terms of the present—and stress the need to recapture the spirit of the times surrounding a study, to comprehend the feelings, persuasions, and emotions that once were real, to grasp how things happened in some past age, or to comprehend the nature of the forces that conditioned life in the past. (pp. 50–51)

Thus, the historian must be immersed in the era, and try to think as the people of that time thought. That requires a passion for history, and an investment of time, because it requires much reading, thought, and study. Once the historian is saturated in the material, it is time to develop a research question—because, as Smith (1989) cautioned: "for want of a research question, many noble attempts at writing history have failed" (p. 318). The research question is essential. It guides the process and helps the researcher find and evaluate the appropriate primary source material. For example, if the research question is what meaning *readers* of a particular era made of community journalism, the primary source material might be (as was Nord's in his study of readers as citizens in 18th-century Philadelphia) the correspondence readers sent to the newspaper, as well as commentary on newspaper reading in diaries and letters (see Nord, 2001, p. 200). If the research question is about the commercialization of news, the evidence might include (as it did in Baldasty's study of 19th-century newspapers) the newspaper content, manuscript collections, government documents, trade journals, proceedings of related associations, newspaper directories, and other publications of the era (see Baldasty, 1992, p. 8). If the researcher seeks to capture the social memory of an era's press (as Dary did in his study of journalism in the Old West), then sources might include not only newspapers of that time, but also books, pamphlets, manuscripts, diaries, and letters (see Dary, 1998, pp. 321–330). If the researcher seeks to provide a case history of a particular organization (as Bosch did, in writing the history of Bush Radio in South Africa), sources might include not only the existing archive, but also in-depth interviews with founders and staff (see Bosch, 2006, pp. 249–265).

Analysis of primary sources must be careful, thorough, and honest. Smith (1989) warned, "A particular caution in weighing credibility of evidence is the effect of language. Like any cultural phenomenon, language changes over time, and modern meanings cannot be imposed on words used two hundred, or even ten, years ago" (p. 323). Startt and Sloan (2003) noted that researchers must compile evidence, evaluate it, understand its "explicit and implicit meanings," and explicate its essence. "To do so requires time, patience, imagination, knowledge, and discipline" (p. 49). Of course, all sources, both primary and secondary, must be given full bibliographic citations so that future scholars can find and access them.

Nord (1990) has called for a foundation of economic and institutional social history of mass media, including studies on the "growing commercial and organizational complexity" of media, and also the "social environments in which mass media messages were received in the past," including "more careful study of readers and the worlds they lived in" (p. 647). Schudson (1997) has warned media historians to avoid certain pitfalls, including "the assumption that the media always are central to a historical event or process" and "the assumption that news media came into existence because they served a popular need" (p. 46).

Is there a need for community journalism? If American journalism has been and will continue to be important to the communities it serves—indeed, if the essence of community journalism is *community*—then serious historians need to continue the important work of trying to understand how and why. They—we—need to focus on the past relationships between local media and the construction and maintenance of communities, and to tell the stories of those communities' storytellers.

❖ REFERENCES

Anderson, B. (1991). *Imagined communities: Reflections on the origin and spread of nationalism.* New York: Verso.

Atton, C., & Hamilton, J. F. (2008). *Alternative journalism.* Los Angeles: Sage.

Baldasty, G. J. (1992). *The commercialization of news in the nineteenth century.* Madison: University of Wisconsin Press.

Baldasty, G. J., & LaPointe, M. E. (2002–2003). The press and the African-American community: The role of *The Northwest Enterprise* in the 1930s. *Pacific Northwest Quarterly, 94*(1), 14–26.

Becker, C. L. (1985). Everyman his own historian. In S. Vaughn (Ed.), *The vital past: Writings on the uses of history* (pp. 20–40). Athens: University of Georgia Press. (Original work published 1932)

Bosch, T. E. (2006). Radio as an instrument of protest: The history of Bush Radio. *Journal of Radio Studies, 13*(2), 249–265.

Brewer, F. (1991). Against all adversities: The pioneer printers of Brookville, Indiana. *Indiana Magazine of History, 87*(4), 303–333.

Brown, R. D. (1989). *Knowledge is power: The diffusion of information in Early America, 1700–1865.* New York: Oxford University Press.

Cash, W. G., & Sterling, E. (2005). *The news in Texas: Essays in honor of the 125th anniversary of the Texas Press Association.* Austin, Texas: Center for American History.

Cebula, J. E. (1979). The new city and the new journalism: The case of Dayton, Ohio. *Ohio History, 88*(3), 277–290.

Copeland, D. A. (1997). *Colonial American newspapers: Character and content.* Newark: University of Delaware Press.

Copeland, D. A. (2000). *Debating the issues in colonial newspapers: Primary documents on events of the period.* Westport, CT: Greenwood Press.

Curti, M. (1959). *The making of an American community: A case study of democracy in a frontier county.* Stanford, CA: Stanford University Press.

Dary, D. (1998). *Red blood and black ink: Journalism in the Old West.* New York: Alfred Knopf.

Emery, M., Emery, E., & Roberts, N. (2000). *The press and America: An interpretive history of the mass media* (9th ed.). Boston: Allyn & Bacon.

Fairchild, C. (2001). *Community radio and public culture.* Cresskill, NJ: Hampton Press.

Fuller, L. K. (1994). *Community television in the United States: A sourcebook on public, educational, and governmental access.* Westport, CT: Greenwood.

Griffith, S. F. (1989). *Home town news: William Allen White and* The Emporia Gazette. New York: Oxford University Press.

Hall, M. W. (1980). Journalism in California: The pioneer period, 1831–1849. *Journal of the West, 19*(2), 46–50.

Hamilton, J. (1999). Common forms for uncommon actions: The search for political organization in Dust Bowl California. *American Journalism, 16*(1), 79–103.

Hilliard, R. L., & Keith, M. C. (2005). *The quieted voice: The rise and demise of localism in American radio.* Carbondale: Southern Illinois University Press.

Hine, R. V. (1980). *Community on the American frontier: Separate but not alone.* Norman: University of Oklahoma Press.

Howley, K. (2005). *Community media: People, places, and communication technologies.* New York: Cambridge University Press.

Hume, J., & Bressers, B. (2009–2010). Obituaries online: New connections with the living—and the dead. *OMEGA: Journal of Death and Dying, 60*(3), 255–271.

Jeffres, L. W., Lee, J.-W., Neuendorf, K., & Atkin, D. (2007). Newspaper reading supports community involvement. *Newspaper Research Journal, 28*(1), 6–23.

Karolevitz, R. F. (1985). *From quill to computer: The story of America's community newspapers.* Washington, DC: National Newspaper Foundation.

Lauterer, J. (2006). *Community journalism: Relentlessly local.* Chapel Hill: University of North Carolina Press.

Lindaman, M. (2004). Heimat in the heartland: The significance of an ethnic newspaper. *Journal of American Ethnic History, 23*(3), 78–98.

Lister, H. (1975). *The suburban press: A separate journalism.* Columbia, MO: Lucas Brothers.

Luconi, S. (1999). The Italian-language press, Italian American voters, and political intermediation in Pennsylvania in the interwar years. *International Migration Review, 33*(4), 1031–1061.

Monti, D. J., Jr. (1999). *The American city: A social and cultural history.* Malden, MA: Blackwell.

Nash, L. (1976). Scott of *The Oregonian*: Literary frontiersman. *Pacific Historical Review, 45*(3), 357–378.

Nord, D. P. (1985). The public community: The urbanization of journalism in Chicago. *Journal of Urban History, 11*(4), 411–441.

Nord, D. P. (1990). Intellectual history, social history, cultural history . . . and our history. *Journalism and Mass Communication Quarterly, 67*(4), 645–648.

Nord, D. P. (2001). *Communities of journalism: A history of American newspapers and their readers.* Urbana: University of Illinois Press.

Pawley, C. (2001). *Reading on the Middle Border: The culture of print in late-nineteenth-century Osage, Iowa.* Amherst: University of Massachusetts Press.

Russo, D. J. (1974). *Families and communities: A new view of American history.* Nashville, TN: American Association for State and Local History.

Russo, D. J. (1980). The origins of local news in the U.S. country press, 1840s–1870s. *Journalism Monographs, 65*, 1–43.

Saum, Lewis O. (1970). Colonel Donan and the image of Dakota. *North Dakota History, 37*(4), 271–291.

Schudson, M. (1991). Preparing the minds of the people: Three hundred years of the American newspaper. *Proceedings of the American Antiquarian Society, 100*(2), 421–443.

Schudson, M. (1997). Toward a troubleshooting manual for journalism history. *Journalism and Mass Communication Quarterly, 74*(3), 463–476.

Shafer, R. J. (1974). *A guide to historical method.* Homewood, IL: Dorsey Press.

Sim, J. C. (1969). *The grassroots press: America's community newspapers.* Ames: Iowa State University Press.

Sloan, W. D. (2002). *The media in America: A history* (5th ed.). Northport, AL: Vision Press.

Smith, M. Y. (1989). The method of history. In G. H. Stempel, III, & B. H. Westley (Eds.), *Research methods in mass communication* (2nd ed., pp. 316–330). Englewood Cliffs, NJ: Prentice Hall.

Startt, J. D., & Sloan, W. D. (2003). *Historical methods in mass communication.* Northport, AL: Vision Press.

Streitmatter, R. (2008). *Mightier than the sword: How the news media have shaped American history* (2nd ed.). Philadelphia: Westview Press.

Tilley, B. B. (1975). A voice in the wilderness: Francis S. Latham and the *Randolph Recorder. West Tennessee Historical Society Papers, 29,* 109-120.

Tocqueville, A. de. (1904). *Democracy in America* (Vol. 2; H. Reeve, Trans.). New York: Appleton. (Original work published 1840)

Wallace, A. (2005). *Newspapers and the making of modern America: A history.* Westport, CT: Greenwood Press.

Reexamine the History of Big-City Community Journalism ●

G. Michael Killenberg

Long before the intriguing, controversial concepts of "public" and "civic" journalism emerged in the 1990s, many urban newspapers of the 1950s and 1960s had built reputations for connecting with citizens and fighting for the welfare of the communities of their cities. Although much of the study of community journalism today is focused on work in small towns or distinct neighborhoods, there is also much to learn from the community journalism practiced through the mid 20th century by the (now mostly defunct) blue-collar newspapers of America's big cities.

The history of big-city community journalism remains fertile ground for researchers, particularly the decades before Watergate and the emergence of New Journalism. Perhaps I am unduly influenced by memories of my childhood, but those decades before the 1970s inspired what felt like *real* journalism. Newsrooms were raucous at times, with both panhandlers and big-name lawmakers dropping in unannounced to kibitz or seek favors, and reporters and editors yelling at each other and occasionally throwing punches. Staffers walked, rode the streetcars, or drove second-hand sedans to work, and when they returned home, they talked to neighbors who, on sultry St. Louis nights, sat outside on what we called "the front stoop." No one needed to remind reporters and editors to "connect" with their communities—they already belonged to it. The blue-collar, common-man orientation of newspapers (and to some degree, local broadcasting, especially radio) helped keep journalists grounded in reality and sensitive to what mattered most to their communities. William Greider, author of *Who Will Tell the People?*, in recalling his introduction to newspapers in 1950s Cincinnati, said, "For all its shortcomings, the *Cincinnati Post* had one great redeeming quality. Like its reporters, the newspaper was frankly and relentlessly 'of the people'" (p. 290). By most accounts, *The Cincinnati Post* maintained that role right up to the end (it was folded in 2007 by the E. W. Scripps Company, making Cincinnati yet another one-newspaper city via the Gannett-owned *Enquirer*).

My interest in community journalism dates back to those days, as I watched my father, in rolled up shirtsleeves, direct news coverage at the *St. Louis Globe-Democrat*, another once-great Midwest newspaper that was "frankly and relentlessly of the people." Dad, who rose to executive editor of the *Globe* before its demise in 1986, teamed with its publisher, Richard H. Amberg, in "Fighting FOR St. Louis," the slogan emblazoned on the newspaper's newsstands and delivery trucks.

Amberg, all but overlooked by journalism historians, dared to lead his community through aggressive front-page crusades and pervasive civic involvement outside the newsroom. I recall that Amberg said, in a 1963 speech at Syracuse University, that newspapers fall into two categories: thermometers and thermostats. "A thermometer simply tells you the temperature and does nothing about it," he said. "The thermostat, on the other hand, tells you the temperature, but converts that information into terms of effective action." Amberg drew accusations of favoritism and boosterism as he led organizations, headed charitable drives, and served on dozens of community boards. In defense of his community involvement, he said, "I believe that a man running a newspaper cannot properly know what goes on in his community unless he is a part of it."

A distinguishing feature of the *Globe-Democrat* and other big-city community newspapers of the day was the "crusade"—a series of articles exposing and attacking a community problem and then pressuring public officials and community leaders into action. The *Globe* mounted more than a hundred major crusades between 1955 and 1967, the year of Amberg's death, and many of them led to legislative reforms and concrete accomplishments.

Even the most nostalgic journalist would acknowledge that the *Globe-Democrat* and other big-city dailies exhibited flaws. Few editors or reporters back then talked about ethics in journalism, although they were ethical by the norms of the day. "Diversity" did not exist by today's standards. In terms of 21st-century journalism and its buttoned-down, politically correct demeanor, Amberg's *Globe-Democrat* might appear intemperate and ill mannered. We study history, however, primarily for the lessons it holds, not necessarily as a model to emulate or celebrate.

What can be learned, then, from newsrooms of the 1950s and 1960s? For one thing, a researcher could test the most obvious hypothesis: Did newspapers of the earlier era truly speak for the people—or even to the people? Was their perspective one that scholar Herbert Gans described as "bottom up?" (p. 313); in other words, did the blue-collar big-city newspapers cover the community through the experience of the common man or woman, or did they rely then, as they do now, on public officials and figures as agenda setters and news sources?

A study of then and now could also explore the oft-heard criticism that today's "civic journalism" (née "public journalism") is nothing more than a marketing-driven repackaging of the traditional "community journalism" that is the focus of this book. Is that true? Would Richard Amberg applaud the variety of public journalism efforts advocated by its pioneering proponents, such as Buzz Merritt and Jay Rosen? Or would he find it a pale imitation of his own philosophy and approach to the craft?

Potential research questions for such inquiry are boundless. Newsroom organization and architecture, for example, offer other compare-contrast possibilities between past and present within the context of community journalism. What did journalism lose and gain when the newsroom, with its open rows of cluttered desks, scuffed floors and loud talk, gave way to an insurance-office model of cubicles, carpeting, and muted conversation? Did big-city community journalism suffer when metal detectors and uniformed guards deterred citizen access to urban newsrooms? Is the self-imposed isolation and detachment today's metro news media have from the public at the root of the current struggles (and in some cities, collapse) of the big-city newspapers of America?

At the very least, researchers who study the history of America's crusading urban newspapers will discover a powerful, exciting variety of community journalism seldom seen today. And perhaps, as big-city newspapers struggle for survival, journalism's past can offer hope and inspiration for a better tomorrow.

❖ REFERENCES

Gans, H. (1979). *Deciding what's news.* New York: Pantheon.
Greider, W. (1992). *Who will tell the people? The betrayal of American democracy.* New York: Simon & Schuster.

G. Michael Killenberg was the founding director of and is a professor in the Department of Journalism and Media Studies at the University of South Florida in St. Petersburg. He also is founder of USF's Neighborhood News Bureau in midtown St. Petersburg.

5

The Challenge of Measuring Community Journalism

Wilson Lowrey

Some have sung praises to community journalism, written poetically about it, admired it, placed it up high and out of reach like an antique urn. And we have tended to view the more personal aspects of community journalism in contrast to those of "big journalism," with its impersonal, bureaucratic entanglements. Community journalism is a haven "far away from the high-pressure, profit-margin-obsessed world of corporate journalism" (Cass, 2005–2006, p. 20). It happens in small, familiar spaces, encouraging citizens and editors to "sit a spell." The flip side of that romantic notion is that neither big-city journalists nor many journalism scholars have tended to take community journalism seriously, considering it either as irrelevant to the "big picture" or as a training ground for "real" journalism. In sampling newspapers for content analyses, many researchers have focused largely on national and global news media because of their presumed influence, and excluded weeklies and small dailies on the assumption that they don't matter so much.

But it's neither useful nor interesting to beatify or brush off the concept of community journalism based on such assumptions, as that blinds us to complexities and variability, and to the ways community journalism is situated socially. By considering its variability and multiple dimensions, we may take a measure of community journalism and its relationship to other well-studied social and psychological concepts—consequences such as civic engagement, social capital, or knowledge gain. We also can consider antecedents such as power structure, demographic makeup, and the resources available to various journalism enterprises. To do that, it helps to see community and community journalism as dynamic and many sided. The concept has many degrees, and ebb and flow. As such, quantitative analysis of community journalism must take place across multiple levels and across time.

Relatively little research published thus far on "community and news" actually mentions the concept of community journalism. Systematic, multivariate research on the relationship between community and media is certainly important, but it is also important for the social scientist to consider community journalism a unified concept, and to recognize its holistic, gestalt-like nature. As John Dewey (1915) observed, "There is more than a verbal tie between the words communion, community, and communication," (p. 4). It should be possible to meld the multivariate and objective with the holistic and normative, to "empirically ground a normative theory of the relationship between democracy and communication" (Friedland & Shah, 2005, p. 252).

This chapter discusses how past and recent scholarship suggest ways to empirically and critically assess community journalism as a dynamic concept operating on multiple levels in correlation with other social variables, while also maintaining a normative vision of communication and community, which are concepts with a common ancestry. This chapter also outlines an effort to produce a valid, reliable measure of community journalism—a multi-item index that assesses different dimensions of a news outlet's orientation toward community. The index measure is an attempt to blend empirical nuance with a vision of journalism's role in fostering community.

❖ COMMUNITY, NEWS, AND MEASUREMENT: A LOOK BACK

Democracy in America, by social philosopher Alexis de Tocqueville (1835/2000), offered an early analysis of the role of the local press, although that is only one of many topics in Tocqueville's expansive study. Tocqueville's approach reflected the methods of his age, as he pursued a master narrative, organizing field notes into a generalizing thesis and pushing "deviant cases along converging trajectories toward a predetermined outcome" (Hochberg, 2007, p. 24). But Tocqueville also recognized variability in social processes, comparing the local American press and its integrative tendencies with the French press and its elite opinion leadership (Friedland & McLeod, 1999).

In some ways, Tocqueville's comparative method offered a more broadly helpful analysis than later work related to community and news. Consider the research conducted by University of Chicago sociologists in the early 1900s: Robert Park, Louis Wirth, and others focused almost exclusively on the media-community relationship in the Chicago area, offering little comparison to such relationships in other communities. The process of immigrants' assimilation into Chicago urban life, via institutions such as the press, was assumed to represent a universal, generalizable process (Kreiling, 1989). Park (1955a) assumed a natural trajectory from simple traditional society to complex, modern urban society, a view influenced by Tönnies's (1887/1963) notions of *Gemeinschaft* and *Gesellschaft*, which refer to the contrasts between idealized communities of shared beliefs and larger societies of people associated only by their proximity to one another. Park believed newspapers could help immigrants socialize by providing content relevant to the immigrant's native culture as well as information enabling their involvement in the complex American society. Degree of complexity of social activities and organization revealed in newspaper content and reader survey responses served as Park's measures of acclimation to social complexities (Park, 1955b), although his data tended to be more anecdotal than systematic. Park charted a presumably natural movement toward American urbanization via spot maps of Chicago that revealed correlations between circulation patterns and the movement and demography of immigrant communities. There was little analysis of individual differences within groups. In that data he saw a "natural" ecology of the city, with subcommunities in primitive "physiological and instinctive" stages competing and integrating into an advanced, pluralistic urban community. He proposed that they achieved that advancement via the rational exchange of ideas, the local press being a major forum for such discourse (Czitrom, 1982; Elsner, 1972; Park, 1922).

Although limited by its narrow geographic focus, a clear strength of the University of Chicago approach lay in its rich, qualitative description and sensitivity to social context. The sociologists' field research was almost anthropological in nature, a common research approach at the time. The Lynds' "Middletown" study of Muncie, Indiana, in the 1920s, used similar techniques (1929). Such a holistic, gestalt-like approach precluded development of precise, replicable procedures, but allowed Park to make broad, forward-thinking arguments: for example, that community news reflects institutional control and shapes attitudes by focusing attention on particular events and topics, and that community news shows tension while fostering meaningful interaction. City mapping techniques also proved valuable, helping researchers track a large, shifting, and conflicting social environment, and revealing connections between community members and the social structures they inhabit. "Urban ecology" methods are still used today (e.g., Jeffres, Atkin, & Neuendorf, 2002; Kim & Ball-Rokeach, 2006).

University of Chicago scholarship regarding news and community would move toward more systematic, positivistic approaches as sociological inquiry across the field began to focus on phenomena that were measurable, specific, and short-term. That trend was influenced by the research of Paul Lazarsfeld at Columbia University. Lazarsfeld and his colleagues viewed individuals as existing within networks, and they focused on ways media messages and interpersonal communication can influence individuals within those networks (Zelizer, 2004). Lazarsfeld and his colleagues developed survey methodology and statistical techniques that shed light on individual-level differences (Friedland & Shah, 2005; Jerabek, 2006; Lazarsfeld, Berelson, & Gaudet, 1944/1968). Their use of panel studies allowed them to observe message movement through communities over time, and that novel approach brought dynamism to the ways scholars study media in communities. Lazarsfeld's work on multivariate statistics and latent analysis encouraged precise understanding of effects, and more precise concept definition (Jerabek, 2006). However, those techniques tended to ignore wider social contexts.

University of Chicago sociologist Morris Janowitz (1967) came to prominence during the Lazarsfeld years, but he inherited the old Chicago School interest in urban ecology and social context. In his analysis of the community press in Chicago's neighborhoods, Janowitz employed a more scientific method than did earlier Chicago scholars, using systematic content analysis and survey research, including random sampling of subcommunities to explore community integration. Janowitz recognized that readership varied according to various sociological and psychological processes, and he valued the individual-level aspects of media effects (Greer, 1967). And he did not assume that the news naturally urged communities toward *Gesellschaft*, but instead viewed the community press and the large daily press as playing distinct but complementary roles, a conclusion reached by other scholars of his time as well (e.g., Edelstein & Larsen, 1960).

Scholars increasingly began to challenge the idea that community cohesiveness and integration must be front and center in such research. Robert Merton, a disciple of Lazarsfeld's, suggested "media use" as a worthy dependent variable, and that notion gained popularity, partly due to funding from media companies (Czitrom, 1982; Zelizer, 2004). Keith Stamm (1985) and his colleagues noted that most research on community and media showed correlation between news use and community attachment, but shed little light on which led to which. He also noted that relationships varied by the way readership was measured, and by which moderating variables were used; he thought longitudinal studies could reveal causal direction as well as influences of moderating variables. We could learn whether news consumption sparks community ties, or whether ties lead to consumption—or perhaps both.

❖ OUTSIDE INFLUENCES

In the 1960s, a number of media scholars began to recognize the relevance of external contexts to the study of community, particularly state and national government agencies and national companies (Greer, 1965; Janowitz, 1967). As discussed in Chapter 3 of this book, Tichenor, Donohue, and Olien (1980) of the University of Minnesota pioneered the systematic examination of the role of institutional power on community media, although the notion was not new (see, for example, Park's discussion of "levers of control" over community media, 1922). Often called the "Minnesota team" because of the number of studies they published together, Tichenor, Donohue, and Olien employed a number of methods to study those issues, most notably content analysis and structured interviews with key individuals. For Tichenor, Donohue, and Olien, conflicts involving institutional power structures within and beyond the community shaped the ways issues were covered in the media as well as the ways communities acquired knowledge. They argued that in complex, "pluralistic" communities, conflict over public issues was likely to be discussed in public forums such as the news media, allowing for change; in smaller, more homogeneous communities, conflict over issues was likely to be downplayed in the press, and deference given to the status quo (Tichenor, Donohue, & Olien, 1980). That research correlated macro and individual levels, using aggregated data to measure the community's institutional structure and data from personal interviews to measure perceptions of community members. To some degree, the Minnesota team's methods echoed the field techniques of the Chicago and Middletown studies, but they also offered cross-community comparison, systematic survey techniques, and tests of effects across levels of analysis.

Concepts of external influence and social conflict and change received more attention as sociology moved away from the dominant functionalist paradigm, which portrayed community cohesiveness as natural (e.g., Parsons, 1960). Mark Granovetter (1973) observed that social learning—and therefore social change—were most likely to come through tenuous "weak ties" from beyond a social group rather than from stronger ties within. Similarly, sociologist Robert Putnam (2000) noted that social capital could help bond groups internally, as well as "bridge" diverse groups; media researchers have since studied the relationship between media and social capital (e.g., Fleming & Thorson, 2008). Such studies have involved comparisons across communities and wider social contexts, leading to greater use of community-level data derived from census reports (e.g., Kim & Ball-Rokeach, 2006), or aggregated from surveys (e.g., McLeod, Scheufele, & Moy, 1999). Also, those analyses allowed a systematic linkage between macro-level social structure and individual cognitions and behaviors— and therefore a link between social control and social change, as change requires human agency.

❖ RECENT SCHOLARSHIP ON COMMUNITY AND NEWS

Those landmark studies offer organizing concepts and methodological practices that are evident in recent scholarship regarding community news. Selections from that scholarship are explored briefly below. Also discussed below are relevant findings from a content analysis my colleagues and I conducted of 10 years of recent academic articles about media and community, to shed light on the pervasiveness of those concepts and practices in the field today.[1]

Multivariate and Multi-Level Research

Positivist multivariate research, conducted at multiple levels of analysis, is common in past community media research, continuing the work of Janowitz; Stamm; Tichenor, Donohue, and Olien; and others. A number of researchers have assumed multiple causes and consequences of variables such as community integration and engagement, and those have been studied across multiple levels of analysis (e.g., Fleming & Thorson, 2008; Friedland & Shah, 2005; Jeffres et al., 2002; Kim & Ball-Rokeach, 2006; McLeod et al., 1996, 1999). Some have suggested that macro-level factors—such as community stability, demographic complexity, and media markets—shape individuals' discussion networks at the middle level ("meso-level"), which in turn shapes cognitive sophistication and civic involvement of individuals (Friedland & Shah, 2005). Similarly, Kim and his colleagues (Kim & Ball-Rokeach, 2006; Kim, Jung, & Ball-Rokeach, 2006) proposed that community structure encourages meaningful discussion about community through interpersonal and media channels, leading individuals to perceive community connectedness. A model by Jeffres, Atkin, and Neuendorff (2002) also works on multiple levels, predicting that community structure, demographics, and distance from the "city center" all shape community media and interpersonal communication, which in turn influence individuals' civic attitudes and behaviors (e.g., Jeffres, Cutietta, & Sekerka, 1999; Jeffres, 2000; Jeffres et al., 2002). Jeffres and his colleagues and Kim and Ball-Rokeach used census data for macro-level measures, focusing on demographic shifts and spatial relationships of urban ecology. Those studies help explain meso-level and micro-level factors, which are measured through surveys of residents.

Research adopting multi-level approaches draws on a wide variety of methodological techniques, including existing community data, surveys and content analyses, and occasionally experimental research

---

[1]Three researchers coded 113 academic articles focusing on news media and community that were published between January 1995 and December 2007. Topics coded were theoretical approach adopted, methods used, nature of content sampled, the way "community" and "community media" were operationalized, and independent and dependent variables investigated, among others.

at the individual cognitive level (e.g., Shah, Kwak, & Holbert, 2001). However, there is little evidence of research using multiple methods, suggesting that few studies are fully investigating multi-level models (Lowrey, Brozana, & Mackay, 2008). Only 12 studies of the 113 we analyzed used some combination of audience survey, survey of professionals, existing data sets, and content analysis.[2]

Interpersonal and Mass Communication

Studies by Lazarsfeld, Katz, and others focused on communication patterns among individuals rather than on community ecology, and we see that emphasis today in the study of relationships among cognitive structures, structures of interpersonal networks, and media information. It is commonly thought that network communication may aid members in making sense of their communities, and community identity may be crafted symbolically through "storytelling" in the media and through interpersonal communication. Ability to "imagine" a community may lead to individual-level effects, such as self-efficacy in civic life, or perceived social capital (Kim & Ball-Rokeach, 2006; Shah, McLeod, & Yoon, 2001).

The dynamics of networked communication may best be assessed through multiple interviews in communities, and so comparative case studies across a limited number of communities may work better than sampling widely. Targeting a handful of communities for comparative study also makes it practical to analyze news content in smaller communities, as archives of content in small community media may not be accessible in online databases (even today, many community media do not have publicly available electronic archives of their content, particularly print-only media and those that have limited online offerings).

News media serve as a forum within which community members negotiate values and norms and make sense of their communities. Media frame that negotiation, such that the decisions by media producers are of key importance. Related to that, the previously mentioned analysis of academic articles (Lowrey et al., 2008) found that 18 of the 113 studies utilized rhetorical analysis of news content, with most focusing on ways news content frames community identity and facilitates negotiation of community meaning. Some studies also touched on ways macro structures influence negotiations by shaping media and interpersonal communication networks (e.g., Shah et al., 2001).

---

[2] Ibid., 8.

❖ NEWS AND NEWS USE AS INDEPENDENT OR
    DEPENDENT VARIABLES?

Many media scholars have struggled with the quandary of which
should come first in the study of media-community relationships—
questions of news use or questions of community attachment. Often,
the relationships are viewed as cyclical (e.g., Stamm, 1985). McLeod
and his colleagues suggested that news and news use operate cyclically
across multiple levels of analysis: "Discussion networks not only serve
as a companion resource for understanding community issues but they
also encourage . . . processing of public affairs [news] content and foster heightened receptivity to mobilizing content" (McLeod et al., 1999,
p. 263). That is, news use fosters interpersonal discussion, and interpersonal discussion fosters news use. However, more studies focus
on media and media use as a predictor rather than a consequence of
community integration. According to the aforementioned analysis of
academic articles (Lowrey et al., 2008), 44 of the 113 studies used media
content or media use as an independent variable to predict social
outcomes, and 25 focused on media or media use as a consequence of
social factors.[3] Only five studies treated media content or media use as
both an independent and a dependent variable, evidence that the full
testing of multi-level community-media models is rare.

    Among the studies using media as a predictor, few addressed
the normative question of what news media *should* be doing to foster
civic engagement, community integration, or change. Even fewer
measured the extent or effectiveness of such efforts, with the excep-
tion of some studies of "civic/public" journalism efforts that also
focused on distinct communities (not all civic/public journalism
efforts are community focused, but even the study of those is useful to
researchers of community journalism). A handful of studies included
multiple-item measures of the degree to which news reflected a civic/
public journalism orientation, with some using content analysis to
assess consequences of such an orientation, and others using surveys
to assess attitudes about journalism's role in community. The following measurement items were found to be common in studies of civic/
public journalism: (a) seeks "citizen's voice" through feedback, articles,
forums; (b) represents diverse views; (c) enables citizen involvement; and (d) helps solve community problems by offering solutions

---

[3]Ibid., 9.

(e.g., Bare, 1998; Jeffres, Cuttieta, Sekerka, & Lee, 2000; Nichols, Friedland, Rojas, Cho, & Shah, 2006).

Social Control and Social Change

Those civic/public journalism studies tended to assess the degree to which media professionals listen to community and enable social change, and the degree to which media shape or narrow a community's agenda, suggesting social control. Research on the power structure of communities also explores both change and stasis in communities, focusing on macro-level predictors. In our own study, we found that 15 of the 25 studies that used community media as a dependent variable adopted the power-structure framework in their analysis (Lowrey et al., 2008). In those studies, community was the unit of analysis, and social control was assessed via an aggregated index measure of "structural pluralism," or the diversity of a community's overall power structure. Other models also have suggested that the structure of power and control within and beyond communities can shape news coverage, news flow, interpersonal discussion, and individual cognition (Jeffres, 2000; Jeffres et al., 2002; McLeod et al., 1996, 1999).

Although the structure of communities and their contexts may offer the *potential* for constructive change, human-level action is needed to bring actual change. To analyze both structure and human agency, aggregated community-level data often are used in combination with surveys to gather individual-level data.

❖ MEASURING COMMUNITY JOURNALISM

The overarching goal of this chapter is to provide researchers with a framework for approaching the study of community journalism using social-scientific methods. With that in mind, the findings from past and more recent literature suggest a set of assumptions that should inform ways to measure community journalism:

1. News media play a role in shaping community and the way a community conceives or "imagines" itself.

2. That role is dynamic, involving ongoing give-and-take between media and community, and allowing both change and control.

3. The media-community "connectivity" concept is complex, operating on multiple levels and crossing multiple dimensions.

4. Structures within and beyond the community shape media and the ability of a community to shape itself.

This chapter's original argument was that it is possible to both explicate *community journalism* as a concept and to anticipate its social benefits in the whole. The objective and normative can and often do coexist.

If we conceive of a community as continuously imagining and re-imagining its own values and norms, we may also take the normative position that journalism plays a role in that process. The degree to which news media foster that *process of community* determines the degree to which media practice community journalism. So, in attempting to study community journalism from a social-scientific standpoint (or any standpoint, for that matter), scholars should keep in mind that community journalism should (a) facilitate the process of negotiating and making meaning about community, and (b) make individuals aware of spaces, institutions, resources, events, and ideas that may be shared, and encourage such sharing, in order to encourage discussion (Lowrey et al., 2008). Community journalism is an ongoing, interactive process involving some degree of both social change and control: community journalists *listen* to disparate, diverse views, and *lead* by responding to feedback by presenting cohesive symbolic representations of the community to the community. A news outlet practicing community journalism should also help clarify *community structure* for community members—including its power structure—thereby making it easier for them to interact and negotiate the meaning of their community.

A review of the literature suggests that *community* and *community journalism* are multivariate, multi-level constructs, and accordingly, any measurement of community journalism would benefit from an index comprising subindices. The higher the score on the overall community journalism index, the more thoroughly a news organization could be said to practice community journalism in a holistic sense. But each of the three subindices includes items measuring different dimensions of community journalism, allowing complexity and nuance within the whole. Dimensions and examples of items include:

1. A *Listening/Change* dimension (e.g., discussion forums, community blogs, letters to the editor)

2. A *Leading/Cohesion* dimension (e.g., special series or sections on local issues, staff-written editorials)

3. A *Community Structure* dimension (e.g., calendars of events, listings of ordinary public information, stories explaining and easing access to community facilities, organizations, and events)

Such measurable dimensions are specifically applicable to quantitative content analysis, but the index may be reworked for other social-scientific approaches, such as surveys, focus groups, and experiments.

My colleagues and I have tested that index in two empirical studies. In one, the index was applied to news websites to see if items in subindices correlated as expected (Lowrey, Woo, & Mackay, 2007). A factor analysis showed some confirmation and some surprises. Some items from the "Explaining Community Structure" dimension loaded with items from the "Listening/Change" dimension. Those items related to interactive online features, indicating that the dimension had more to do with the technology available to news outlets than to newsroom decision-making. Also loaded together were several items that indicated journalists considered readers' needs in their reporting—for example, by using "everyday people" as sources, and explaining how to take advantage of community services. Neither community size nor news outlet size seemed to influence the likelihood of finding such "community journalism" features (Lowrey et al., 2007).

The index was used a second time in a study of news outlets' efforts to maintain "sports community" in communities fragmented by local college sports affiliations (Lowrey & Woo, 2009). It was thought journalists would work harder to help their communities make sense of the community's collegiate-team affinities if the community had competing sporting teams. But the opposite was discovered, with news outlets scoring higher on the community journalism index in cohesive communities with only one dominant college sports team. News outlets scored especially low in communities split between a dominant college and a historically black college. Across all community types, "listening" scores were low. Those findings suggest some news outlets may be working to strengthen already cohesive communities, but are doing relatively little to aid "bridging" across diverse groups, at least in sports communities (Lowrey & Woo, 2009).

Both studies indicated that news outlets may not be making enough effort to listen to their communities. Findings from the first study suggest decisions about online news features and content may be shaped more by routines and resources of the news outlet than by needs specific to the community, while the second study suggests some news outlets are responding in cohesive communities, but are making less effort to aid communication in fragmented communities.

❖ MEASURING COMMUNITY JOURNALISM: LOOKING AHEAD

The community journalism index offers an approach that embraces the complexity and variation of communities. Its ratio-level measurement can allow examination of the process of community journalism within the context of structural constraints and motivators. It allows for comparison across communities and across news outlets, making it possible to generalize, which is not possible in one-shot case studies. The index does not assume that community journalism happens only in small-town newspapers, but allows consideration of such factors as size, corporate ownership, and multimedia delivery of news, and also allows scrutiny of relationships between large and small media operating in the same markets.

Unlike a scale, which requires measurement items to "hang together," an index derives validity from its plurality and comprehensiveness. The challenge is to make sure an important item is not left out, and that items are not duplicated (Diamantopoulos & Winklhofer, 2001). Indices also can be dynamic, adjusted from study to study as new contexts are encountered. The variations of the structural pluralism index are evidence of that.

The index suggested here is appropriate for analyzing other media forms, such as blogs and online discussion sites; those may offer ways to lead and listen, as well as explanation for navigating the online community's structure (e.g., instructions for use, policies and rules, notifications of upcoming discussions). All communities, whether geographically bounded or not, work to maintain and evolve identity in the face of external changes, relying on a shared, mediated forum to aid meaning-making.

That may be even truer for communities of shared interest and identity communities, which may be weakly supported by structures and institutions. It appears the "meso-level"—where interpersonal, networked communication takes place—is becoming more central to the process of community and to communication's role in that process. Communication and information through social networking sites assist the creation and dissolution of social networking communities, which capriciously appear and disappear. It would be interesting to adjust the community journalism index to measure the degree to which social networking mediums are oriented toward community, and which dimensions are more evident. For example, does the relative absence of structure and sense of location in those environments raise the importance of explaining community structure to community members? What macro-level factors are at play, and how might they shape communication and community in those environments?

The functionalism of an earlier age—viewing community as a contained, natural "biotic order"—should be avoided in the social-scientific study of community journalism. Each community's wider social context must be considered, as a diminished community may signal a wider realignment—dysfunctional for the community, but perhaps beneficial in a larger context.

We have seen the virtue of a normative vision of communication and community from the rich work of the University of Chicago, but we have also seen the dangers of oversimplification from assumptions of functional order. Likewise, we have seen the nuance and rich detail of multivariate individual-level analyses, but we have also seen the tendency for such research to lack unifying vision and purpose. Community journalism researchers should acknowledge the complexity of empirical detail and context in order to study communication and community, and that is especially true in a rapidly changing and increasingly complex media environment. The simple fact that media and communities are connected only sets the stage for more robust and rigorous study of the intricacies of those connections.

❖ REFERENCES

Bare, J. (1998). A new strategy. In E. B. Lambeth, P. E. Meyer, & E. Thorson (Eds.), *Assessing public journalism* (pp. 88–108). Columbia: University of Missouri Press.

Cass, J. (2005–2006). Wonderful weeklies. *American Journalism Review, 27,* 20–29.

Czitrom, D. J. (1982). *Media and the American mind: From Morse to McLuhan.* Chapel Hill: University of North Carolina Press.

Dewey, J. (1915). *Democracy and education.* New York: Macmillan.

Diamantopoulos, A., & Winklhofer, H. (2001). Index construction with formative indicators: An alternative to scale development. *Journal of Marketing Research, 38*(2), 269–277.

Edelstein, A. S., & Larsen, O. N. (1960). The weekly press' contribution to a sense of urban community. *Journalism Quarterly, 37,* 489–498.

Elsner, H., Jr. (Ed.). (1972). Introduction. In *Robert E. Park: The crowd and the public and other essays* (pp. vii–xxv). Chicago: University of Chicago Press.

Fleming, K., & Thorson, E. (2008). Assessing the role of information-processing strategies in learning from local news media about sources of social capital. *Mass Communication and Society, 11,* 398–419.

Friedland, L. A., & McLeod, J. M. (1999). Community integration and mass media: A reconsideration. In D. Demers & K. Viswanath (Eds.), *Mass media, social control and social change: A macrosocial perspective* (pp. 197–228). Ames: Iowa State University Press.

Friedland, L., & Shah, D. V. (2005). Communication and community. In S. Dunwoody, L. B. Becker, D. M. McLeod, & G. M. Kosicki (Eds.), *The evolution of key mass communication concepts* (pp. 251–272). Cresskill, NJ: Hampton Press.

Granovetter, M. (1973). "The Strength of Weak Ties," *American Journal of Sociology, 78,* 1360-1380.

Greer, S. (1965). *The emerging city: Myth and reality.* New York: Free Press.

Greer, S. (1967). Postscript: Communication and community. In M. Janowitz (Ed.), *The community press in an urban setting* (pp. 245–270). Chicago: University of Chicago Press.

Hochberg, L. J. (2007). Reconciling history with sociology? Strategies of inquiry in Tocqueville's *Democracy in America* and the Old Regime and the French Revolution. *Journal of Classical Sociology, 7,* 23–54.

Janowitz, M. (1967). *The community press in an urban setting* (2nd ed.). Chicago: University of Chicago Press.

Jeffres, L. W. (2000). Ethnicity and ethnic media use. *Communication Research, 27,* 496–535.

Jeffres, L. W., Atkin, D., & Neuendorf, K. A. (2002). A model linking community activity and communication with political attitudes and involvement in neighborhoods. *Political Communication, 19,* 387–421.

Jeffres, L. W., Cutietta, C., & Sekerka, L. (1999). Differences of community newspaper goals and functions in large urban areas. *Newspaper Research Journal, 20,* 86–99.

Jeffres, L. W., Cutietta, C., Sekerka, L., & Lee, J. (2000). Newspapers, pluralism, and diversity in an urban context. *Mass Communication and Society, 3*(2–3), 157–184.

Jerabek, H. (2006). *Paul Lazarsfeld's research methodology.* Prague: Karolinum Press.

Kim, Y.-C., & Ball-Rokeach, S. J. (2006). Community storytelling network, neighborhood context, and civic engagement: A multilevel approach. *Human Communication Research, 32,* 411–439.

Kim, Y.-C., Jung, J.-Y., & Ball-Rokeach, S. J. (2006). "Geo-ethnicity" and neighborhood engagement: A communication infrastructure perspective. *Political Communication, 23,* 421–441.

Kreiling, A. (1989). The Chicago School and community. *Critical Studies in Mass Communication, 6,* 317–321.

Lazarsfeld, P. F., Berelson, B., & Gaudet, H. (1968). *The people's choice: How the voter makes up his mind in a presidential campaign* (3rd ed.). New York: Columbia University Press. (Original work published 1944)

Lowrey, W., Brozana, A., & Mackay, J. B. (2008). Toward a measure of community journalism. *Mass Communication and Society, 10,* 1–26.

Lowrey, W., & Woo, C. W. (2009, April). *Journalism's role in bridging fragmented community: The case of college sports communities.* Paper presented at the Scholarly Conference on College Sport, Chapel Hill, NC.

Lowrey, W., Woo, C. W., & Mackay, J. B. (2007, August). *A test of a measure of community journalism.* Paper presented at the annual convention of the Association for Education in Journalism and Mass Communication, Washington, DC.

Lynd, R. S., & Lynd, H. M. (1929). *Middletown: A study in contemporary American culture.* New York: Harcourt, Brace.

McLeod, J. M., Daily, K. A., Guo, Z., Eveland, W. P., Bayer, J., Yang, S., et al. (1996). Community integration, local media use and democratic processes. *Communication Research, 23,* 179–209.

McLeod, J. M., Scheufele, D. A., & Moy, P. (1999). Community, communication and participation: The role of mass media and interpersonal discussion in local political participation. *Political Communication, 16,* 315–336.

Nichols, S. L., Friedland, L. A., Rojas, H., Cho, J., & Shah, D. V. (2006). Examining the effects of public journalism on civil society from 1994 to 2002: Organizational factors, story frames and citizen engagement. *Journalism and Mass Communication Quarterly, 83,* 77–100.

Park, R. E. (1922). *The immigrant press and its control.* New York: Harper & Brothers.

Park, R. E. (1955a). *Societies.* Glencoe, IL: Free Press.

Park, R. E. (1955b). The sociological methods of William Graham Sumner, and of William I. Thomas and Florian Znaniecki. In E. C. Hughes, C. S. Johnson, J. Masuoka, R. Redfield, & L. Wirth (Eds.), *Robert Ezra Park: Society.* Glencoe, IL: Free Press.

Parsons, T. (1960). *Structure and process in modern societies.* New York: Free Press.

Putnam, R. (2000). *Bowling alone.* New York: Simon & Schuster.

Shah, D. V., Kwak, N., & Holbert, R. L. (2001). "Connecting" and "disconnecting" with civic life: Patterns of Internet use and the production of social capital. *Political Communication, 18,* 141–162.

Shah, D. V., McLeod, J., & Yoon, S.-H. (2001). Communication, context and community. *Communication Research, 28,* 464–506.

Stamm, K. R. (1985). *Newspaper use and community ties.* Norwood, NJ: Ablex.

Tichenor, P. J., Donohue, G., & Olien, C. N. (1980). *Community conflict and the press.* Beverly Hills, CA: Sage.

Tocqueville, A. de. (2000). *Democracy in America* (H. Mansfield & D. Winthrop, Trans.). Chicago: University of Chicago Press. (Original work published 1835)

Tönnies, F. (1963). *Community and society* (C. P. Loomis, Trans.). New York: Harper & Row. (Original work published 1887)

Zelizer, B. (2004). *Taking journalism seriously.* London: Sage.

Methodological Choices Offered From the Study of the Norwegian Press ●

Sigurd Høst

For researchers and journalists who are interested in community newspapers and community journalism, there is much to be learned from the Norwegian situation. We have a newspaper system dominated by local dailies, but also a successful group of local non-dailies. Despite a marked decrease since 1999–2000, total newspaper consumption is still high, with a circulation of more than 1.2 newspapers per household. The decrease has affected only the dailies; the local non-dailies have had almost two decades of continuous growth.

Although all parts of Norway are covered by dailies with a local character, the distribution of non-dailies is more restricted. One third of the Norwegian population now live in a *commune* (municipality) with a paid-for, non-daily paper. Those municipalities are also covered by a daily paper that is published in the nearest town. In most cases, the household penetration of the non-daily is higher than 50% (Høst, 2005).

Although some of the newspapers were founded in the 19th century, Norway's system of local non-dailies is a product of the last 40 years. In the 1950s and 1960s, that group of newspapers was clearly on the decline. The largest of them became dailies, while the others remained small, poor, and understaffed. Four broadsheet pages per issue was the norm, and local material was combined with wire telegrams, material copied from other papers, and so forth.

The turning point came in about 1970 and was caused by a combination of several different factors. Higher incomes and a better economy made it possible for small non-daily papers to employ full-time journalists in addition to their editors. That economic growth was caused mainly by an expansion of local advertising, but press subsidies introduced in 1969 also played a part. The 1960s also marked the beginning of a series of municipal reforms that made local democracy and administration more important, and therefore strengthened the newspapers in their role as channels of information and arenas for local debate. A third factor was the technical revolution with offset printing and, later, personal computers, which made the production of small local newspapers much easier.

The cultural climate in the years around 1970 also was beneficial. In our country, the debate in connection with the 1972 referendum on the European Economic Community (now the European Union) was most important. That debate, which had a very strong center versus periphery dimension, gave new confidence to small, local communities. It also inspired people in such communities to start their own newspapers. The establishment of new newspapers is risky business, with failures as well as successes, but the net result was that the number of paid-for, non-daily local papers in Norway has increased from 99 in 1969 to more than 140 today.

Our research on local or community newspapers is dominated by two different approaches. One is the systematic description of the newspaper system. Because Norway is a homogeneous country with a population of less than 5 million, the "Norwegian newspaper system" is a meaningful unit for analysis. In addition to the newspaper system itself, it is possible to study the interconnection between the newspaper system, the system of cities and other local communities, and our system of local government.

Many of those studies have been inspired by the umbrella model of American economist James Rosse (see Compaine, 1980; Gustafsson, 1996; Høst, 1991, 1999; Rosse & Dertouzos, 1978). Instead of viewing newspapers from different geographic layers as competitors, however, our research is more concerned about the functions filled by local dailies and non-dailies and by geographic variation. The main conclusion is that the local non-dailies are usually found in small communities with clear geographic borders and a strong local identity, located in districts also covered by large or medium-sized local dailies. Suburban non-dailies are not an established part of our system.

The other important methodological approach for us is quantitative studies of newspaper content. Some of them are general descriptions of a representative group of newspapers, usually a mix of local dailies and non-dailies (Allern, 2001; Roppen, 1991). Variables studied include the types of content, the number and kind of sources used, the geographic focus of the stories, journalistic genres, and the amount of material produced by news services and other external sources. The general impression is that the local non-dailies cover a wide range of topics, but with special attention to municipal politics and the quality of services provided by the municipality (such as health care and education), the activities of local associations, and hard news such as crime and accidents. The newspapers speak to their readers as citizens and voters, and as members of the local community, while the reader as consumer seems less important.

In addition to the cross-sectional studies, we also have a few longitudinal studies of local non-dailies. They confirm that there has been a tremendous development from the 1960s to the 1990s. The editorial volume has increased, the journalistic presentation is more professional, and the content is purely local. Most small papers dropped their subscriptions to the national wire service NTB in the 1980s and did not substitute it with other sources of syndicated material.

One crucial question is whether work in small local papers is a special kind of journalism, or just ordinary journalistic work conducted in a small community. Today, most researchers will stress the similarities between local dailies and non-dailies, but also acknowledge that the content of the newspaper is influenced by the size and character of the community. The task of criticizing local authorities is usually not undertaken by the local non-dailies themselves. Instead, they give plenty of room for politicians, organized interest groups, and concerned individuals.

The most recent wave of debate started in 2007, when author and former editor Ingar Sletten Kolloen told the delegates at a yearly conference for small local newspapers that they wrote far too much about cozy topics such as local cultural events, anniversaries, and the like, and neglected their role as local watchdog. Although his description was exaggerated, "the curse of Kolloen" has been an important inspiration to Norwegian journalists and editors in small papers—many want to prove him wrong.

❖ REFERENCES

Allern, S. (2001). *Nyhetsverdier. Om markedsorientering og journalistikk i tinorske aviser* [News values. Market orientation and journalism in ten Norwegian Newspapers]. Kristiansand, Norway: IJ-forlaget.

Compaine, B. M. (1980). *The newspaper industry in the 1980s.* New York: Knowledge Industry.

Gustafsson, K. E. (1996). *The umbrella model—Upside-down. Nordicom Review,* 17(1), 181–193.

Høst, S. (1991). The Norwegian newspaper structure. In H. Rønning & K. Lundby (Ed.), *Media and communication* (pp. 281–301). Oslo, Norway: Norwegian University Press.

Høst, S. (1999). Newspaper growth in the Television Era: The Norwegian experience. *Nordicom Review, 20*(3), 107–128.

Høst, S. (2005). *Det lokale avismønsteret* [The local newspaper pattern] (IJ-rapport 2/2005). Fredrikstad, Norway: Institutt for Journalistikk.

Roppen, J. (1991). *Kva står i avisa* [What's in the paper]. Volda, Norway: Møreforsking.

Rosse, J. N., & Dertouzos, J. N. (1978). *Economic issues in mass communication industries* (Studies in Industry Economics Report No. 99). Stanford, CA: Stanford University.

Sigurd Høst *is a professor of media and journalism at Volda University College on the western coast of Norway. He has also worked as a researcher at the Institute for Press Research (now the Department of Media and Communication) at the University of Oslo, and as director of research at the Norwegian Institute of Journalism in Fredrikstad.*

6

Drawing From the Critical Cultural Well

Bill Reader

For scholars looking to test the waters of community journalism research, critical cultural studies offers a fairly approachable (yet adequately rigorous) starting point. That is because critical cultural studies (CCS) offer the researcher considerable flexibility to explore the concept of community journalism by taking an open-ended, yet still empirical, approach to investigating the interactions between community culture and journalism. The "cultural studies" aspect of that approach is particularly ripe for new research in community journalism; the acceptance of cultural studies into the journalism-studies discipline is a relatively recent development (Zelizer, 2004), and thus a wide-open frontier for researchers.

Without question, CCS's roots in Marxist theory and its interpretive, rather than scientific, approach challenges many traditions of 20th-century professionalism and science. CCS approaches can make some traditionalists uncomfortable, whether they be veteran community journalists or veteran journalism scholars; tenderfoot scholars who are drawn to the light of CCS may be warned not to fly too close lest they fall into the flame—or, as cultural critic Neil Postman observed two decades ago, the more advanced scholars who consider themselves social scientists "are apt to deprive others of the right to proceed in alternative ways, for example, by denying them tenure" (Postman, 1988, p. 10). Postman's critique is certainly dated, as quite a few CCS scholars have enjoyed success, earned tenure, and now are among the most important scholars in the journalism and mass communication discipline. But Postman's core observation remains most apt: because communication is a creative endeavor of humans, it often defies being studied in the same manner as planetary forces or the melting points of various minerals. Communication in all forms, including scholarly research, is essentially storytelling, Postman argued; communication scholars tell stories about how stories are told. Postman wrote,

> The words "true" and "false" do not apply here in the sense that they are used in mathematics and science, for there is nothing universally and irrevocably true or false about these interpretations. There are no critical tests to confirm or falsify them. There are no postulates in which they are embedded. They are bound by time, by situation, and above all by the cultural prejudices of the researcher. (1988, p. 13)

As I often tell my own students, the goal of CCS is not about testing hypotheses and finding answers, but rather about discovering new and more interesting questions. And there are many questions about community journalism that we have yet to discover.

This chapter is not, and cannot be, comprehensive, as the theories and methods employed by CCS scholars are numerous, diverse, and ever changing; instead, it is offered as a starting point for scholars who may be new to CCS and/or its application to community journalism research.

❖ ORIGINS, CONTROVERSIES, AND JUSTIFICATIONS OF CCS

The amalgamated term "critical cultural studies" is derived from two different traditions of scholarship: cultural studies as practiced at the Birmingham Centre for Contemporary Cultural Studies of the 1960s, and its predecessor from the Continent, the critical theory traditions established in the 1930s most often aligned with the "Frankfurt School." The cultural studies tradition of Canada and the U.S. is considered a derivation from the British model. Knowing those distinctions is important to some extent, as the critical-theory tradition focuses more on sociopolitical structures and an overarching goal to effect positive social change (Macey, 2001, p. 75), whereas the cultural studies traditions take a broader approach to study culture in all its complexity, from major social movements to mundane and passing fads in popular culture (Macey, 2001, p. 77). But the overlap in the foundations and key works of those traditions cannot be ignored: they both evolved from the theories of Marx and others concerned with social divisions of class, wealth, and power. In fact, the early cultural studies efforts of the 1960s and 1970s drew heavily from the works of critical theorists from earlier decades. The pioneers of both traditions also had in common an objection to the idea that a positivistic, scientific approach to scholarly inquiry was the only legitimate means to study and understand society.

Collectively, those traditions introduced and by the end of the 20th century legitimized a new paradigm of social research. That paradigm embraced and mixed various forms of critical analysis as research methods, and it introduced and advanced theories that challenge (and may even defy) scientific measurement. It also encouraged pluralistic and often polysemic interpretations of cultural phenomena. And it eventually gave rise to and solidified the concept of post-structuralism across multiple disciplines (and enabled the development of some newer disciplines, such as film studies, gender studies, and fan studies, to name but a few). Today, many graduate-level textbooks mention the same pioneering theorists as setting the foundations for critical cultural studies—Marx, Gramsci, Horkheimer, Adorno, Althusser—as well as the contributions of more modern theorists from both traditions, including Williams, Habermas, Barthes, Benjamin, Marcuse, Hall, Foucault, bell hooks, Friedan, McLuhan, Pollock, Carey, and many others. The approaches apply to the entire catalog of the humanities, from anthropology to women's studies. For students and scholars new to the paradigm, there are a number of useful edited volumes that pull together key works from many of those and other CCS scholars, such as collections edited by Durham and Kellner (2001) and Malpas and Wake (2006).

In terms of media studies, the CCS approach has largely been applied to study of entertainment media. Examples include observations by Larry Gross (1989) of how sexual minorities had been "invisible" in mainstream media; Herman Gray's examination of the various ways African Americans are portrayed on network television (1995); and a more recent study by Carol A. Stabile (2009) of the representations of gender in superhero stories.

To a somewhat lesser degree, critical cultural inquiry has been applied to journalism specifically, as the news media are generally viewed as institutions of cultural ideology and therefore are a common target of critical analysis. Antonio Gramsci (1985) remarked that the press of his time (the early 20th century) was the "most prominent and dynamic part" of the ideological structure of society (p. 389). Those ideas have been expanded and refined through the years by other scholars, such as Chantal Mouffe and Ernesto Laclau (see Carpentier & Cammaerts, 2006). The slow and sometimes contentious acceptance of CCS in journalism-studies circles may have a lot to do with the tensions between the two disciplines: one (journalism) traditionally devoted to the scientific approach of "objectively" recording observed "reality," the other (CCS) rejecting the possibility of objective observation or the existence of universal meanings. The tensions between the two can sometimes lead to open feuding. Consider the following from Australian scholar and publisher Keith Windschuttle:

> The body of work called media theory does not deserve the academic standing it has and . . . it has no place in professional education of journalists. Moreover, it is self-contradictory and intellectually incoherent. Its success derives from academic fashions and politics rather than logic and scholarship. In fact, of the two, the underlying principles of journalism education have by far the greater intellectual and scholarly integrity. (2000, p. 146)

A more balanced consideration of the apparent incompatibilities between cultural studies and journalism studies was offered by American media scholar Barbie Zelizer:

> Cultural inquiry forces an examination of the tensions between how journalism likes to see itself and how it looks in the eyes of others, while adopting a view of journalistic conventions,

routines, and practices as dynamic and contingent on situational and historical circumstance. (2004, p. 103)

Zelizer continued, "The uneasiness with which cultural analysis encounters journalism's predilection for facts, truth, and reality has been reflected in an ambivalence toward journalism in cultural studies" (p. 105). As such, CCS research reports can be hard to find in journalism-studies journals, although more have been published in those journals over the past decade. Examples include Karin Wahl-Jorgensen's (2005) critique of "journalism-on-the-cheap" and lack of political coverage in the local weekly newspapers in Britain, and Wendy Weinhold's (2008) ethnographic study of how community journalists in America often adapt their professional values to the profit motives of their employers. Of particular interest is the work of Kitty van Vuuren of the University of Queensland's Centre for Critical and Cultural Studies, who has studied rural community newspapers (van Vuuren, 2007) and community radio (van Vuuren, 2006) in Australia.

The advantages of taking a CCS approach to study community journalism make it a challenge worth undertaking. Community journalists must have strong, reflexive knowledge about the communities they serve, and the journalism they produce is influenced by the cultures of those communities. The unique aspects of a specific community, and the news media serving that community, can be discovered and explained quite effectively with critical cultural inquiry, and the results would be useful not only to journalism scholars, but also to journalists and the members of their communities.

❖ APPLYING CCS TO COMMUNITY JOURNALISM: METHODS

A critical cultural study of community journalism must begin with a recognition that the CCS approach is in many ways inverse to the social-scientific approach. Both begin with identifying a phenomenon worthy of study and reviewing any existing literature related to that phenomenon, but after that, the two approaches differ greatly. Social-scientific studies are generally carefully structured and meticulous in terms of developing hypotheses, research questions, and sampling and analysis schemas, often using some experimental or quantitative method that leads to statistical analysis or qualitative means that are generally objective and descriptive (such as the social-scientific approach to history). CCS studies often are more like open-ended explorations. Both approaches certainly lead to discovery, but in profoundly different ways. As Switzer and Ryan (2002) explain,

> critical-cultural scholars challenge the assumptions, premises, conditions, texts, and contexts of journalism and mass communication practice, teaching, and scholarship. They are not bound to any single method. Many employ approaches that have been influential in other disciplines (e.g., history, sociology, anthropology, literature), and they subject the methods themselves to critical analyses. (p. 213)

The open methodological structure in the CCS approach may be intimidating and/or confusing to some scholars, but to others it can be liberating. As with other approaches to media research, however, a credible report from a CCS study must be rigorous, scrupulously accurate, and intellectually honest. Such a study may be less confining than one carried out using social-scientific methods, but CCS approaches still require hard work.

A critical cultural study of community journalism, then, might begin with the scholar first learning as much as possible about the community in question and then explaining it to others. Consider a recent study by Leela Tanikella (2009), which analyzed Indo-Caribbean media in New York City. Tanikella's article includes background about that "twice migrant" population of various New York neighborhoods, explaining how they largely emigrated from Trinidad and Tobago or Guyana and are descended from indentured laborers brought there from India in the 1800s. Many Indo-Caribbeans live in New York neighborhoods alongside immigrants from India, which creates an interesting mix of cultures that have common ethnicities but different cultural backgrounds. Tanikella opened the article with a first-person account of her visit with an Indo-Caribbean man who lived in New York but visited his home country every year to attend an Islamic ritual event, and described how he took with him an article printed in the New York–published *Caribbean Daylight Global News*; the article originally had been published in the online version of a major Guyanese daily newspaper. The study itself focused on how Indo-Caribbean media in New York (several radio stations and many free weekly newspapers) linked Indo-Caribbean New Yorkers to each other but also provided news from their home countries, as well as Hindu teachings and Bollywood news (p. 172). The analysis of such community media draws upon the author's deep understanding of the complexities of the communities those media serve.

Conceptualizing a CCS research project also will utilize any number of methods that are generally considered under the "qualitative" umbrella. If the study will focus on published works—such as community newsletters or online discussion threads—then the scholar will likely use some form of *textual analysis*. A textual analysis could follow a loosely structured approach, such as that suggested by McKee (2003). Or it could take a more focused approach, such as semiotics as suggested by Chandler (2002), discourse analysis as suggested by Fairclough (2003), or various approaches to visual research as suggested by Emmison and Smith (2000).

If the study will focus on information that needs to be gathered from community citizens, then some form of *qualitative interviewing* would be appropriate. Qualitative interviewing is not to be confused with polling or survey research, as the goal is not to assess broad public opinions, but rather to consider many different individual opinions and ideas. The specific method of interviewing should be compatible with both the information sought and the theory that is to be used to guide the analysis, but should not be based on preconceptions or prejudices. As one researcher wrote, "One has to be able to change the viewpoint, lens and focal distance as freely as possible, not to gather data that consist of observations made through a single methodological lens" (Alasuutari, 1995, p. 42). The interview approach could involve open-ended conversations stemming from basic prompts ("Let's talk a little bit about your newspaper's role in the community"), or a series of predefined, carefully worded, and strategically organized questions. The responses could be refined into data within a similarly broad range of rigor, from isolation of particular words and phrases repeated by many different respondents to open-ended consideration of every minute detail captured in the interview (including every word, pause, hesitation, facial expression, etc.).

A time-consuming approach that tends to offer rich analysis is the *ethnographic approach*. Ethnography is, according to Schwandt (2007), "a particular kind of qualitative inquiry distinguishable from case study research, descriptive studies, naturalistic inquiry, and so forth by the fact that it is the process and product of describing and interpreting cultural behavior" (p. 96). In general, ethnography uses both textual analysis and qualitative interviewing, but adds a third dimension of firsthand observation by the scholar, or "fieldwork," sometimes in a detached, fly-on-the-wall manner, sometimes through active participation. Ethnographic studies can be sizable undertakings, taking months or years of observation, note-taking, recording, mid-study analysis, method modification, and so on; examples include the noteworthy studies of newsroom culture by Warren Breed (1955) and Gaye Tuchman (1978). Ethnography can be dauntingly complex. The method is the subject of a four-volume text (Bryman, 2001), although some experts in the method have created more manageable reference works for researchers who are new to ethnography, such as the step-by-step guide by Fetterman (2009). The richness of the analysis is well worth the effort, as an ethnographic study of journalists at work in a specific community would certainly provide useful insights to both the community and the journalists working within it (and for the researcher, more than enough data for a doctoral thesis, a series of peer-reviewed journal articles, or even a scholarly book).

❖ USING CCS THEORY TO STUDY COMMUNITY JOURNALISM

Although the type of data to be analyzed is the dominant factor in choosing a general method, refining the method into a specific research strategy requires the researcher to develop an appropriate theoretical framework as well. Theoretical frameworks in CCS studies can be broadly defined (e.g., "hegemony theory") or narrowly focused on a particular scholar's definition of a concept (e.g., "Habermas's concept of 'the public sphere'"). What follows are but a few examples of broad theoretical frameworks that can be applied to community journalism research. These examples are intended to provide guidance to those new to CCS, and as such may seem overly simplified to scholars more familiar with these and other critical cultural theories.

Marxist theory. The theories of Karl Marx (1818–1883) essentially are focused on the influence of economic power on all other aspects of society, especially politics, education, and culture. In CCS circles, "Marxists" are scholars who focus on the distributions of material wealth in society and how those distributions create inequities with regard to socioeconomic class (Durham & Kellner, 2001, p. 31; Tyson, 2006, pp. 53–54). For the study of community journalism, Marxist theory can be useful in analyzing the role of news media among the various socioeconomic classes in a community. For example, in a medium-sized city with multiple news outlets, a scholar might attempt to identify which news outlets align with the *bourgeoisie* (the "haves") and which align with the *proletariat* (the "have nots") by analyzing how different community media cover broad social issues that affect various socioeconomic classes in different ways (health care policy, public education, economic development, etc.). Another tactic might be to apply Marxist theories to the internal workings of a community newsroom. Kaul (1986), for example, suggested that journalists of the modern era are a sort of "technical white-collar proletariat" (p. 53), who through the 20th century rose to the status of "professionals" while remaining relatively low-paid and expendable workers in "news factories" (p. 47). That assertion could be adapted to community journalism studies, such as projects assessing where journalists fit into community structure (are they "haves" or "have nots"?) or class conflicts within community news organizations themselves (do the sports reporters identify with the blue-collar proletariat of their communities while publishers and business editors align with the bourgeoisie?). A great number of basic questions about community journalism have yet to be asked through a Marxist lens, making that branch of critical inquiry ripe for new research.

Hegemony theory. "Hegemony theory" is shorthand for any number of different theories concerned with the interplay of dominant culture and ideology. The concept is most often attributed to the writings of Italian Marxist theorist and activist Antonio Gramsci (1891–1937), and is focused on not just the inequitable distribution of wealth and power, but also the construction of popular culture, or *dominant ideology*. Gramsci made a distinction between the organs of the state (government) and the powerful organs of civil society (privately held institutions, such as banks, schools, and, of course, news media), which he argued worked collaboratively to ensure that "the mass of the population 'spontaneously' consents to the general direction imposed upon social life by the ruling group" (Macey, 2001, p. 176). Because Gramsci identified the press as the most powerful instrument of distributing and maintaining dominant ideology, that framework clearly can be useful in studying the complex role of community media in reinforcing the power structure within a community. One example is a study by Norton and Sadler (2006), in which the authors analyzed how residents of a rural Midwestern town debated and articulated the pros and cons of a proposed highway project that would change the character of the community. Different individuals within a community might view their community news media from very different perspectives. As Stuart Hall (1980) suggested, one might interpret a televised message (such as a local TV news report about plans to build a new highway through a rural community) from the dominant-hegemonic position (ostensibly, that the highway project would be good for the local economy), from an oppositional position (that the highway project would harm the environment and/or destroy the community's small-town character), or from a negotiated position (that the highway is going to be built regardless, so it may as well be built to minimize harm). An even more sophisticated framework might be to apply Celeste Condit's concept of hegemonic "concordance" (Condit, 1994) to suggest that the dominant ideology about the highway project might be created by the most powerful factions debating the issue (such as the most vocal proponents and opponents of the highway project, who are quoted in news stories and who debate the issue via local letters to the editor); concordance suggests that the most vocal factions can drown out minority opinions or ideas.

The hegemony framework also could be used to analyze alternative news media created by communities to supplement or compete with established media outlets—such as "synagogue pamphlets" published in Israel (Cohen, 2000) that "oppose secular and liberal hegemony by providing alternative interpretations of current events, solidifying group identity, defining boundaries of the community, and boosting the religious community's self image" (p. 247). Along those same lines, the hegemony framework could be applied to any number of alternative journalistic media, such as community newsletters, zines, community blogs, and community podcasts.

Ritual of communication. American cultural theorist James Carey's concept of the "ritual view" of communication is another framework well suited to the study of community journalism. Carey (1992) argued that the role of communication in society "is directed not toward the extension of messages in space but the maintenance of society in time . . . not the act of imparting information or influence but the creation, representation, and celebration of shared even if illusory beliefs" (p. 43). The ritual view stands in contrast to the more traditional "transmission view" of communication, in which communication is viewed as a means to transmit distinct bits of information from one party to another. Carey suggested that the transmission view reflects 19th-century efforts to use transportation and communication to "extend influence, control, and power over wider distances and greater populations" (p. 43). To Carey, the view of communication as the transmission of information turned communication into a mere commodity to be accumulated and distributed for purposes of political power, economic wealth, and social influence, and the media that engaged in such communication in turn sought ever larger audiences, ever more money, and ever more influence within the power structures of society. Evoking Raymond Williams, Carey argued that what was missing from such an approach was the consideration that communication "also includes the sharing of aesthetic experience, religious ideas, personal values and sentiments, and intellectual notions—a ritual order" (p. 34).

Applied to the archetype of community journalism—the small-town weekly newspaper—Carey's ritual view can be easily observed. Regardless of the "quality" of the journalism within such a newspaper, the fact remains that it serves as the central medium for its community. Although members of that community certainly read the newspaper to learn about local news and events, the very act of picking up and reading the paper every week could be seen as a ritual of community engagement. And the reading of content in the community newspaper that is uncommon or absent from larger media outlets (comprehensive obituaries, school lunch menus, results of local youth and amateur sporting events, etc.) becomes an important component of that ritual. A model for such studies of community media could be Vivian Martin's study (2008) of "news attending" rituals among people living in and around urban central Connecticut. Her ambitious project involved scores of lengthy interviews with community residents and analysis of all manner of public and informal written communications, all within months of the attacks of 9/11. Overall, Martin observed what she termed an "awareness-relevance-attending" loop (p. 90) with regard to how people use and react to various news media. That approach could be replicated on a smaller scale to study how more distinct communities ritualize "news attending."

Imagined communities. International-studies scholar Benedict Anderson put forward the concept of "imagined communities" in a book of the same name first published in 1983. In that work, Anderson argued that the printed media of a nation (particularly books, but also newspapers and other media) were highly influential in the construction of national identity in new countries in the 18th through the 20th centuries. Anderson (1991) suggested that a "nation" is an "imagined political community" because "the members of even the smallest nation will never know most of their fellow-members, meet them, or even hear of them, yet in the minds of each lives the image of their communion" (p. 6). With particular regard to newspapers, Anderson also suggested that the "ceremony" of daily newspaper reading is a powerful cohesive force of imagined communities:

> The significance of this mass ceremony—Hegel observed that newspapers serve modern man as a substitute for morning prayers—is paradoxical. It is performed in silent privacy, in the lair of the skull. Yet each communicant is well aware that the ceremony he performs is being replicated by thousands (or millions) of others of whose existence he is confident, yet of whose identity he has not the slightest notion. (p. 35)

In the early 21st century, the fracturing media landscape has provided a way to apply Anderson's concept to identifying and studying communities that exist only through media—the so-called "virtual" communities of the Internet age. To that end, scholars have applied the concept of imagined community to studies of a variety of subcultures, including a study of lesbians in Japan (Frank, 2002), a study of conservative rural women in the United States (Webb, 2006), and this author's own study of letters to the editor published in niche magazines devoted to such varied topics as sustainable agriculture and Western-style "engaged Buddhism" (Reader & Moist, 2008). Such studies suggest that individuals may identify themselves with virtual communities via books and newspapers in much the same way Anderson envisioned people identifying themselves with the nations in which they lived. That is particularly fertile ground for the study of community journalism, as the concepts of both *community* and *journalism* are modified to fit the realities of an increasingly mediated world, one in which a person may feel more connected to somebody living on the other side of the planet than with the people who live next door.

❖ CONCLUSION

Critical cultural studies is a mature paradigm of research rich with both tradition and diversity of thought, and its growing acceptance in the mainstream of journalism studies makes it an appealing approach for researchers looking to expand their understanding of the reflexivity of communities and their news media. Many of the theories developed by CCS scholars through the 20th century have been adapted and refined to better explain the ever-increasing complexity of mediated communication in the early 21st century, particularly journalism. What's missing is a substantive body of work in which CCS approaches are applied to community journalism.

That lack of CCS research devoted to community journalism is not an obstacle, but an opportunity. There is no lack of published CCS works focusing on other media that creative scholars can adapt to the community journalism subdiscipline; community journalism scholars also should consider CCS studies in other disciplines that have given short shrift, or overlooked entirely, the role of news media in community life.

Thanks to the hard work and perseverance of a generation of scholars, CCS is a legitimate alternative for journalism research. New CCS studies of community journalism that are well grounded in theory, use sufficiently rigorous methods, and provide new insights, should have little trouble finding acceptance at academic conferences, in research journals, and in scholarly volumes—and along the way, of course, greatly expanding our collective understanding of community journalism.

❖ REFERENCES

Alasuutari, P. (1995). *Researching culture: Qualitative method and cultural studies.* Thousand Oaks, CA: Sage.

Anderson, B. (1991). *Imagined communities: Reflections on the origin and spread of nationalism* (Rev. ed.). New York: Verso.

Breed, W. (1955). Social control in the newsroom. *Social Forces, 33,* 326–335.

Bryman, A. (2001). *Ethnography.* London: Sage.

Carey, J. W. (1992). *Communication as culture: Essays on media and society.* New York: Routledge.

Carpentier, N., & Cammaerts, B. (2006). Hegemony, democracy, agonism, and journalism. *Journalism Studies, 7*(6), 964–975.

Chandler, D. (2002). *Semiotics: The basics.* New York: Routledge.

Cohen, J. (2000). Politics, alienation, and the consolidation of group identity: The case of synagogue pamphlets. *Rhetoric and Public Affairs, 3*(2), 247–275.

Condit, C. M. (1994). Hegemony in a mass-mediated society: Concordance about reproductive technologies. *Critical Studies in Mass Communication, 11*(3), 205–230.

Durham, M. G., & Kellner, D. (2001). *Media and cultural studies: Keyworks.* Malden, MA: Wiley-Blackwell.

Emmison, M., & Smith, P. (2000). *Researching the visual.* Thousand Oaks, CA: Sage.

Fairclough, N. (2003). *Analyzing discourse: Textual analysis for social research.* New York: Routledge.

Fetterman, D. M. (2009). *Ethnography: Step-by-step.* Thousand Oaks, CA: Sage.

Frank, H. (2002). Identity and script variation: Japanese lesbian and housewife letters to the editor. In K. Campbell-Kimbler, R. J. Podesva, S. J. Roberts, and A. Wong (Eds.), *Language and sexuality: Contesting meaning in theory and practice.* Stanford, CA: CSLI Publications.

Gramsci, A. (1985). *Selections from cultural writings* (D. Forgacs & G. N. Smith, Eds.; W. Boelhower, Trans.). London: Lawrence & Wishart.

Gray, H. (199.5) *Watching race: Television and the struggle for "blackness."* Minneapolis: University of Minnesota Press.

Gross, L. (1989). Out of the mainstream: Sexual minorities and the mass media. In E. Seiter, H. Borchers, G. Kreutzner, & E.-M. Warth (Eds.), *Remote control: Television, audiences, and cultural power* (pp. 130–149). New York: Routledge.

Hall, S. (1980). Encoding/decoding. In S. Hall, D. Hobson, A. Lowe, & P. Willis (Eds.), *Culture, media, language* (pp. 128–138). London: Hutchinson.

Kaul, A. J. (1986). The proletarian journalist: A critique of professionalism. *Journal of Mass Media Ethics, 1*(2), 47–55.

Macey, D. (2001). *The Penguin dictionary of critical theory.* New York: Penguin Books.

Malpas, S., & Wake, P. (2006). *The Routledge companion to critical theory.* New York: Routledge.

Martin, V. B. (2008). Attending the news: A grounded theory about a daily regimen. *Journalism, 9*(1), 76–94.

McKee, A. (2003). *Textual analysis: A beginner's guide*. Thousand Oaks, CA: Sage.

Norton, T., & Sadler, C. (2006). Dialectical hegemony and the enactment of contradictory definitions in a rural community planning process. *Southern Communication Journal, 71*(4), 363–382.

Postman, N. (1988). *Conscientious objections: Stirring up trouble about language, technology, and education*. New York: Vintage Books.

Reader, B., & Moist, K. (2008). Letters as indicators of community values: Two case studies of alternative magazines. *Journalism and Mass Communication Quarterly, 85*(4), 823–840.

Schwandt, T. A. (2007). *The SAGE dictionary of qualitative inquiry*. Thousand Oaks, CA: Sage.

Stabile, C. A. (2009). "Sweetheart, this ain't gender studies": Sexism and super-heroes. *Communication and Critical/Cultural Studies, 6*(1), 86–92.

Switzer, L., & Ryan, M. (2002). The acceptance of critical-cultural scholarship in mass communication education. *Journalism and Mass Communication Educator, 57*(3), 213–229.

Tanikella, L. (2009). Voices from home and abroad: New York City's Indo-Caribbean media. *International Journal of Cultural Studies, 12*(2), 167–185.

Tuchman, G. (1978). *Making news: A study in the construction of reality*. New York: Free Press.

Tyson, L. (2006). *Critical theory today: A user-friendly guide*. New York: Routledge.

van Vuuren, K. (2006). Commercial trends in community radio: Sponsorship, advertising and John Laws. *Southern Review, 39*(2), 26–43.

van Vuuren, K. (2007). Contours of community: A snapshot of the independent community press in south east Queensland, 2006. *Media International Australia, 124*, 96–107.

Wahl-Jorgensen, K. (2005). The market vs. the right to communicate: The anti-political local press in Britain and the journalism of consensus. *Javnost* [The Public], *12*(3), 79–93.

Webb, S. (2006). The narrative of core traditional values in Reiman magazines. *Journalism and Mass Communication Quarterly, 83*(4), 865–888.

Weinhold, W. M. (2008). Newspaper negotiations. *Journalism Practice, 2*(3), 476–486.

Windschuttle, K. (2000). The poverty of cultural studies. *Journalism Studies, 1*(1), 145–159.

Zelizer, B. (2004). When facts, truth, and reality are God-terms: On journalism's uneasy place in cultural studies. *Communication and Critical/Cultural Studies, 1*(1), 100–119.

Asian and American Perspectives on Community Journalism •

Crispin C. Maslog

As I sit down to write this essay, it dawns on me, after half a century in journalism and journalism/mass communication teaching in the United States and Asia, that I essentially have lived in two journalistic worlds—the American and the Asian. Translating that into community journalism, one might say that I have been exposed to two journalistic traditions—that of Asian community journalism and that of American community journalism.

The community press in the United States is libertarian and competitive and subscribes to free enterprise. The archetypal community newspaper publishes in a small town, but its circulation is relatively big in proportion to population (such as a circulation of 500 copies per week in a town of 1,000 or less). The picture in Asia is more kaleidoscopic: the papers range from controlled and crummy to sophisticated and free. But their circulations are uniformly small in proportion to population because of poverty and illiteracy (such as 1,000 copies per week in a city of 100,000 or more).

I came from another world of international journalism as an Agence France-Presse news editor, but after getting a Ph.D. in mass communication at the University of Minnesota, I returned to my country, the Philippines, and my first job was to train journalists for the Philippine community press. I remember that my first research project was a survey of the Philippine community press in 1967—probably the first of its kind. Since the beginning, my research has focused more on the practical than the theoretical side of journalism.

I had so many questions. What makes community newspapers and radio stations in the Philippines tick? What factors make for success or failure? Who are the people behind those small-town media? What are their personal and professional profiles? What are their perceptions of their roles in society? Who trains them in journalism? What are the profiles of the journalism and mass communication schools that train them?

My 1971 paper on Philippine journalism and communication education was also probably the first of its kind in the country. The main research methods were surveys, case studies, content analysis, and in-depth interviews.

One of the earliest running debates I had was with an expatriate radio journalism trainer from Germany. At many journalism seminar-workshops we conducted, we would debate whether *community* in community journalism was a geographic community or a community of interests, such as science or environmental issues. It was an endless, entertaining debate until we decided it could be both. To my mind, however, community journalism still refers more to geographic community than to communities of interests, although with the onset of the Internet, community journalism serving communities of interest is becoming more common.

The field of community journalism and community journalism research has expanded since then. With the advent of the Internet and decreased production costs, community newsletters have sprouted all over the place, beckoning the new, Internet-savvy generation of journalism researchers as a promising area of study. The *OhmyNews* of Seoul, South Korea, which at one time had a staff of 40,000 volunteer citizen journalists using cell phones to report the news (Min, 2005), comes to mind as a new media model ripe for research.

In 1993, my book, The *Rise and Fall of Philippine Community Newspapers*, was published in celebration of 25 years of personal involvement in community journalism research and teaching. Since then, I have switched to the study of development journalism. Development journalism is journalism with a purpose—to help promote community development. The concept was first developed in Asia, which is understandable because that continent is where we find so much underdevelopment. Community journalism and development journalism merge at the point where practitioners analyze their roles: are community newspapers and radio stations expected to contribute to community development purposively? It is interesting to note that a parallel movement in the United States started in the 1990s, called citizen journalism, or civic journalism. It has faint resemblance to development journalism because it seeks to involve citizens in the identification and reporting of issues that affect the community.

My most recent research interest has turned to peace journalism. Peace journalism has been advanced as an alternative, or complement, to conflict reporting. Peace journalism focuses on the areas of agreement, rather than on disagreement, in any confrontation. It rejects the journalistic obsession with conflict as a news value. Like development journalism, peace journalism has a purpose—to promote peace.

One will notice that the common thread in those three variations on the theme of journalism—development journalism, civic journalism, and peace journalism—is advocacy. The new buzz word is advocacy journalism, which runs counter to the age-old (decrepit?) concept of objective journalism. Community journalism also involves a degree of advocacy. That is a new area where debate is brewing, and it will make for exciting new research.

❖ REFERENCES

Maslog, C. C. (1993). *The rise and fall of Philippine community newspapers.* Manila, Philippines: Philippine Press Institute.
Min, J. K. (2005). Journalism as conversation. *Nieman Reports, 59*(4), 17–19.

Crispin C. Maslog is the senior consultant at the Asian Institute of Journalism and Communication in the Philippines. He worked for decades as a newspaper editor and journalist in the Philippines. He received his Ph.D. from the University of Minnesota and is the author of 5 Successful Asian Community Newspapers *(Asian Mass Communication Research and Information Centre, 1985).*

7

A View From Outside

*What Other Social Science Disciplines Can
Teach Us About Community Journalism*

John A. Hatcher

The concept of community journalism, from a theoretical perspective, is a vagabond, wandering among geography- and
identity-based definitions applied by scholars from myriad disciplines.
Discussions of "community" struggle to distinguish concepts such as
identity, place, culture, governance, ideology, and social values. Such
investigations share a desire to explain how individuals form and maintain groups, and within that broad scope, scholars often ponder the role
journalism plays in community structure. That scholars in varied disciplines are asking similar questions at the same time is probably not an
accident (assuming any of those questions are new ones: the thinking of
Aristotle and Tocqueville suggest they aren't). In an age of technological and global transformation, scholars are envisioning new forms of
communities and are wondering what the impact of those social reorga-
nizations will be on traditional social structures, including news media.

The goal of this chapter is to offer some ways to think about community journalism that may parse out the nuances of an increasingly complex social world, but to do so by looking at research conducted in disciplines other than mass communication. It asks many of the same questions found elsewhere in this book; the difference is that the answers are provided by political scientists, philosophers, geographers, and sociologists, as well as cross-cultural and social psychologists. Presently, much of that work in other disciplines is happening without community journalism scholars, and that is unfortunate because we have much to add to the dialogue. We also have much to learn from it. To open that door, I've gone back and looked at ideas from various disciplines that pose and inspire important questions about community journalism. The chapter concludes by using those ideas to ask research questions that I hope some of us will explore in greater depth.

❖   DEMOCRATIC THEORY AND COMMUNITY JOURNALISM

Community journalism of course lends itself well to the study of political science, especially democratic theory, within which community politics plays an important role. Aristotle (350 BCE) described a community as composed of politically engaged citizens who contribute to the construction of a government that seeks the good life for all. A community, in other words, is not just a collection of disparate individuals living their lives in proximity to one another, but a group of people actively involved in a public discussion of their shared existence and their visions of their community. That line of thought forms the foundation of much democratic theory—that a society (and its governance) is built on a shared conversation, whether at the national (or even global) level or at the community level. In democratic theory, the power of government resides in the people, and the people work together to create an understanding of what is right and good for the entire community. Those ideas are the natural starting point for discussing the role of community journalism, because in its idealized form, journalism serves the societal role of providing a means for common dialogue in a democracy (Mill, 1869/1978). Mill described mass media as instruments with which an individual may peruse the ideas and perspectives of a society, exposing the individual to the complete spectrum of information and ideas. It could be argued that community journalism comes closer to that idealized role than its increasingly globalized and homogenized cousins in the larger, broadly focused media.

Tocqueville (1835/2001) concluded that the local and independent press allows small groups of citizens to join together and voice their opinions in an association that gains strength in the face of the imposing majority. Each independent community newspaper serves only a unique, isolated place that has its own priorities and interests. The content of those newspapers often is focused on the mundane and trivial matters of the local community, rather than on the concerns of a broader region or an entire nation. Tocqueville saw the community newspaper as virtually incapable of fostering a homogenous national voice: "They cannot form those great currents of opinion which sweep away the strongest dikes" (p. 94).[1]

It is in the relationship between the newspaper and the formation of associations that Tocqueville found a dynamic and interactive partnership. A newspaper can help a group of individuals with like-minded concerns find one another and form associations. Sometimes those associations are fleeting relationships, such as when people are drawn together to deal with a specific issue or event; when the issue is resolved or the event concludes, the community disperses. Other times those associations may be more permanent, such as when the issue that joins them lingers, or the event that joins them becomes recurring. By serving as a conduit for publicly discussing such issues, a newspaper (or other news medium) facilitates associations, and, in return, the newspaper gains vitality from the activities of those associations.

A universal requirement of community is that a group of individuals share something in common. It's that verb *share* that begins the discussion of the role of journalism in a community. Communities of place *share* a common geographic identity, and, with it, a shared sense of the goals and issues common to the residents of that place—a *telos*, according to MacIntyre (1984). MacIntyre, known for espousing a communitarian philosophy, described a view of the "good life" as a place in which all residents enjoy a shared vision, much like the passengers of one ship have a common destination and a shared journey. Community

---

[1] Although there was no national press in the U.S. in 1835, that would later become one of the earliest arguments not only that community journalism has both strengths and weaknesses, but more important, that its social role is fundamentally different from that of national and global news media.

journalism, it could be argued, is the place where the discussion of that vision happens and where consensus of those ideas is reached.

However, there is a strong critique in political philosophy of that concept of community, and the same argument could be used to implicate community journalism. The most dangerous assumption to make in any study of community journalism is that the individuals that comprise a community are equals. Differences in class, education, ideology, and ethnicity among community members inevitably mean that not all of them enjoy the same rights, freedoms, and access to community benefits. The ramifications of how those differences play out in the relationship between the community and the journalist can be profound.

Robert Dahl's description of the Athenian *polis* (1989), for example, could be used to build an argument that true democracy can occur only in a community with few differences among individuals. Individuals must feel their voices will be heard and heeded. The citizen, as described in Dahl's vision of the Greek democracy,

> is a whole person for whom politics is a natural social activity not sharply separated from the rest of life, and for whom the government and the state—or rather, the *polis*—are not remote and alien entities distant from oneself. (p. 19)

To maintain order in such a setting, Dahl wrote, a community must be unified in its vision and composed of a population that is largely homogeneous. The proper functioning of a *polis* would be largely disturbed by differences in income, race, ethnicity, religion, or language. Diversity, Dahl suggested, is not congruent with democracy.

So what becomes of those who are different in one or all of those ways? In a Greek democracy, Dahl noted, those who are different are simply excluded. Women, foreigners, and slaves living within the Greek city-state were denied access to the dialogue that defined the vision of the city-state.

Although Tocqueville (1835/2001) saw the community newspaper (and during his time there was no other kind of newspaper in America) as a filter against the oppressive voice of the majority, he also saw the local journalist, generally a printer/editor, as being very much at the mercy of the community. The public discourse of a community has a limiting effect as well—setting the boundaries that define the opinion of a community's newspaper editor.

Before publishing his opinions, he imagined that he held them in common with others; but no sooner has he declared them, than he is loudly censured by his opponents, whilst those who think like him, without having the courage to speak out, abandon him in silence. (Tocqueville, 1835/2001, p. 117)

A newspaper that strays from community boundaries takes a grave risk, which is yet another challenge to practicing community journalism in more homogenous communities, where the boundaries are both clear and rarely in flux.

The needs of minorities in communities inevitably lead to questions about justice and impartiality. Iris Marion Young (1990), a feminist scholar and political philosopher, challenged the ideal of impartiality defined by scholars such as John Rawls (1993, 1971/1999) as a means of promoting justice. No theory that assumes impartiality in the distribution of justice can realistically address the oppression that occurs when group difference is not recognized, Young asserted. She wrote that justice using impartiality as its foundation allows the values and decisions of privileged groups to dominate in a process she described as "cultural imperialism" (p. 10).

Young argued not just that difference must be recognized, but also that difference must be thought of in a completely new way. A key definition of Young's is that of the social group. Although Tocqueville described an association as a group of individuals united for one purpose, Young (1990) showed how the social group plays a part in defining an individual both to herself and to others: "A person's particular sense of history, affinity, and separateness, even the person's mode of reasoning, evaluating and expressing feeling are constituted partly by her or his group affinities" (p. 45).

Young's ideas are exciting because they take on the challenge of Dahl (1989), who questioned whether democracy and justice are possible in complex societies. Young began by demanding that we recognize that each member of a democracy—or, for the sake of this discussion, each member of a community—is not equal to each of the others. That may seem obvious, but, she pointed out, most theories of justice do not account for that. Differences inevitably lead to privileges afforded to some and not to others. Young accounted for that by describing the city as a complex and thriving urban environment defined in many ways by its differences in faith, ethnicity, and language. Young (1990) saw the urban city as a setting where social group differences are celebrated: "City life is composed of clusters of people with affinities—families, social group networks, voluntary associations, neighborhood networks, a vast array of small 'communities'" (p. 238).

With regard to community journalism, those ideas suggest that more complicated communities require more of their news media. Young's vision materialized for me during my visits to community newspapers in the boroughs of New York City, which contain some of the world's most socially diverse and complex neighborhoods. Walk into any neighborhood market and the first thing you see are the newspapers. Yes, there are the big-city dailies and international papers, but there are also countless community papers. The Independent Press Association–New York estimated that in 2004 there were 300 local magazines and newspapers, serving more than 60 ethnic groups, published in 42 languages ("Many Voices, One City," 2004). Neighborhood newsstands are indicators of community life: there are newspapers for groups who share common neighborhood bonds, newspapers for specific language groups, newspapers for different faiths, and newspapers for immigrants who share a common homeland.

Imagine yourself as a newspaper editor striving to create one publication that will satisfy the needs of the members of even one small neighborhood in such a socially complex place. It's easy to facilitate a shared community discussion if everyone enjoys equal status and agrees on what's important to talk about—take, for example, the small rural villages of northern Minnesota, where I now reside. But what happens when some members of a community have different privileges? What happens when they share different values and worldviews? What happens when there are great socioeconomic divides? Suddenly, the shared vision of community becomes fragmented, and so do beliefs about what should be the subject of public discourse. The community journalist immediately faces a daunting, if not futile, challenge in trying to create a forum in his work where a truly open and egalitarian public discourse occurs for all of the stakeholders in the community of place.

❖ GEOGRAPHY: COMMUNITY JOURNALISM
    AND A SENSE OF PLACE

It's likely no coincidence that some of the great geographers were journalists before they became scholars. Geography and journalism share a strong familial bond. Before urban geographer Jane Jacobs wrote her influential book, *The Death and Life of Great American Cities* (1961/1993), she was a reporter at the *Scranton Tribune* in northeastern Pennsylvania. As an urban journalist for Louisville, Kentucky's *Courier-Journal*, Grady Clay hungered for ways to better understand the patterns, connections, and clues that would help him to explain the urban neighborhoods he wrote about, and the result is a must-read for scholars of urban community journalism: *Close-Up: How to Read the American City* (1980).

For urban geography scholars, the word *place* is often preferred over *community*, but the concepts are closely linked. Urban geographers do a delightful job of pondering which ingredients combine to create a "place" (and exploring what *place* means, for that matter). For the geographer, a sterile, empty "space" becomes a "place" when it is ascribed meaning by the humans who inhabit it (Relph, 1976; Tuan, 1977). That conceptualization comes from varied sources—the structures and layout of the landscape, the history and the narratives of those who settled and live there—that simmer and yield a complex soup of meaning (Clay, 1980).

Naturally, one ingredient in that soup of "place" is the news organization, and a number of geographers have examined the role news organizations play in defining a place. Parisi and Holcomb (1994) described newspapers as "local economic institutions whose business might be said to be the symbolic construction of place" (p. 377). Buchanan (2009) also used the concept of "local" to explore the ways a newspaper contributes to the meaning of a place.

As Martin (2000) noted, much of the research involving the role of media in place identity has focused on the larger mainstream press; little work has been done examining the role of the local or community press. Martin argued that major media define urban neighborhoods from the outside in a hegemonic relationship, while the local press provides a means by which the hegemonic view of the mainstream media is "contested by local actors, who, through their own discourses and activism, demand a voice in constructing inner-city neighborhood identities" (p. 380). In an analysis of how the major daily newspaper in St. Paul, Minnesota, reported on the urban neighborhood of Frogtown compared to the local *Frogtown Times*, Martin noted that the community newspaper did not ignore the problems of the community, but its approach was decidedly different from that of the metro daily: the community paper talked about the actions being taken to address those problems and provided the community a place to define itself. Martin's work is noteworthy for its ability to parse out important distinctions in the function of the community press in urban settings:

> This examination of media reporting on vice in the neighborhood illustrates how local discourses in the alternative neighborhood newspaper consistently offer a more positive view of residents, who directly influence the dominant media through the actions and discourses of their neighborhood organizations. Thus we cannot view the media as a singular entity with an inflexible, purely hegemonic power over place portrayals. (p. 401)

❖ SOCIOLOGY: QUESTIONS OF IDENTITY AND COMMUNITY

Ideas from political philosophy suggest that a citizenry will be dissatisfied with media that cater only to geographic definitions of community. Citizens who do not feel their voices are heard in traditional community media may seek out or create other channels through which to express viewpoints and keep up with community happenings. Many types of communities do not share geographic place, which makes their community media all the more important for community cohesion. In some cases, new communities may evolve as reactions to disenfranchisement from traditional communities and dissatisfaction with established community media.

The study of non-proximate communities is thriving, driven by research in many social science disciplines related to questions of technology, globalization, and identity. In some sense, such identity-based communities have always existed (as exemplified by immigrant and ethnic communities), but the seeming transformation of society through new and more accessible communication technologies has meant those communities have received more attention from scholars in the past two decades than ever before. A question to ponder is whether those kinds of communities will eventually supplant more traditional, proximate communities, as some have suggested, and what role journalism will play in those new communities. Some mass communication scholars are already applying those ideas and using them to think about new definitions of community. David Morley (1995, 2000), for example, has theorized that technology is reshaping culture on a global scale. Time and space were once crucial aspects of how individuals saw their identities and their positions in proximate communities. Now, Morley argues, mobility and media have diminished time and space as parameters of identity. Individuals define themselves not by their neighbors, but by those who see the world as they do.

A growing body of work in political science sees the modern individual as behaving in ways that bypass traditional images of geographic community. Scholars of comparative political behavior foresee a great transformation in the way individuals participate in a democracy (Dalton, 2000; Topf, 1995). Dalton has argued that we are "living through a period of significant cultural change" (p. 918). He envisions the citizen as a free thinker, not motivated by traditional parties or political elites, but rather oriented toward a set of issues based on individual tastes and preferences. Dalton's citizen participates in a form of "direct democracy" (p. 932) that may include involvement in community groups or social movements and accessing media channels that cater to those interests. Such a citizen is motivated by an expanding array of issues and concerns that transcend proximity, and that would suggest great selectivity in media use that may not be connected to traditional community ties.

Sociologist Manuel Castells (2004) took that argument a step further, writing that traditional institutions of democracy are being "bypassed by global networks of wealth, power, and information" (p. 419). Many individuals no longer see themselves as residents of physical neighborhoods with common governments and media. Rather, Castells believed, individuals now use media to "commune" with people who think like they do but who are not tied to place. Castells described groups called *resistance identities* that make irrelevant traditional conceptions of community derived from a democratically constructed civil society. Fueled by technology and globalization, resistance identities unite individuals into communal groups based on shared faiths, ethnicities, nationalities, and social movements (e.g., the women's movement or environmental activism). Those groups do not behave in the same way as the traditional institutions; Castells believed they bypass traditional democratic institutions and are leading to a shift in power toward groups defined by the identities of individuals.

Community journalism is often seen as a way to unite and empower groups. However, social identity theory offers ways to think about how community journalism may also exclude and disenfranchise individuals within communities. Although it does not deal specifically with media, social identity theory helps explain how an individual's sense of self can influence the information he would be drawn to in the mass media. Social identity scholars have explicated three ways to explain the individual in relation to society: self-esteem (Tajfel, 1978), uncertainty reduction (Hogg, 2001), and the simultaneous creation of differentiation and belonging (Brewer, 2001). Tajfel (1978) first used social identity theory to explain how a person's affiliation to a group or groups builds self-esteem. That identification might include a sense of pride in being a member of an ethnic group, but could just as likely be a feeling of worth resulting from an affiliation to a sports team. Hogg (2001) added the dimension of "reducing uncertainty" to social identity. A strong affiliation with a church, for example, gives an individual guidance for how to behave and to perceive the world; that affiliation reduces the individual's uncertainty about how to act or how to respond to complex issues. It also means that a threat to that group's credibility is, indirectly, viewed as a threat to the individual. Brewer (2001) added a third dimension: membership in a group allows an individual to feel both unique from the general population, and also gives the individual a feeling of being part of a group of like-minded people.

If, as has been asserted in other chapters of this book, community journalists are not just objective third-party observers, but rather active members of communities, then social identity theory posits that a sense of belonging will have profound effects on how such a journalist makes decisions in every phase of the news gathering process: determining what warrants coverage, determining how news is framed, and deciding which voices participate in the explanation of news events. Those journalists also have a role in determining what proposed solutions are published when social problems are discussed. How a journalist reacts to those important roles would seem to be determined by that journalist's identity within a particular community.[2]

---

[2]Social identity theory seems strongly related to ideas suggested by much of the work of Minnesota scholars Olien, Tichenor, and Donohue, including their "guard dog" theory of journalism in which there is a tendency to blame problems on someone or something outside the community (see Donohue, Tichenor, & Olien, 1995; Olien, Donohue, & Tichenor, 1968). Their work is summarized in Chapter 3.

❖   SOCIAL CAPITAL AND CIVIC LIFE

From communication studies, we know that Habermas (1962/1989, 1992) saw community as being created through public exchange of serious ideas among individuals—what Habermas dubbed the "public sphere." Public life and communication with others is where individuals work to define and understand the set of rules, values, and beliefs that define a community. To simplify, public life is where we meet our neighbors and talk about our understanding of the way things are in our community. The public sphere, for the sake of that discussion, can be seen as a place (physical or virtual) where individuals partake in public discussion in which other (ideally all) members of a community can participate and collectively strive for new understanding.

In other disciplines, and specifically in the political sciences, Habermas has inspired great discussion about issues related to civic life. If public life is a discussion and community journalism is a place where that discussion occurs, then the *actions* inspired by such discussion are what scholar Robert Putnam (2000) meant when he referred to "social capital"[3]—this is basically the idea that the activities of community that create and maintain connections have value. Some scholars have voiced concern about the diminished importance of such activities in modern life. Putnam's book *Bowling Alone* (2000) suggests a decline of civic life in America by noting a decrease in collective activities such as bowling leagues, voting, and participation in civic organizations. He found a correlation between that perceived decline and a decrease in newspaper readership, coupled with an increase in television viewing at home. Putnam also believed that some communities enjoy much higher social capital than others, characterized by their higher voter turnouts and greater involvement in social and community activities.

Putnam made a distinction that is potentially significant for those who study community journalism—the difference between "bridging" and "bonding" social capital. *Bonding* capital is the kind of public work that contributes to the strengthening of relationships within a

---

[3]Putnam was not the first to discuss social capital, but his more positive use of the concept is the focus of this discussion. Jane Jacobs (1961/1993) and Pierre Bourdieu (1985) were probably the first to use the concept in social science research.

community. *Bridging* capital, as the name suggests, reaches across groups or even attempts to build capital in a disparate or pluralistic community. For scholars and activists interested in community development (see Gittell & Vidal, 1998)—especially in poor, urban neighborhoods—bridging capital can be seen as a crucial component of civic life because of its ability to extend the benefits of community to a broader group.

It's easy to see examples of bonding capital occurring in community journalism. Community newspapers, for example, are known for the kind of news that families cut out of newspapers and stick onto their refrigerator doors to celebrate themselves, their community, and civic life in general. In that fashion, community journalism builds the self-esteem of individuals in the group. That kind of journalism promotes civic life and gives the whole community a stronger, positive sense of itself.

Finding examples of bridging capital in community journalism may be more problematic. For the traditional community news outlet, one of the goals is to focus on news from within the community, and to add or find local angles to news from outside the community. For example, news about a statewide increase in a sales tax might be "localized" by getting comments from local lawmakers and business owners about the legislation. Bridging capital may therefore be contrary to the mission of a community newspaper. With that consideration in mind, it becomes clear just how challenging it is to practice community journalism in a more diverse, pluralistic community—a caution that harks back to Dahl's argument (1989) that effective democracy requires a certain level of homogeneity.

Putnam's work is used as evidence to bemoan the end of democracy and the engaged citizen; Michael Schudson (1998), on the other hand, believed both are alive and well, but that civic engagement has simply changed from previously observed modes. Civic and private life both have morphed into a complicated web of activity that is hard to measure, but perhaps is also more powerful, Schudson wrote, noting that "civic participation now takes place everywhere. . . . It exists in the microprocesses of social life" (p. 298).Those ideas pose a fascinating challenge for community journalism scholars, who could explore whether journalism has made a similar shift, either through changes in the content of individual news organizations or through a more complicated web of community journalism channels.

❖ SOME QUESTIONS FOR MOVING FORWARD

We began by envisioning individuals as equal and homogeneous and defining themselves based on their proximate community—the "place" in which they live. Although that definition is part of who they are, scholars such as Castells (2004), Dalton (2000), and Young (1990) have urged us to see individuals as much more complex than we have viewed them in the past, each holding multiple views of community and residing in cultural situations that further influence their visions of community and of journalism.

In these turbulent times, the evidence would suggest that citizens may now attach less importance to where they live and, with that change, see the local community newspaper (and its equivalents) as being less relevant to their lives. In such a milieu, could community journalism be dying? Or is our understanding of community and journalism just changing? For optimists and pessimists alike, this is an exciting time to study community journalism.

This chapter has attempted to shed light on work from disciplines other than mass communication that can be useful to the study of community journalism. Based on this cursory review, the following research questions are possible paths for community journalism scholars to consider and explore:

Does a transformation of community mean an end to or a loss of relevance for the more traditional community press?

One view of the current community journalism landscape is bleak. News media in general have become interactive and diffuse, allowing individuals to self-select the news they access and even the people they interact with based on the communities for which they feel strong affiliation. If Dalton (2000) was correct and citizens have become more "complex and individualistic," then they will not be satisfied by media designed for mass consumption, for the nonexistent idea that there exists an average citizen. To the contrary, a citizen will seek out a medium largely specialized and responsive to the issues salient in her individual life.

It is likely that the changes in what defines a community do not foretell the end of the community press, but a restructuring and a greater diffusion of the power of the gatekeepers. After all, as much as community journalism may present itself as another public place, it isn't a true public forum. It's a mediated discussion, controlled by journalists who themselves are complex individuals, and who are influenced by many factors as they make decisions about how to interpret and present the news.

There is great potential here for modern community journalism to return to Tocqueville's vision. Community media could become even more insulated from the homogenizing voice of the mainstream because the number of channels of communication have become too numerous and diverse for one voice to permeate. That suggests that traditional community journalism (adapted, of course, to modern technology and cultural norms) can remain a significant part of the increasingly complicated web of media channels. Each strand is independent, largely because it is focused around specific issues and frames that are defined by the individuals it serves. Community media do not have to attempt to serve the general public in either the issues they cover or in the ways that coverage is framed. Rather, community media could become the tools of existing and emerging social movements, of places experiencing rapid cultural change, and of groups of individuals who identify with specific issues or sets of ideals. For political scientists especially, focused research on community media may be more telling about political processes than analysis of larger media serving expansive regions or nations.

How much does technology foment new concepts of community?

If a community is a collection of individuals who have shared ideas, then a requirement of community is to have public places where citizens can meet and exchange ideas. Those can be physical places such as meeting halls and public schools, or virtual places such as newsletters or online forums. Mass communication scholar Lewis Friedland believed that democracies require communities and, further, that group creation is enhanced through communication (Friedland, 2001). Advancing communication technology pushes us to make a crucial modification of the definition of community journalism offered by Tocqueville (1835/2001). Community journalism no longer requires a geographic focus but can now be defined by shared interests; it can now encompass multiple communities with which an individual may identify (Davis, Elin, & Reeher, 2002). Moreover, community journalism no longer requires the expertise or equipment required to produce traditional news media. Citizens in a democracy motivated by one issue—and by a particular point of view on that issue—are able as never before to access and create media that are responsive to them. What's more, those citizens are able to mobilize and communicate on a global level.

But is technology really driving that transformation of community journalism? For many, identifying with an ethnic diaspora may mean more than being active in the neighborhoods in which they live, and such people will seek out or create media that serve those ethnic interests. Those kinds of identity communities are not new, though. In the early 20th century, Robert Park's studies of the immigrant and ethnic press (1922) described how immigrants with shared ethnic backgrounds relied on one another to navigate a new society. Park found that the immigrant press that galvanized ethnic groups in America was successful because it drew on its readers' common bonds—those of language, tradition, and culture. Thus, in today's complicated media landscape, we may find that what drives the creation of new community media may have more to do with the desire for community than with the accessibility of communication technology.

Can increased specialization of community media lead to polarization of groups?

It seems that one concern about the increase in specialized community media is that broad public dialogue at the provincial or national level, such an important component of democracy, will vanish as individuals tend to communicate with and access the messages of only people who think as they do. A distinct possibility is that such specialization will lead to greater segmentation of the population (Davis et al., 2002). Specialized community media could lead to a homogenizing and polarizing of groups that would impede a healthy exchange of dissenting views, information, and innovation. The metaphor of the Tower of Babel is often invoked here: it's not hard to envision a collection of individuals who live in the same physical place, but are so insulated from their proximate communities and so engaged in their virtual communities that they do not participate in discussions of what's important and good in the place where they live. However, to see those changes as having only negative effects on communities and, ultimately, on democracy itself, requires accepting the assumption that a "one size fits all" media channel—the vaunted "marketplace of ideas"—ever truly was a place where all members of a community could freely participate.

There is a convincing argument that traditional community journalism, as part of the institutional design of a democracy, is not truly representative. Instead, it is critiqued as being sympathetic to the majority and as dismissing or ignoring the voices of others (Young, 1990). Media specialization may offer minorities in communities new opportunities to define their issues and even to define themselves on their own terms—that is to say, more individual opinions may now "count," or, at minimum, not go unnoticed. Communities may seek definitions of membership that are more inclusive and media that allow greater participation. In other words, a more complicated community and a correspondingly complicated array of community media may mean stronger communities and a stronger democracy. It would seem that there is potential for the new media landscape to invite more voices into the creation of community and to make the media of various communities available to the broader public, expediting community discourse and bringing it closer to the interpersonal discourse of democracy imagined by Aristotle.

Can community journalism create bridging capital?

In some ways, the work of journalism within a community is the easy part. A more intriguing question is whether such journalism has an influence outside a community—and, further, whether journalism is up to the task of building or expanding community. Part of the role of journalism is to unite a community in a shared discussion, but what happens when a community has a complex mix of values, interests, and desires that are not shared by all members? Can it be called a community? Community journalism seems inherently good at responding to and even enhancing the strength of established and/or homogeneous communities. However, the great challenge for journalism in an increasingly diverse society is how to serve those same functions in pluralistic and/or heterogenous communities.

The issue of homogeneity has come up in many places in this book about community journalism, which isn't surprising, considering how society is at once moving toward being more diverse and being more divided. As Putnam (2000) argued, migration to mega-cities is creating a largely centralized, largely diverse culture. However, at the same time, Putnam believed bridging capital is not occurring, depriving civic engagement to large segments of society.

The question of communication in complex societies is explored in detail in the diffusion of innovation research conducted by Everett Rogers (2003). Rogers asked how information spreads and what factors speed that up and slow it down, and he found that group-level factors, including the heterogeneity of a society and divisions by class, have an impact on innovation. Sociologist Mark S. Granovetter (1973) is credited for developing a theory of "the strength of weak ties" based on how stratified groups interact. It describes a heterogeneous networking that allows information to flow vertically in a society.

So, what role do community media play in all of that? A long line of communication research (going back to Katz & Lazasfeld, 1955, and Rogers, 1962) suggests media are limited to providing only knowledge, and that true attitude change can happen or mostly happen only in interpersonal networks. Even so, community journalism appears capable of mediating those interpersonal networks, most obviously in computer-mediated communities, for which the Internet is the primary communication tool for bridging capital and creating stronger communities (Kavanaugh, Reese, Carroll, & Rosson, 2003).

❖ CONCLUSION

This chapter has drawn on research primarily from outside the mass communication discipline to explore and inspire new research in community journalism, and it concludes by urging community journalism scholars to take a lead in the current scholarship in their own fields. The opportunity is there to establish an emerging field of community journalism research that shatters the stereotype of community journalism scholarship as simply the work of former practitioners extolling the virtues of their profession. The next logical step is to create research that is not just informed by other disciplines, but shows scholars in other disciplines the great variation that exists within the journalism profession.

Although one can't ignore the globalizing, homogenizing media monolith that has been prophesized by many, the media landscape is far more dynamic than that. Community journalism scholars have long recognized that, and other scholars are starting to understand it as well. Across social science disciplines, there is passionate discourse about the power of the citizen and the role of the individual. Scholars are interested in the loss of the power of entrenched democratic institutions and the increased power of groups based on transnational identity. They are interested in the power of media to influence society in a time of unprecedented media turmoil based on fracturing audiences, changing media platforms, and rapid shifts in media ownership and management. Community journalism scholars are perfectly poised to be at the forefront of research in all of those areas, because they see "the media" as more than a monolith. Community journalism scholars also see communities as more than just fixed, geographically defined places of relatively small size. Community journalism scholars see the complexity of both *journalism* and *community*, and it is that subdiscipline of communication studies that has the most promise for making sense of our increasingly complex society.

Despite decades of effort, community journalism scholarship is only now beginning to make notable inroads into the mass communication discipline. It's now understood that *journalism* and *media* no longer refer only to large daily newspapers and national or global news broadcasts, and many journalism schools are changing their curricula to prepare students for the new media environment. The next step is to expand the definition of *news media* for scholars in other fields. It is up to the community journalism scholar to parse out the intricate connections between communities and journalism. The key is to be skeptical of generalization and rather to focus on variation. There is variation in community on scales of size, complexity, and endless cultural nuances. There is variation in journalism based on readership, community climate, and modes of delivery. And between those two concepts, there is a dynamic and fascinating two-way relationship that is never fixed and rarely predictable. If nothing else, community journalism scholars should give pause to scholars in all disciplines who build research based on the assumption that all media fit into one convenient definition, or who see "big media" as the sole actors in the media landscape. If anything, in the presently changing media landscape, large media are experiencing a rapid decline of power and influence, while community media are gaining greater recognition.

The great questions regarding the role of journalism in community have been revived and refreshed, and there has never been a more exciting time to explore the relationships that community and journalism share. Ultimately, we are still interested in how we relate to our neighbors and how we communicate within our "community," but the ways of defining community and of using journalism to enhance those relationships appear open to the imagination of the individual. It is no exaggeration, I think, to say that it is our time. Here's hoping we seize the opportunity.

❖ REFERENCES

Aristotle. (350 BCE). *Politics*. Retrieved August 4, 2009, from http://classics .mit.edu/Aristotle/politics.html.s

Bourdieu, P. (1985). The forms of capital. In J. G. Richardson (Ed.), *Handbook of theory and research for the sociology of education* (pp. 241–258). New York: Greenwood.

Brewer, M. B. (2001). Ingroup identification and intergroup conflict: When does ingroup love turn to outgroup hate? In R. D. Ashmore, L. Jussim, & D. Wilder (Eds), *Social identity, intergroup conflict, and conflict* (pp. 17–41). New York: Oxford University Press.

Buchanan, C. (2009). Sense of place in the daily newspaper. *Aether, 4,* 62–84.

Castells, M. (2004). *The power of identity*. Malden, MA: Blackwell.

Clay, G. (1980). *Close-up: How to read the American city*. Chicago: University of Chicago Press.

Dahl, R. A. (1989). *Democracy and its critics*. New Haven: Yale University Press.

Dalton, R. J. (2000). Citizen attitudes and political behavior. *Comparative Political Studies, 33*(6–7), 912–940.

Davis, S., Elin, L., & Reeher, G. (2002). *Click on democracy*. Boulder, CO: Westview Press.

Donohue, G. A., Tichenor, P. J., & Olien, C. N. (1995). A guard dog perspective on the role of media. *Journal of Communication, 45,* 115–132.

Friedland, L. A. (2001). Communication, community, and democracy. *Communication Research, 28*(4), 358–391.

Gittell, R., & Vidal, A. (1998). *Community organizing: Building social capital as a development strategy*. Thousand Oaks, CA: Sage.

Granovetter, M. (1973). The strength of weak ties. *American Journal of Sociology, 78*(6), 1360–1380.

Habermas, J. (1989). *The structural transformation of the public sphere: An inquiry into a category of bourgeois society* (T. Burger with F. Lawrence, Trans.). Cambridge, MA: Polity. (Original work published 1962)

Habermas, J. (1992). Further reflections on the public sphere. In C. Calhoun (Ed.), *Habermas and the public sphere* (pp. 421–461). Cambridge: Massachusetts Institute of Technology.

Hogg, M. A. (2001). A social identity theory of leadership. *Personality and Social Psychology Review, 5*(2), 184–200.

Jacobs, J. (1993). *The death and life of great American cities*. New York: Random House. (Original work published 1961)

Katz, E., & Lazasfeld, P. (1955). *Personal influence*. New York: Free Press.

Kavanaugh, A., Reese, D., Carroll, J. M., & Rosson, M. B. (2003). Weak ties and collective efficacy in networked communities. In M. Huysman, E. Wenger, & V. Wulf (Eds.), *Communities and technologies* (pp. 265–286). Amsterdam: Kluwer Academic.

MacIntyre, A. (1984). *After virtue: A study in moral theory*. Notre Dame, IN: University of Notre Dame Press.

Many voices, one city: The IPA-NY guide to ethnic press of New York and New Jersey. (2004). Retrieved March 10, 2008, from http://www.indypressny .org/directory.shtml

Martin, D. G. (2000). Constructing place: Cultural hegemonies and media images of an inner-city neighborhood. *Urban Geography, 21,* 380–405.

Mill, J. S. (1978). *On liberty*. Indianapolis, IN: Hackett. (Original work published 1869)

Morley, D. (1995). *Spaces of identity: Global media, electronic landscapes and cultural boundaries*. New York: Routledge.

Morley, D. (2000). *Home territories: Media, mobility and identity*. New York: Routledge.

Olien, C. N., Donohue, G. A., & Tichenor, P. J. (1968). The community editor's power and the reporting of conflict. *Journalism Quarterly, 45,* 243–253.

Parisi, P., & Holcomb, B. (1994). Symbolizing place: Journalistic narratives of the city. *Urban Geography, 15*(4), 376–394.

Park, R. (1922). *The immigrant press and its control*. New York: Harper & Brothers.

Putnam, R. (2000). *Bowling alone: The collapse and revival of American community*. New York: Simon & Schuster.

Rawls, J. (1993). *Political liberalism*. New York: Columbia University Press.

Rawls, J. (1999). *A theory of justice*. Cambridge, MA: Belknap Press. (Original work published 1971)

Relph, E. (1976). *Place and placelessness*. London: Pion Limited.

Rogers, E. M. (1962). *Diffusion of innovations*. New York: Free Press.

Rogers, E. M. (2003). *Diffusion of innovations* (5th ed.). New York: Free Press.

Schudson, M. (1998). *The good citizen: A history of American civic life*. New York: Free Press.

Tajfel, H. (1978). Interindividual behavior and intergroup behavior. In H. Tajfel (Ed.), *Differentiation between groups: Studies in the social psychology of intergroup relations* (pp. 27–60). London: Academic Press.

Tocqueville, A. de. (2001). *Democracy in America*. New York: New American Library. (Original work published 1835)

Topf, R. (1995). Beyond electoral participation. In H.-D. Klingemann & D. Fuchs (Eds.), *Citizens and the state* (pp. 52–92). New York: Oxford University Press.

Tuan, Y. (1977). *Space and place: The perspective of experience.* Minneapolis: University of Minnesota Press.

Young, I. M. (1990). *Justice and the politics of difference.* Princeton, NJ: Princeton University Press.

Community Journalism
as Metropolitan Ecology ●

Lewis Friedland

The central problem of community journalism is the rapidly changing structure of community itself. In the realm of journalism today,
communities always have two aspects: they are geographic places and
they are networked collectives.

We can assume that where traditional communities of place are
strongest, more traditional forms of community journalism (including
actual newspapers) are most likely to continue to flourish. That is evident in the small dailies and weeklies, often in rural or exurban communities, that continue to be essential and vital local resources in 2011.
We are also more likely to see Web startups that flourish either in the
absence of print journalism (in many rural areas, exurbs, and suburbs,
and some city neighborhoods) or where only glorified advertising–
focused "shoppers" exist.

But one of the most important social and urban shifts in the past
20 to 30 years has been from communities of place to communities as
"networks of networks." Most sociologists see that as a long process,
going back at least to the urbanization that grew in the latter part of the
19th century. But it has become more acute in the past decade with the
rise of the Internet, for two reasons.

First, the Internet makes the formation of small niche communities nearly costless. Whereas before the limits of communication made
it necessary to live with at least some "unlike-others" in the same
place, now it is possible for people to opt out of proximate communities and focus on niche communities on the Internet. Of course, no one
does that completely—everyone still lives someplace. But increasingly
we can associate much of the time with like-minded others elsewhere.

Second, life online in networked communities is more appealing
to and stronger among the young—exactly those who have all but
stopped reading metropolitan newspapers.

The biggest challenge for journalism in this era is with metropolitan journalism, the news media produced in and for expansive urban
areas. Some might say that a large metro area is either too big to be "a"
community, or is really a patchwork of smaller communities. Both of

those things are true in some sense. But a metropolis is an imagined community (to use Benedict Anderson's [1991] term). Even though only a small fraction of its residents will ever meet, they share a common imagined life of place: for example, an imagined "Milwaukee," even though many people who identify with that city live outside the city limits, reaching to the suburbs of Ozaukee and Waukesha counties. Such large imagined communities provide much of the social, economic, and cultural structure for the many smaller communities contained within it (Kaniss's *Making Local News* [1991], while dated, explains that process very well). And as the imagined community of the "metro daily" starts to disintegrate, the smaller communities within it and their news coverage suffer as well.

Smaller communities are not islands, even though they often imagine that they are or wish to be. They are integral parts of the larger urban metropolitan ecology, and that is precisely what the traditional metropolitan daily newspaper, at its best, reinvents every day—the imagined metropolitan community. With the decline of the metro daily, many forms of community and community journalism supported by such newspapers are threatened, just as a single species can't survive when its habitat disappears.

Research on that problem will need to be multidimensional. First, it will have to be ecological, modeling the change structures of community urban and social ecologies, the emerging structures of niche communities, and the complex relations between those two layers. It will also have to be practical. In Madison, Wisconsin, we created a community news site called Madison Commons (2011), and as our experiments with that project have demonstrated, it is not easy to reweave those two layers, particularly because one is in rapid decline and transformation while the other is emerging and growing just as quickly. Finally, it should be multimethodological, combining the richness of qualitative research with every layer of those communities; the ability of network models to pattern complexity; and the strength of quantitative models to demonstrate what is truly effective, and what is not.

Lewis Friedland is a professor in the School of Journalism and Mass Communication at the University of Wisconsin–Madison and is director of the Center for Communication and Democracy. His publications include three books: Public Journalism: Past and Future (Kettering Foundation Press, 2003); Civic Innovation in America: Community Empowerment, Public Policy and the

Movement for Civic Renewal *(with Carmen Sirianni; University of California Press, 2001), and* Covering the World: International Television News Services *(Twentieth Century Fund Press, 1993).*

❖ REFERENCES

Anderson, B. (1991). *Imagined communities: Reflections on the origin and spread of nationalism.* Brooklyn, NY: Verso.

Kaniss, P. (1991). *Making local news.* Chicago: University of Chicago Press.

Madison Commons. (2011). *Who we are.* Retrieved April 28, 2011, from http:// madisoncommons.org/?q=about

PART III

Multimedia and Global Considerations

8

Considering Community Journalism From the Perspective of Public Relations and Advertising

Diana Knott Martinelli

One look through the local Morgantown, West Virginia, newspaper demonstrates the importance of public relations work in keeping that community informed. The number of articles with the byline "Submitted to *The Dominion Post*" are numerous, and represent information from local law firms, university programs, hospitals, government agencies, civic groups, animal rights organizations, religious groups, the Chamber of Commerce, and more. In its Sunday issue, *The Dominion Post* publishes regular columns by hospital community-relations directors, chiropractors, and real estate practitioners. Its mix of community- and reporter-generated news is mirrored in the local television and radio programming.

Advertisers and public-relations practitioners in such communities are not just customers and news sources, but also neighbors, church members, youth-soccer coaches; they are fellow citizens who represent and/or buy advertising for local banks, retail shops, restaurants, and car dealerships, including those that reporters, publishers, and station owners frequent. Yet, as noted in the first chapter of this book, even small newspapers have been publicly reproved for their frequent use of public-relations materials or their close ties to local advertisers. At the community level, such relationships are often mutually beneficial; in some communities, they are essential.

Such local information partnerships can be found the world over. For example, recent scholarly literature has discussed the importance of local media to the U.K. construction industry as a means of educating and safeguarding audiences, building positive community relationships, and engaging the next generation of industry professionals (Smith, 2003). Likewise, a Spanish scholar (Capriotti, 2009) has described how local communities are the primary audience for museums, which as such initiate a great deal of media-relations activities. Capriotti's study found that 85% of museums used press releases, press conferences, and personal relationships with local media personnel to reach large numbers of locals at low costs. Nearly 62% of the museums in his study also advertised in local media outlets.

This chapter explores the interconnectedness of community journalism with advertising and public relations, and discusses relevant theoretical perspectives from those fields that might be employed in the study of community journalism. The conclusion argues that researchers should consider that such interconnectedness may not always be problematic to journalists, but that there could be many journalistic benefits to establishing positive, mutually beneficial relationships with businesses (i.e., advertisers) and organizational advocates (i.e., PR practitioners).

❖ TRADITIONAL NEWS AND THE "DARK SIDE"

The tension between journalism and strategic communications is not just in external relationships. The sometimes idealized separation of the newsroom from advertising and marketing departments of a news organization has never been the norm for community news media.

In such operations, advertising sales representatives, circulation/ audience marketing directors, and newsroom personnel have long shared relatively small physical workplaces and company budgets. As described in Chapter 1, sometimes the news staff and the business staff of a community newspaper are the same people. That reality of the news business is often given short shrift in journalism school curricula.

Likewise, students in many leading journalism schools often are not taught about the symbiotic relationships between journalists and advertisers and public-relations practitioners. Advertisers, of course, make news dissemination possible through the revenue they provide, and, as business owners and community leaders, advertisers often are also news sources with whom reporters and editors must have professional rapport. The relationships are much more pronounced with PR practitioners. PR professionals provide "information subsidies" such as news releases, pitch story ideas, and facilitate access to public officials and corporate executives (Gandy, 1982). Yet some journalism scholars and professionals may view advertising as a necessary evil and PR as just evil.

Denise DeLorme and Fred Fedler (2003) argued that the animosity between journalism and PR arose after World War I, when newspapers feared decreased advertising revenue because of the availability of "free publicity" through PR efforts (p. 102). They analyzed nearly 500 autobiographies, biographies, and magazine articles by and about early U.S. newspaper editors and reporters, and outlined the historical roots of the modern-day mistrust between the two professions. They found it to be the result of a number of factors, including the methods and criticism of early PR practitioners—which, one might argue, became part of the journalism field's collective consciousness, handed down through the generations. Public-relations scholar James Grunig (1990) suggested that the conflict continued throughout the 20th century because many public-relations practitioners showed little regard for the ethical norms of journalism and would "do whatever it takes to gain exposure for their client organizations in the media" (p. 18). Lingering distrust between the two groups was documented 25 years ago in a Florida study (Kopenhaver, Martinson, & Ryan, 1984) and has been confirmed and reconfirmed several times since. For example, journalists and editors at more than 650 daily newspapers were surveyed in a study by Lee Bollinger (2003); Bollinger confirmed a persistent, generally negative perception of the public-relations field among journalists.

However, the negativity cannot be attributed solely to historical roots. A 2002 *Public Relations Quarterly* article reported journalists were flooded with hundreds of emails each day, many of which were reported to be "distracting nuisances" from PR people (Marken, 2002). In a 2004 article, Trudie Richards and Denel Rehberg-Sedo argued that news in general has largely become propaganda generated by the PR industry. Organizations such as the Center for Media and Democracy, with its PRWatch Web page, as well as books such as *Toxic Sludge Is Good for You: Lies, Damn Lies, and the Public Relations Industry* (Stauber & Rampton, 1998), have reinforced those prejudices with examples of government and corporate public-relations efforts that were not necessarily conducted ethically or in society's best interests. Still, journalism relies heavily on PR to produce news. Lynn Sallot and Elizabeth Johnson (2006) found in their survey of 418 U.S. journalists that, on average, the reporters estimated 44% of news content is influenced by PR work. In the U.K., a similar dependence on public-relations practitioners has been documented (Lewis, Williams, & Franklin, 2008). Interestingly, the most experienced journalists in the Sallot and Johnson study reported having better relationships with PR practitioners than those with fewer years of experience, perhaps reflecting both the veteran group's confidence in their own knowledge and journalism skills and their rapport with the PR practitioners with whom they'd developed working relationships.

Researchers Jon White and Julia Hobsbawm (2007) acknowledged that although PR is a "child of journalism," a "love-hate relationship" exists between the two professions. However, the authors argued that both professions face similar threats and, as such, must come together to address them:

> When the public makes the news via mobile phone footage . . . greater and greater commitment should be made to providing "trusted truth"— information which the public knows is sourced properly, accounted for properly, and has truly the "public interest" at its core. (p. 289)

Even today, with shrinking advertising revenues and reporter pools—arguably a time when journalists looking to keep their jobs should be softening their views toward potential allies in advertising and PR—many journalists still express largely negative sentiments toward strategic communicators (Supa & Zoch, 2009). Attitudes toward PR practitioners among 122 Florida reporters were found to be similar to or worse than attitudes in Kopenhaver and her colleagues' 1984 sample. A West Virginia study that examined the perceived value of PR practitioners to journalists during crisis situations also found such negative attitudes among journalists (Waugh, 2007). Despite those lingering prejudices, it's apparent that advertising revenues and information subsidies are essential to the news business, and it's likely their importance has long been realized and appreciated more fully in community-focused enterprises that are heavily reliant on personal knowledge and professional relationships.

❖   CONSIDERING THE "BRIGHT SIDE"

Advertisers are a recognized element in traditional news outlets' business models, and they also play an important role in educating the community about bargains, sales, and available products and services. Public-relations practitioners play a more extended "boundary spanning" role across group agendas in communities, serving as the liaisons between various stakeholders and their own community organizations. Because of that liaison role, some describe public-relations counselors as the "social conscience" of organizations. However, some scholars continue to balk at the notion that PR and advertising serve societal roles, noting that by their nature they serve private, not public, interests. Bruce Berger (2005) wrote, "There is little doubt that public relations has effectively served capitalism and powerful economic producers for many years, but whether it has served or can serve stakeholders and society as well . . . is a contested issue" (p. 6).

Perhaps today's social-media environment has changed some of that. It has forced companies to realize they no longer control the conversations about them through their paid advertising and strategic public relations conveyed via legacy media. Today, organization managers understand that if their communications are not authentic, they surely will be confronted by critics, and the ramifications of such criticism are amplified within small communities. Community journalists and their strategic-communications counterparts have long recognized the power of word of mouth and social networks at the community level; they therefore have acted accordingly to maintain credibility and positive relationships within the close-knit social structures in which they ply their trades.

Longtime public-relations scholar Robert Heath (2006) wrote,

> Many have never doubted the role of public relations in business, but others see it as being very much alive in the planning and execution of nonprofits, NGOs . . . , even activists . . . and governmental agencies. The corporate . . . role in public relations is the essence of modern public relations where organizations have replaced single individuals in the citizenship roles needed for a fully functioning society. . . . At their best, these organizations employ tactics to increase awareness and attract others—whether followers, supporters, or customers—to participate in a coordinated enactment based on shared meaning . . . that leads to and results from enlightened choice. (p. 94)

Few can argue the important role that public-affairs specialists and public-information officers (PIOs) play in their communities. Their role as liaisons between government entities and the press requires them to supply critical information about and access to all manner of governmental processes, such as policy development, law enforcement, and court decisions. That is especially true when localized health issues and public-safety crises are involved (Avery, 2010). When an industrial disaster strikes a small town, PIOs are in the spotlight to keep the community informed, whether directly or via the community news media. Even in today's social-media environment that allows direct communication strategies, Avery and her colleagues' (2010) research found that local health department personnel still rely on community media. Their spring 2009 survey of 48 U.S. states found only 17% of public health departments using social media to disseminate information.

Of course, the partnership between local media and organizational spokespersons to benefit communities extends well beyond government and health departments. When superintendents decide to close schools because of severe weather, local television and radio stations air repeated announcements while also posting the news on their websites. When power outages occur, utility spokespersons provide localized information about affected areas and service restoration timetables.

Corporate communicators also value the importance of community engagement and journalism's role in facilitating it. One recent study explored communicators' sense of obligation regarding risk and community right-to-know legislation (Palenchar & Motta, 2008).

> In a nutshell, community right to know is the principle that community residents, activists, nongovernmental and governmental agencies, businesses and industries make better collaborative decisions through transparent discourse, and at the core of transparency is community residents' right to know about health, safety and environmental risks their community faces or does not face. (p. 2)

That study included a national Web-based survey and in-depth interviews of risk and environmental communicators; the authors found strong and consistent support for providing and widely disseminating such information. One respondent was quoted as saying, "That's why we are here, to provide information to the media, mayor's office, commissioners, school districts, local businesses, anyone who wants to know what we are doing" (Palenchar & Motta, 2008, p. 25). Other studies (e.g., Heath & Palenchar, 2000) have found that community engagement in risk and crisis planning generates higher trust in the company and in local government officials, making such dialogue beneficial for all parties. That line of research could be extended to community journalism to determine whether facilitating such engagement generates higher trust among close-knit audiences as well.

When local scandals or crises do arise, existing community and media relationships also can help strategic communicators to mitigate organizational damage. Heath, Lee, and Ni (2009) found in a survey-based study in Houston that people are more likely to feel prepared to respond to local emergencies if the information is provided to them by "sources similar to them and stated in messages that are sensitive to them" (p. 123). For example, Loyola University in New Orleans was able to avoid institutional stigma in the early 2000s when its president, Rev. Bernard Knoth, resigned after being charged with sexual misconduct (Murphree & Rogers, 2004). Scholars noted that by using a community-focused approach, the university was able to deal with the situation in a manner that did not affect student enrollment or fundraising efforts. "Much of this success likely evolved from the ongoing relationships that the university had forged for years with students, faculty, staff, alumni, benefactors, and the media" (p. 34).

Advertising also provides information crucial to local communities, which is another topic ripe for media researchers. For example, the 2008–2010 recession precipitated going-out-of-business and bankruptcy sales; automobile dealers affected by the bankruptcies of Chrysler and General Motors had to aggressively promote their inventory and markdowns to local audiences. With the continued expansion of large chain stores into relatively small communities and the explosion of Internet commerce, advertising in community media is more important than ever to small, geographically limited businesses. A 2005 study found that local advertisers still regarded local newspapers and radio stations as the most effective media for advertising (Reid, King, Whitehill, Hugh, & Soh, 2005).

As online communication becomes more ubiquitous among media outlets, the outlets' ability to provide advertising and public-relations announcements in various forms holds promise for all parties. The use of social media and viral, buzz, and word-of-mouth marketing have become part of the nomenclature of the field, and strategies include Twitter, YouTube, Facebook, and correspondence with both amateur and professional bloggers. Those tools allow for inexpensive, timely, and potentially international engagement, thus expanding the possibility of reaching communities. For example, people can use social media to easily remain in touch with friends and family in their hometowns, even if they are moving around the world. Soldiers can listen to their hometown radio stations, follow their high school or college sports teams, read news reports concerning their home regions, and order goods from their favorite hometown shops. Community journalists cannot ignore the fact that they no longer provide the only forums for community discourse and interaction; audiences and advocates can bypass legacy news media entirely and seek out and publish information of their own choosing among self-selected communities.

❖ DEFINING COMMUNITIES AND RELATIONSHIPS

One thing that community journalism has in common with community-level strategic communication is a reliance on the work of building relationships, and that seems to be more pressing than ever in the age of social media. That phenomenon may be reversing what many scholars lamented as the decline of community life through the 20th century. Dean Kruckeberg and Kenneth Starck (1988) traced that lament to the Chicago School of Social Thought in the late 19th and early 20th centuries. Then, such scholars as John Dewey believed the decline of community was due to mass communication, transportation, industrialization, and urbanization. Kruckeberg and Starck wrote,

> Ironically, the Chicago School sought to restore community primarily through the original culprit—communication. The widespread use of mass media, which was impersonal in nature . . . altered people's relations to one another. One solution, the scholars felt, was . . . to open up new and replace old channels of communication. (p. 29)

Today, via social media, communication can be both mass and interpersonal, and the concept of community is far broader as well. Be it defined by geography, advocacy, issue, cause, passion, or values, community implies relationships and interdependency, much like the interdependency of PR practitioners, advertisers, and journalists to collectively tell the stories of people, products, services, accomplishments, tragedies, and issues of importance.

The two-way symmetrical model of communication—discussed in the foundational book *Excellence in Public Relations and Communication Management* (Grunig, 1992)—has at its core egalitarian dialogue for the mutual benefit of organizations and publics. Recent studies have shown that when organizations engage their communities in dialogue, people perceive the organizations more positively (Bruning, Dials, & Shirka, 2008). Other scholars (Culbertson & Knott, 2004; Leeper, 2005) have looked at communitarianism and its public-relations implications. Some view it as mirroring Grunig's two-way symmetrical model; others say the communitarian position sees the "public at the center of activity, directing the actions of institutions . . . and not the other way around" (Leeper, 2005, p. 178).

One might point to the example of the weekly California newspaper *Point Reyes Light*, which was owned by a local citizen for 30 years until its 2005 purchase by an "outsider." As discussed in a 2008 *Columbia Journalism Review* article, the newspaper's ensuing external perspective alienated readers and resulted in the development of a competing community weekly that was more in tune with the community (Rowe, 2008). The *Light*'s owner acknowledged the "'discord' that grew between himself and the West Marin community" (Walsh, 2010) after the newspaper's sale to Marin Media in May 2010. The new owners expressed hopes to create a "hybrid of a 'traditional newspaper' and a nonprofit that will foster 'community education and communication in a variety of media and formats'" (Walsh, 2010).

A valid focus of research might thus consider the degree to which symmetrical communication plays a role in modern community journalism. A recent study (O'Neill & O'Connor, 2008) looked at nearly 3,000 sampled news stories in four U.K. community newspapers to examine the sources used. They found that the papers relied less on readers for news, and that single-source stories, which omitted alternative perspectives, accounted for 76% of the articles; in many cases, articles were based on statements or releases given to the newspapers by media-relations specialists in local government, the police department, businesses, schools, and other newsworthy institutions. Such research sheds considerable light on, first, the strong interconnectedness of PR/advertising and the community press and, second, that media aimed at a particular community are not necessarily establishing relationships with the publics of that community.

Additionally, research into organizational relationships, strongly rooted in the PR and advertising disciplines, has great potential for use in studying community journalism. Stephen Bruning and John Ledingham (1999) developed a scale that examines organizational relationships on three meso-levels: personal organizational relationships, professional organizational relationships, and, most pertinent to this discussion, community/public organizational relationships. Those scholars discussed five dimensions that seem to operate within that last level: trust, openness, commitment, investment, and involvement. Others have found evidence to support duration of relationship as a sixth dimension (Ledingham, Bruning, & Wilson, 1999). When viewed as organizations that are not necessarily connected to their communities simply by virtue of being called "community media," such media could benefit from recognizing and adopting tactics used by other organizations to establish and strengthen community/public organizational relationships.

Scholars who study the PR subfield of community relations also explore relationships between organizations and communities.

Community-relations practitioners are expected to be connected to and aware of local political, business, environmental, religious, and philanthropic organizations, as well as local trends, values, and sentiments, to help their organizations engage in "corporate social responsibility" (CSR) activities. Advertising research also has found that corporations who do good deeds can sell products at prices more than 6% higher than those of their competitors (Kelleher, 2007).

Today's interactive social-media environment provides the public with the opportunity to more easily learn of CSR activities and to establish relationships with journalists and their communities through hyperlocal dialogue. Likewise, it offers opportunities for community journalists to strengthen relationships with their audiences, including strategic communicators. When the gatekeeper is removed from the equation, anyone can report to multitudes of others, and the old message-control rules no longer apply. Instead, more cooperative dialogues among those groups should be fostered to better represent— and thus better serve—the community and its varied interests.

White and Hobsbawm (2007) also recognized those dramatic changes:

> Against this background, there is a need for a new realism in the relationship between public relations practitioners and journalists. . . . The transparency that is a feature of social media and is changing social communication needs to be embraced rather than "worked around." (p. 289)

They further argued,

> Both groups need to recognize the responsibilities they share in the shaping of perceptions of social reality. The more their role in this is exposed and examined, the greater the possibility for understanding the sources of views of what is real and true in society. (p. 291)

❖ THE QUESTION OF SOCIAL NETWORKING

The *community* in *community journalism* no longer is limited by geographic boundaries, and that applies to community relations as well. Another theoretical lens that could be employed in this new, fluid media environment is that of social network analysis, or SNA. According to Fortunata Piselli (2007), the field of classical sociology referred to the concept of community as based on common residence, willingness to cooperate, and shared feeling, whereas anthropologists defined it as a territorial unit with defined geographic boundaries that included its institutions and corporations and held commonly prescribed norms. In both cases, physical proximity was paramount. Piselli wrote,

> The problem at hand was . . . called the "community question": How does the structure of large-scale social systems influence the composition, structure, and contents of interpersonal relations? And conversely, . . . [h]ow do personal bonds affect the large-scale social systems in which they are embedded? (p. 868)

Thus, Piselli explained, network analysts have gone beyond definitions of place to define community in terms of interpersonal relationships, focusing on the individual as the network center of diversified interaction that transcends physical space.

In that sense, one might view strategic communicators as being at the center of their respective communities, owing to their myriad connections as liaisons between organizations and various constituents and as businesses that cater to people with similar wants or needs. Community newspapers and broadcast outlets also might be deemed "individuals" in terms of being entities at the center of community, and thus they also are entities that benefit from having good working relationships.

Piselli (2007) noted that American scholars of network structural analysis have primarily used quantitative methods (typically, large random surveys) and have demonstrated that "diverse patterns of relations structure diverse opportunities and resources" (p. 876) for network members, whereas British social scientists have used qualitative methods (e.g., participant observation and in-depth interviews). Both lines of inquiry have shown that communities are constantly being redefined and that they merge economic and political dimensions beyond the boundaries of singular groups or places (Piselli, 2007). Such analysis is similar to what author Albert-László Barabási described in his book *Linked: How Everything Is Connected to Everything Else and What It Means* (2003). Just as there are major "hubs" of information on the Internet through which most other nodes are linked, so too there are hyperlocal physical and electronic hubs of community media. By encouraging broadly defined community voices to be part of the dialogue, a true "marketplace of ideas" develops—a place that community journalism and community-focused strategic communications are uniquely situated to foster.

In a 2007 article in *Nieman Reports*, Rick Edmonds noted the Gannett Company's move toward multiple specialty publications and its edict that its newspapers and broadcast stations become "information centers" with multiple local databases, rather than focusing exclusively on its daily print newspapers. Similarly, a Swedish media company composed of print, online, and production components created a community around itself "with the purpose of becoming important and in the end profitable" (Johansson, 2002, p. 10). It did that by employing a "cognitive dominance" strategy, gaining continuous attention through public debate and storytelling to create a common reality with its audience. Certainly, community journalism also maintains a sort of cognitive dominance within the communities it serves. In a NewsLab publication titled "What It Takes: Cultivating Quality in Local TV News" (Geisler, 2000), "understanding the community" was viewed as one of the keys for local broadcast success. Few would argue that mainstream journalism's "parachute" style—in which a reporter descends on a newsmaker or event, "gets the story," and then moves on to the next issue—is superficial journalism. Unless one has an intimate relationship and engagement with a community (including listening, observation, and dialogue), the articles about the issue or crisis being reported will have little historical context, nuance of place, or respect for long-term consequence. Most local PR practitioners and advertisers have command of such nuanced context, as do most local and specialized journalists.

Those types of issues need to be studied much more by media scholars. Community journalism as a whole differentiates itself from the big-media model by understanding its psychic and geographic place, by being sensitive to audiences' different tastes and values, and by actively engaging all of its constituents—including advocacy professionals and advertisers—in the public-opinion agora. As such, research that sheds light on community journalism's active relationships is an important area of scholarship for the future.

❖ FUTURE RESEARCH

Although the symbiotic relationships between community journalism and advertising/public relations seem clear, few have studied
their specific interdependencies or extrapolated and extended existing
scholarship to fully examine them. Therefore, studies that focus on
those relationships within community journalism would help fill an
important void in the research literature.

Such studies could include experiments to test the aforementioned
Swedish company's "cognitive dominance" success, which basically
constructed and comprehensively publicized its brand by becoming
part of the cultural consciousness (Johansson, 2002). Or they could focus
on the convergence of corporate PR, advertising, and marketing functions and its news implications for community journalists. The community relations and CSR literature (e.g., Kim, Brunner, & Fitch-Hauser,
2006; O'Connor, Shumate, & Meister, 2008) also might be useful to
scholars who want to study the importance of community journalism to
larger PR and advertising goals. Relationship and SNA literature could
provide a rich foundation by which to explore the quality of a news
entity's relationships with and connections to its audience.

In addition, the relatively recent addition in some newspapers of a
"submitted to" byline for all published news releases could be studied
in terms of audience attention and perceived credibility. Many community newspapers have filled a lot of space with such submissions,
but are they effective from a public-relations or a community journalism perspective? For example, if such pieces are not read, trusted, or
believed, is the paper serving its audience, and is the PR practitioner
serving his or her employer or client? And how does the quality of relationships among PR practitioners, advertisers, and community journalists differ, if at all, from relationships at larger media entities, about
which most studies are conducted? Are PIOs/public-affairs specialists
and corporate/nonprofit/agency communicators viewed the same
or differently among community journalists? Do times of economic
uncertainty and challenge alter those relationships in any way?

According to British journalist and journalism scholar John
Plunkett (2006), such relationships warrant exploring:

> The normal journalistic approach to PR . . . is grossly self serv-
> ing from the point of view of journalists. It glosses over, ignores

or even denies the fact that much of the current journalism, both broadcast and press, is public relations in the sense that stories, ideas, features and interviews are either suggested, or in the extreme actually written by public relations people. Until that becomes open and debated between PR people and journalists, we will continue to have this artificially wide gulf where journalists pose as fearless seekers of truth and PRs are slimy creatures trying to put one over on us. It is not remotely like that. (p. 3)

Perhaps, then, studies that examine objectively the professional similarities between advertising and public-relations practitioners and community journalists might yield the most revealing and helpful information of all. Information about sources, discovery, audiences, objectives, and standards of truth and ethics could help establish commonalities to build additional trust and foster strategic collaboration, which could ultimately be employed to serve not just distinct communities, but the broader society.

❖ REFERENCES

Avery, E. (2010). Contextual and audience moderators of channel selection and message reception of public health information in routine and crisis situations. *Journal of Public Relations Research, 22*(4), 378–403.

Avery, E., Lariscy, R., Amador, E., Ickowitz, T., Primm, C., & Taylor, A. (2010). Diffusion of social media among public relations practitioners in health departments across various community population sizes. *Journal of Public Relations Research, 22*(3), 336–358.

Barabási, A.-L. (2003). *Linked: How everything is connected to everything else and what it means for business, science, and everyday life.* New York: Plume.

Berger, B. K. (2005). Power over, power with, and power to relations: Critical reflections of public relations, the dominant coalition, and activism. *Journal of Public Relations Research, 17*(1), 5–28.

Bollinger, L. (2003). Public relations, business and the press. *Public Relations Quarterly, 48*(2), 20–23.

Bruning, S. D., Dials, M., & Shirka, A. (2008). Using dialogue to build organization-public relationships, engage publics, and positively affect organizational outcomes. *Public Relations Review, 34*(1), 25–31.

Bruning, S. D., & Ledingham, J. A. (1999). Relationship between organizations and publics: Development of a multi-dimensional scale. *Public Relations Review, 25*(2), 157–171.

Capriotti, P. (2009, May). *Cultural heritage and public relations: How museums establish relationships with their local community.* Paper presented at the annual meeting of the International Communication Association, Chicago.

Culbertson, H., & Knott, D. L. (2004). Communitarianism: Part of a world view for symmetry in communication. In *Eighth International Public Relations Research Conference Proceedings.* South Miami, FL: University of Miami.

DeLorme, D., & Fedler, F. (2003). Journalists' hostility toward public relations: An historical analysis. *Public Relations Review, 29*(2), 99–125.

Edmonds, R. (2007). The "local-local" strategy: Sense and nonsense. *Nieman Reports, 61*(4), 34–36.

Gandy, O. (1982). *Beyond agenda setting: Information subsidies and public policy.* New York: Ablex.

Geisler, J. (2000). *What it takes: Cultivating quality in local TV news.* Washington, DC: NewsLab.

Grunig, J. E. (1990). Theory and practice of interactive media relations. *Public Relations Quarterly, 35*(3), 18–23.

Grunig, J. E. (Ed.). (1992). *Excellence in public relations and communication management.* Hillsdale, NJ: Lawrence Erlbaum.

Heath, R. L. (2006). Onward into more fog: Thoughts on public relations' research directions. *Journal of Public Relations Research, 18*(2), 93–114.

Heath, R. L., Lee, J., & Ni, L. (2009). Crisis and risk approaches to emergency management planning and communication: The role of similarity and sensitivity. *Journal of Public Relations Research, 21*(2), 123–141.

Heath, R. L., & Palenchar, M. J. (2000). Community relations and risk communication: A longitudinal study of the impact of emergency response messages. *Journal of Public Relations Research, 12*(2), 131–161.

Johansson, T. (2002). Lighting the campfire: The creation of a community of interest around a media company. *International Journal on Media Management, 4*(1), 4–12.

Kelleher, K. A. (2007). "Good" matters to consumers. *Advertising Age, 78*(49), 4–5.

Kim, S. H., Brunner, B. R., & Fitch-Hauser, M. E. (2006). Exploring community relations in a university setting. *Public Relations Review, 32*(2), 191–193.

Kopenhaver, L. L., Martinson, D. L., & Ryan, M. (1984). How public relations practitioners and editors in Florida view each other. *Journalism Quarterly, 61*(4), 860–884.

Kruckeberg, D., & Starck, K. (1988). *Public relations and community: A reconstructed theory.* New York: Praeger.

Ledingham, J. A., Bruning, S. D., & Wilson, L. J. (1999). Time as an indicator of the perceptions and behavior of members of a key public: Monitoring and predicting organization-public relationships. *Journal of Public Relations Research, 11*(2), 167–184.

Leeper, K. A. (2005). Communitarianism. In R. L. Heath, *Encyclopedia of Public Relations* (Vol. 1). Thousand Oaks, CA: Sage.

Lewis, J., Williams, A., & Franklin, B. (2008). A compromised Fourth Estate? UK news journalism, public relations and news sources. *Journalism Studies, 9*(1), 1–20.

Marken, G. A. (2002). Trade shows + email + PR people = journalists' wrath. *Public Relations Quarterly, 47*(2), 29–31.

Murphree, V., & Rogers, C. (2004). "A hell of a shock": When a Jesuit university faces a presidential sex allegation. *Public Relations Quarterly, 49*(3), 34–40.

O'Connor, A., Shumate, M., & Meister, M. (2008). Walk the line: Active moms define corporate social responsibility. *Public Relations Review, 34*(4), 343–350.

O'Neill, D., & O'Connor, C. (2008). The passive journalist. *Journalism Practice, 2*(3), 487–500.

Palenchar, M., & Motta, B. (2008, November). *Community right to know and environmental justice: Public relations practitioners are neither getting nor using the message.* Paper presented at the national convention of the National Communication Association, San Diego, CA.

Piselli, F. (2007). Communities, places, and social networks. *American Behavioral Scientist, 50*(7), 867–878.

Plunkett, J. (2006, April 10). Press and PR partnership—Networking or not working. *MediaGuardian,* p. 3.

Reid, L. N., King, K., Whitehill, M., Hugh, J., & Soh, H. (2005). Local advertising decision makers' perceptions of media effectiveness and substitutability. *Journal of Media Economics, 18*(1), 35–53.

Richards, T., & Rehberg-Sedo, D. (2004). Journalists rely too heavily on spinmeisters. *Media, 10*(4), 18–38.

Rowe, J. (2008). The language of strangers: How a hotshot editor with big ideas failed to comprehend the soul of community journalism. *Columbia Journalism Review, 46*(5), 36–40.

Sallot, L. M., & Johnson, E. A. (2006). Investigating relationships between journalists and public relations practitioners: Working together to set, frame and build the public agenda. *Public Relations Review, 32*(2), 151–159.

Smith, A. (2003). Community relations: How an entire industry can change its image through proactive local communications. *Journal of Communication Management, 7*(3), 254–264.

Stauber, J., & Rampton, S. (1998). *Toxic sludge is good for you: Lies, damn lies, and the public relations industry.* Monroe, ME: Common Courage Press.

Supa, D. W., & Zoch, L. M. (2009, March). *Maximizing media relationships through a better understanding of the public relations–journalist relationship: A quantitative analysis of changes over the past 23 years.* Paper presented at the International Public Relations Research Conference, Coral Gables, FL.

Walsh, J. (2010, May 27). Nonprofit buys *"Point Reyes Light." Pacific Sun.* Retrieved November 10, 2010, from www.pacificsun.com/news/story_print.php?story_id=1824

Waugh, C. A. (2007). The relationship between journalists and public relations practitioners during crises. *Master's Abstracts International, 46*(04). (UMI No. 1451685)

White, J., & Hobsbawm, J. (2007). Public relations and journalism. *Journalism Practice, 1*(2), 283–292.

The Economics of Community Newspapers ●

Stephen Lacy

All newspapers share certain economic realities. They must provide valuable services to the people in their markets, and they must make enough profit to stay in business. They face risks and uncertainties. But the economic factors faced by community newspapers differ from those faced by the large-circulation newspapers that seem to dominate people's ideas of what constitutes "real" journalism.

A journalism professor once told me that the difference between big-city newspapers and community newspapers is that when you work at a community newspaper, you drink coffee with your sources and readers. Community journalism is more intimate, and the relationship with community members often more resembles a familial than a professional relationship.

Community members demand that their newspapers deliver information and news about the people and institutions in their community. They also see the newspaper as a way to bring local buyers and sellers together through advertising. But they expect more. They expect the newspaper to connect community members not as customers, but as equal members of a group of people with shared values and experiences.

When I edited weekly suburban newspapers outside Dallas, Texas, another editor told me that community newspaper editors had to enjoy being at the center of a community's activities because that was their job. For example, he said he didn't mind covering the Friday night high school football game because he would have been there anyway.

Community newspapers must meet the demand for news and information in a way that recognizes a special relationship with those demanding the news. A community journalist must report on events and people not as a doctor or lawyer delivering a diagnosis or advice, but as a family member explaining the meaning of what another family member said or did. Connecting community members is a prime function of a quality community newspaper. How much people will pay for a newspaper reflects the value they place on it. A newspaper that connects a community has much higher value than one that does not, and it will be worth the price of subscription to most community members.

But what about advertising? Isn't that just about attracting as many eyeballs as possible and selling that to advertisers, regardless of the type of newspaper? Not necessarily. If a newspaper is meeting a community's demand for news, information, and connectedness, people who want to sell products and services to that community will want to be identified with the central role community newspapers play. That is especially true of businesses that are competitive in the community. Having an advertisement in a newspaper read by many community members can differentiate those businesses from the competitors that do not advertise in the newspaper.

Today's technological shifts are creating new challenges for community newspapers' ability to stay in business and make profits, but, again, their central role in community life gives those newspapers many advantages. Large metropolitan dailies have viewed the Internet as a threat to their business. The role community newspapers serve—that of connectors—creates a great opportunity for them to use the Web to enhance those connections. On the Web, big local stories do not have to wait for the print version (which could appear only once weekly), and as such community news can be timelier. Local advertising can become more interactive. The Web is perfect for connecting people, and community newspapers that allow citizens to participate in a wide range of online activities can create a higher degree of community connectedness using online communication tools. A community newspaper's website should become a portal to news, information, advertising, discussion and any other form of communication that defines the community. That approach should work whether the community is geographic or topical.

It may not maximize profits, but serving a community well can provide a good income and a rewarding career for modern journalists, and the study of community newspapers can provide interesting research opportunities for media economists.

Stephen Lacy *is a professor and associate dean for graduate studies in the College of Communication Arts and Sciences at Michigan State University. He has written or cowritten more than 85 refereed journal articles, more than 50 refereed conference papers, 10 book chapters, and four books. He has coedited two other books and written numerous other articles. He is currently coeditor of the* Journal of Media Economics.

9

Broadcasting and Community Journalism

George L. Daniels

Around the world, many communities are served by local broadcast media that provide local news and public information—community journalism—along with arts and entertainment programming. Those radio and television stations that produce local entertainment programs as well as local news programs are the archetypes of "community broadcasters," as they often reflect community culture more holistically than news-only or entertainment-only media. Even entertainment-only stations provide at least a rudimentary form of community journalism by offering local weather forecasts, traffic reports, calendars of events, and local public service announcements; in times of crisis, such as natural disasters, entertainment programming may be interrupted or replaced with important safety and recovery information (see Tanner, Friedman, Barr, & Koskan, 2008). For those reasons and more, broadcast media play an important, if often overlooked, role in the broader phenomenon of community journalism.

Broadcast news has been a part of our society for nearly a century. Beginning with radio in the 1920s, followed by television in the 1950s, news delivered over the airwaves has been an important source of information that is relevant, up-to-date, and, thanks to many new technologies, remains relatively inexpensive to distribute to wide audiences today. Some historians have identified major national or international news events—such as the assassination of U.S. president John F. Kennedy and the first man to land on the moon—as defining moments for the broadcast TV news medium. Local news, both on radio and TV, have been defined far more by their influence on communities. As others have noted, local television news programming is the most visible element of local TV stations in U.S. broadcasting (Rosengard, 2004); many stations are affiliated with national networks, such that the bulk of their entertainment or educational programming is not as distinct as local news. Thus, it would behoove researchers studying community journalism, especially when using a geographic definition of community, to carefully consider the role of local broadcast news in community life.

When studying contemporary broadcast news through the lens of community journalism, it is virtually impossible to separate an over-the-air radio or television station from its corresponding content on the Internet. Some have even suggested that a local broadcast licensee today has at least two stations: one over the air, the other online. In fact, some television station managers in 2009 were talking about a "three-screen" strategy—referring to over-the-air broadcasts, content for the Internet, and content for mobile devices (the third screen). More recently, the term "TV 2.0" has come into vogue as a reference to television offering the "four A's"— any content, watched anytime, anywhere, on any device (Morabito, 2010). Indeed, the World Wide Web has accelerated the fragmentation of the broadcast audience for more than a decade, just as it has the audiences for print media. But, for the researcher, that redefinition of a local broadcaster in Web terms as well as over-the-air terms provides an opportunity for studying a broader definition of community journalism. Yet over-the-air broadcasting has been and remains an important source of community journalism, particularly in developing regions of the world. This chapter focuses on over-the-air media considerations; online media are discussed more broadly in the next chapter.

Given the fact that broadcasting ushered in many opportunities for new forms of community journalism, it bears repeating that until fairly recently community journalism research has been mostly "newspaper-centric." Only a relative handful of researchers have produced community journalism scholarship relating to broadcast news. The concept of *community* in *community journalism* is really concerned with the relationships between journalists and communities through any medium, whether it be the Internet or a radio or television broadcast, but the practices of broadcast journalism add distinct dimensions to such inquiry. Because much of the literature to date related specifically to "community journalism" has focused on newspapers, the study of community journalism in other media forms must cast a broader net and apply more liberal interpretations of published studies. Therefore, some of the literature reviewed for this chapter may use the term *public journalism* or *civic journalism* rather than *community journalism*, which reflects the considerable overlap of those distinct concepts. As expressed in Chapter 1, community journalism is about community connectedness and not necessarily restricted by the media platforms used or the form of community served (geographic, ethnic, professional, etc.). When studying broadcast media as players in community life, scholars should consider all of the literature focusing on how the producers of news messages link up or connect with their communities (including studies of "civic" or "public" journalism). And although television is often the focus of contemporary studies of broadcast journalism, it should be noted that in much of the world, radio remains much more exemplary of community journalism than TV, although TV is worth studying through a community journalism lens.

❖ COMMUNITY JOURNALISM IN TELEVISION

Because of its high operating costs, local television news tends to originate from stations in only major cities or large geographic regions, and as such TV news is often not focused on distinct communities as other media forms (such as newspapers, radio, and websites) frequently are. Yet local television news often places a great deal of emphasis on its "local" or "hometown" interests, which suggests that even without distinct communities to focus on, local television journalism often does exhibit characteristics of community journalism. Studies of local and regional TV news provide some basis for new research focused much more on the "community" aspects of TV journalism.

Scholar David Kurpius (2004) has done some of the most important recent work in civic/public journalism in broadcast media, and his findings certainly can inform new studies of community journalism. A former broadcast journalism and television news director himself, Kurpius spent the better part of a decade doing content analyses, in-depth interviews, and ethnographic observations to study the inclusion of stakeholders and communities missing in television news coverage. Rather than staking out a methodological specialty, Kurpius let his research questions guide the different methods he chose. In one of his early studies, Kurpius (2000) conducted more than 90 interviews (most at least 30 minutes long) and spent countless hours observing broadcast journalists at work, which led him to identify the key elements of what he called "community-conscious" television stations—different stations that exhibited similar characteristics in regard to market position, organizational structure, norms and routines of journalistic work, and commitment to public journalism. That study informed a later project, a content analysis of 184 entries for a TV civic journalism award (Kurpius, 2002), which generated hard evidence of the impact of civic journalism routines (such as encouraging television journalists to get to know and trust people in diverse communities) in community journalism. Such community-mindedness resulted in greater racial and gender diversity among sources (Kurpius, 2002). Another content analysis of calls to C-SPAN's *Washington Journal* program provided empirical evidence of how a call-in show can help foster meaningful dialogue with regard to consciousness raising, working through issues, and reaching resolutions (Kurpius & Mendelson, 2002). Even though that study was focused on a national program with a national audience, the findings also suggest that call-in shows exhibit many of the characteristics of community journalism. More directly related to community journalism, the data Kurpius (2004) has collected over the years has allowed him to make a convincing argument that journalists who spend time in lower-class neighborhoods will more accurately reflect the realities of lower-class life in their coverage.

Another important starting point for studies of community journalism in electronic media is consideration of the late Phyllis Kaniss's book-length studies of metropolitan broadcasting. For part of her landmark book *Making Local News* (1991), Kaniss analyzed the content of three network-affiliated stations' newscasts for two single-week periods, all in Philadelphia, Pennsylvania, one of the largest media markets in the U.S. In addition to finding similarity among the newscasts of the three stations in their balancing of government stories with stories about crimes, fires, and accidents, the study found 37% of all newstime was devoted to covering the city of Philadelphia, while news from the surrounding suburbs received attention just 18% of the time (p. 126). In the second study, Kaniss (1995) followed Philadelphia media's coverage of the city's 1991 mayoral race. Compared to the city's major newspapers,

> the typical local television station appears less concerned with social responsibility and less willing to spend the money necessary to improve the quality of information provided to voters. . . . [T]he low-budget approach to local television news coverage seems to have grown even stronger, resulting in more tabloid-like coverage of sensational crimes, more canned reports picked up from the satellites, and less local campaign coverage than ever. (p. 378)

John H. McManus's *Market-Driven Journalism* (1994) also provided some in-depth research of broadcast journalism in distinct communities. McManus focused primarily on how market logic in producing broadcast news influenced the product, which journalists suggest reflects the highest journalistic standards. His model of commercial news production is useful in understanding at a theoretical level how local stations may make newsroom decisions that are much more products of community market forces as broader standards of professional journalism. McManus built his argument upon the "gatekeeper" process as applied in local news, by which certain individuals in the television station decide which stories end up in newscasts and which do not.

Other scholars have considered the gatekeeping aspects of community broadcast media. Berkowitz (1990) used a combination of qualitative and quantitative observation techniques to study stations in the Indianapolis market, which at the time was the 24th-largest market in the U.S. A decade earlier, Bantz, McCorkle, and Baade (1980) had looked at some of those same issues using participant observation. Both studies provided groundbreaking research not only in defining the news making process, but also in beginning to study the role of broadcasters in community journalism. Generally, such studies are based on analyzing the content of broadcast news stories, with the implicit assumption that the TV broadcast medium is often criticized for its superficial delivery of complicated news stories.

Community journalism researchers interested in television news content also would be well served to consider the body of work about journalistic routines, sometimes referred to as "news making" or "news work." One example of such inquiry came from Berkowitz (1992), who conducted research on how broadcast newsrooms covered big breaking stories, or what Berkowitz termed the "what-a-story." In that research, Berkowitz did a case study of a major-market station's coverage of a plane crash for its evening newscast. Included in that coverage were interruptions of regular programming with such things as news bulletins and commentary by public officials, all putting the story into bigger context locally.

Community journalism scholars interested in TV news also should read the work of Tony Atwater and his colleagues. Atwater (1984) was among the first to explore story "sameness" and "consonance" by analyzing the evening television newscasts in three markets in the same region—Detroit and Lansing in Michigan, and Toledo, Ohio. Atwater found that unique news stories made up half the stories in his sample; the larger-market stations, with their longer newscasts, were more likely to have such stories than those in other markets (p. 760). In another article, Atwater (1986) focused on the sameness or consonance among the stories from stations in those same markets. Defined as the percentage of stories broadcast by two or more television stations within a market, consonance was found to be as common in local markets as at the network level, with one of every two stories having been aired on another TV station (Atwater, 1986). A decade later, Davie and Lee (1996) built on Atwater's research using recorded newscasts from three major markets in Texas: Dallas, San Antonio, and Austin. They found that the highest percentage of unique stories from stations in those markets was sports stories. In their study, 70% of so-called "sensational" stories (stories regarding sex or violence) appeared on more than one station (p.134). That line of inquiry is certainly worthy of further exploration.

The "civic journalism" movement of recent decades has fostered a number of newsroom efforts that also exhibit community journalism. Kurpius (2001) combined content analysis strategies with semi-structured interviews with news workers to indicate that foundation-funded efforts such as Best Practices 2000—which involved partnerships among local commercial and public television stations—worked best because they created new airtime for stories and specials focused on politics and community issues. That contrasted with earlier findings by McManus (1994), which suggested that market-driven TV journalism provided the least expensive mix of content and protected the interests of the sponsors and investors while garnering the largest audience and, as such, attracting more advertising revenue (p. 85). The merits of such market-driven decisions may correlate with results from a later study, a mail survey of 283 television journalists from all 214 U.S. television markets, which showed a perceived downward trend in coverage of local government news (Coulson, Riffe, Lacy, & Charles, 2001). Smaller markets, however, were where local television was doing the best job of covering city hall news (p. 90).

Another area for scholars to consider is the role of local TV news in providing health and science information to communities. Corbett (1998) built on Berkowitz's expansion of the gatekeeping metaphor by examining the environmental news coverage of a Minnesota television station. The station devoted a recurring segment to environmental news, and Corbett found that scientists were used as sources in only 6% of stories, whereas government sources were the most prevalent among those presented on-camera. Also, the largest number of stories focused on governmental policy and regulation rather than the science of environmental studies (Corbett, 1998). The origins of science and health story ideas also are an area worthy of study. Tanner (2004) used a nationwide survey of local-television reporters to examine the link between agenda building and health news delivered by local television stations. More than half of the local-TV reporters surveyed received ideas for their health reports from public-relations professionals who contacted them, but

other popular manners in which the health reporters said they receive story ideas included a phone call or e-mail from a viewer or information from other media outlets, such as the newspaper or wire services. This suggests the reporters are learning of story ideas through a "passive news discovery process" in which reporters find story ideas without ever leaving the newsroom. (p. 25)

That study suggests that community connections may play only a minor role in how local TV news covers community health and environment issues. Miller, Augenbraun, Schulhof, and Kimmel (2006) found that science and health stories in local television newscasts may enhance viewers' existing schemas for considering science/health information.

Many of the studies mentioned above have been produced in the past 10 years, suggesting that TV community journalism is receiving more attention from scholars. Likewise, researchers have in recent years identified better ways of capturing local television content for the purpose of conducting research (Hale, Fowler, & Goldstein, 2007); newer technology makes the study of TV news much easier than it was in the videotape era. Dramatic changes in the TV industry also are worth studying, such as the recruitment of "community correspondents" to provide content after massive staff cutbacks in television newsrooms during the recession of 2008–2010. For example, the community correspondent idea was pursued by Pappas Telecasting, owner of more than two dozen television stations in the U.S (Niekamp, 2009). The online components of local TV news operations also are getting some attention from researchers. For example, Niekamp (2009) analyzed online posts to websites of television stations in three communities; in terms of journalistic values, he found that neither attribution nor bias was evident in many of the citizen-produced stories. Likewise, few of the contributors tried to mimic professional reporters (p. 50).

Postrecession television station groups, such as NBC's Nonstop digital channels for local news (Malone, 2010a) and Raycom Media's television stations, generated local news for a national syndicated show, *America Now* (Malone, 2010b). Those new models showcase community TV news in an unconventional manner, even with the online complements in the form of companion websites. It will be interesting to study how local TV news changes its on-air practices in light of those developments.

❖ COMMUNITY JOURNALISM IN RADIO

No one studying community journalism should overlook radio. In much of the world, radio remains a significant part of the community news sector, although in many developed nations community radio has seen sharp declines. In the United States, for example, a few noncommercial outlets—NPR (formerly National Public Radio) and its program competitors, American Public Media and Public Radio International—have seen audiences grow, but many commercial radio outlets still providing local news have turned to outsourcing to gather and deliver community news. Hood (2010) combined content analysis with in-depth interviews and field observations to compare remotely delivered news produced for multiple stations in a regional "hub" with locally delivered news. That study of 454 stories aired between 2004 and 2007 showed that decisions about local news content had been taken away from producers in the community, which may have led to news that was not really "local" in focus (Hood, 2010).

Community radio is quite important in the developing world, particularly for communities in Africa, Asia, and South America. Studies of community radio provide excellent opportunities for international research, cross-cultural collaboration, and perhaps even funded research by governments and non-governmental organizations. That is not to say that studies of community radio in the developed world are not useful or needed. There have been a number of important studies along those lines in the past decade. Hardyk, Loges, and Ball-Rokeach (2005) used a case study of storytelling practices of two Los Angeles radio stations, one a commercial hip-hop station and the other a public radio station. By analyzing ratings and financial data from the stations as well as conducting interviews with key individuals, the authors found both stations were successful as storytellers because they found a way to include local community issues in their programs. They balanced the stations' financial interests against their interest in community building (p. 179). In addition to studies on community radio such as Dunaway's (2005) examination of Pacifica radio, Sussman and Estes (2005) conducted a case study of a community radio station in Portland, Oregon: KBOO. The study found that KBOO devoted its attention to promoting community-based initiatives and providing training for local residents in regard to public transmission, radio news production, political education, and mobilization (p. 235). Even news that simply "sounds" local can slightly improve listeners' attitudes toward news (Hubbard, 2010).

One developed nation that has benefited from study of its community radio landscape is Australia. Forde, Foxwell, and Meadows (2003) looked at the Australian community radio sector to understand the role of community (or "public arena") journalism in offering different frameworks by which audience members make sense of the world around them. The research team used surveys and focus group discussions of community journalists to better understand the cultural role they play in providing communities with a "local voice" (p. 332). Furthermore, the team found that the news and current affairs coverage of the Australian community radio sector relied heavily on local meetings, conversations, regular contacts, and local newspapers for story ideas. In a follow-up article, Meadows, Forde, Ewart, and Foxwell (2009) called community radio the "foundation for community journalism." Their research suggested that traditional definitions of news and newsworthiness in Australia have been renegotiated when one talks about community journalism in terms of radio (p. 167). A more recent study found that only one quarter of Australian community radio stations offered their own original news service (Forde, 2010). That gap, researchers found, was being filled by the community media sector with a model of "citizen journalism," or news provision that engaged members of the local community in on-air discussions about upcoming events, politics, and social concerns (p. 188).

The study of community radio in developed nations may be a small niche for additional research, but it is an important niche. Several useful studies have explored community radio in Europe, such as a study of radio for ethnic Turks in the Netherlands (Cankaya, Güney & Köksalan, 2008), a study of the decline of community radio due to commercialization pressures in the Flanders region of Belgium (Evens & Hauttekeete, 2008), and a study of intercultural programming for various ethnic communities in Switzerland (Borger & Bellardi, 2010). Hallett and Hintz (2010) suggested that the advance of digital radio creates both challenges and opportunities for community radio across Europe. Cammaerts (2009) argued that community radio has often struggled in the West due to not only market forces, but also regulations written for larger commercial broadcasters. Cammaerts found that in the U.S., U.K., and Belgium, community radio is often positioned as an amateurish and/or "rogue" element of the broader industry, and as such tends to be marginalized. The study of regulatory issues as they relate to community radio is certainly worthy of additional research, not only in the developed West, but around the globe.

There has been a flurry of recent research focused on community radio in the developing world. When taking a more global approach to studying community radio, researchers must consider that different countries (and different regions within countries) may exhibit different relationships between broadcast journalism and communities. Radio in particular can be an important medium in developing nations for communities with low literacy rates, for communities that need specialized information, or for communities in rural regions with dispersed residents and little to no infrastructure, which combined make other forms of community journalism, including newspapers and online media, unfeasible.

One area that has already seen some important research is the role of community radio in serving specific subgroups or achieving socioeconomic progress. Such studies cover a broad range of cultures and topics. Some examples include a study of the role of radio in helping to establish civil society in post–civil war El Salvador (Agosta, 2007) and another focusing on the potential for community radio to serve rural communities in South Africa (Megwa, 2007). One study considered the difficulties faced by development-communication radio in rural Nigeria (Ojebode, 2008), and yet another compared the effectiveness of radio to other media forms among women's self-help groups in rural parts of southeast India (Prathap & Ponnusamy, 2009). Community radio is also important for population centers, of course, which is why more research is needed of community radio projects such as Koch FM, which serves the Nairobi ghetto of Korogocho (Koch FM, n.d.).

There also are any number of regulatory, economic, and cultural topics that can be explored via the study of community radio. Ownership issues in particular have been studied in recent years. For example, Elliott (2010) considered grassroots community radio in Thailand and found that locally controlled radio stations offer a promising alternative to state- or corporate-owned radio. Conversely, Mhlanga (2009) found that a radio station created by the South African Broadcasting Corporation aimed at creating a "community" among two distinct ethnic groups did not adequately serve the intended community but rather served as an extension of the national system. Ojebode and Akingbulu (2009) suggested that the democratization of Nigeria has not resulted in the development of truly community-based radio stations as hoped; rather, autocrats and governmental officials have maintained regulatory control over the radio airwaves similar to when the nation was governed by the military.

The role of community radio in cultural development also has been the topic of some recent study. For example, McKay (2009) discussed how direct dialogues among community radio personnel and local residents has the potential to improve the communities' management of natural resources, such as fisheries and timberland. Leal (2009) studied community radio around the Federal District of Brazil to assess the role of those stations as forums for cross-community debate and/or advocacy for distinct communities. A number of the studies have considered the role of community radio in post-revolutionary situations, such as the previously mentioned study that found a lack of community radio in democratic Nigeria (Ojebode & Akingbulu, 2009) and another study focusing on the rise of clandestine community radio in post-independent Zimbabwe (Moyo, 2010).

One overarching question that arises from the plethora of community radio studies is whether "community radio" is synonymous with "radio community journalism." Perhaps some distinctions could be made between the two, particularly when considering programming that is more akin to entertainment than to news and opinion. There does appear to be significant overlap, however, just as there is considerable overlap of "civic journalism" and "community journalism" in regard to local TV news. A broad-minded approach to the topic of community radio may be more appropriate and beneficial than drawing and defending strict delineations between community radio and radio-borne community journalism.

❖ CONCLUSION

The examples offered above reflect just some of the many approaches scholars can take if they wish to research community journalism within the broadcasting industry. Indeed, because the area is under-researched compared to many other aspects of journalism and mass communication, there is considerable opportunity here for scholars to develop and test new approaches, to advance existing theories or suggest new concepts, and also to examine issues that have been overlooked for decades. Even as research of newer digital and Internet-based media sometimes eclipses research of more traditional broadcast media outlets (or as, to some extent, the two become indistinguishable), there is value in conducting community-focused research about just localized broadcast news media and their audiences. That is certainly true with research in rural and/or underdeveloped regions, where broadcast news (particularly radio) is very much woven into community life and structure.

Another challenge of studying community journalism in electronic media is the considerable crossover, or convergence, of different media forms in the early 21st century. The so-called "legacy" media of community journalism—local newspapers and local broadcasting stations—have largely embraced online communication, and the flexibility of online delivery means of course that traditionally "print" media (newspapers and magazines) can produce broadcast-style video and/or audio content, while traditionally "broadcast" media are providing content online that is very similar to print content (articles intended to be read, along with still photographs and informational graphics). Scholars studying contemporary community journalism should not overlook the role of convergence in today's media environment.

Even as online communication becomes more ubiquitous in society, it is important to remember that over-the-air broadcasting remains a large segment of the journalism industry. Television news dominates the landscape as people's major source of news. When respondents in a 2006 study by the Radio-Television News Directors Foundation were asked to name up to three sources for their news, 65% identified local TV news, and TV news was identified as the "first choice for news" by those in every demographic group (Papper, 2006). Even though television stations today are reportedly airing more local newscasts than ever, with 4:30 a.m. newscasts available in 44 out of 56 metered markets (Malone, 2010c), a State of the News Media (2010) study showed that audiences continued to decline for newscasts across all time slots. After cutting back and positioning themselves for more newsroom high-definition upgrades (Winslow, 2010), over-the-air broadcast stations anticipate a vastly improved advertising market (Albiniak, 2011) and the opportunity for locally produced community journalism across multiple platforms. Those industry conditions suggest that broadcast news will continue to be a major player in the journalism industry, and as such a topic of interest for community journalism scholars.

❖ REFERENCES

Agosta, D. E. (2007). Constructing civil society, supporting local development: A case study of community radio in postwar El Salvador. *Democratic Communiqué, 21*(1), 4–26.

Albiniak, P. (2011). Time to step up: Stations have (some) money again. Now syndicators have to earn it. *Broadcasting and Cable, 141*(4), 10–11.

Atwater, T. (1984). Product differentiation in local TV news. *Journalism Quarterly, 61*(4), 757–762.

Atwater, T. (1986). Consonance in local television news. *Journal of Broadcasting and Electronic Media, 30*(4), 467–472.

Bantz, C. R., McCorkle, S., & Baade, R. C. (1980). The news factory. *Communication Research, 7*(1), 45–68.

Berkowitz, D. (1990). Refining the gatekeeping metaphor for local television news. *Journal of Broadcasting and Electronic Media, 34,* 55–68.

Berkowitz, D. (1992). Routine newswork and the what-a-story: A case study of organizational adaption. *Journal of Broadcasting and Electronic Media, 36*(1), 45–60.

Borger, A., & Bellardi, N. (2010). From coexistence to cooperation: Experiments in intercultural broadcasting in Swiss community radios. *Telematics and Informatics, 27*(2), 182–186

Cammaerts, B. (2009). Community radio in the West. *International Communication Gazette, 71*(8), 635–654.

Cankaya, Ö., Güney, H. S., & Köksalan, M. E. (2008). Turkish radio broadcasts in the Netherlands: Community communication or ethnic market? *Westminster Papers in Communication and Culture, 5*(1), 86–106.

Corbett, J. B. (1998). Media, bureaucracy, and the success of social protest: Newspaper coverage of environmental movement groups. *Mass Communication and Society, 1*(1–2), 41–60.

Coulson, D. C., Riffe, D., Lacy, S., & Charles, C. R. (2001). Erosion of television coverage of city hall? Perceptions of TV reporters on the beat. *Journalism and Mass Communication Quarterly, 78*(1), 81–92.

Davie, W. R., & Lee, J.-S. (1996). Sex, violence and consonance/differentiation: An analysis of local TV news values. *Journalism and Mass Communication Quarterly, 72*(2), 128–138.

Dunaway, D. K. (2005). Pacifica radio and community broadcasting. *Journal of Radio Studies, 12*(2), 240–255.

Elliott, P. W. (2010). Another radio is possible: Thai community radio from the grass roots to the global. *Radio Journal: International Studies in Broadcast and Audio Media, 8*(1), 7–22.

Evens, T., & Hauttekeete, L. (2008). From hero to zero: How commercialism ruined community radio in Flanders. *Radio Journal: International Studies in Broadcast and Audio Media, 6*(2–3), 95–112.

Forde, S. (2010). The lure of local: "News" definitions in community broadcasting. *Pacific Journalism Review, 16*(1), 178–191.

Forde, S., Foxwell, K., & Meadows, M. (2003). Through the lens of the local: Public arena journalism in the Australian community broadcasting sector. *Journalism, 4*(3), 314–335.

Hale, M., Fowler, E. F., Goldstein, K. M. (2007). Capturing multiple markets: A new method of capturing and analyzing local television news. *Electronic News, 1*(4), 227–243.

Hallett, L., & Hintz, A. (2010). Digital broadcasting: Challenges and opportunities for European community radio broadcasters. *Telematics and Informatics, 27*(2), 151–161.

Hardyk, B., Loges, W. E., Ball-Rokeach, S. J. (2005). Radio as a successful local storyteller in Los Angeles: A case study of KKBT and KPCC. *Journal of Radio Studies, 12*(1), 156–181.

Hood, L. (2010). Radio recentered: Local news returns home. *Journal of Radio and Audio Media, 17*(2), 151–166.

Hubbard, G. T. (2010). Putting radio localism to the test: An experimental study of listener responses to locality of origination and ownership. *Journal of Broadcasting and Electronic Media, 54*(3), 407–424.

Kaniss, P. (1991). *Making local news.* Chicago: University of Chicago Press.

Kaniss, P. (1995). *The media and the mayor's race: The failure of urban political reporting.* Bloomington: Indiana University Press.

Koch FM. (n.d.). *About Koch FM.* Retrieved April 30, 2011, from http://kochfm.org/about/

Kurpius, D. D. (2000). Public journalism and commercial local television news: In search of a model. *Journalism and Mass Communication Quarterly, 7*(2), 340–354.

Kurpius, D. D. (2001). *A report for Best Practices 2000 on election coverage innovations.* Madison, WI: Best Practices 2000.

Kurpius, D. (2002). Sources and civic journalism: Changing patterns of reporting? *Journalism and Mass Communication Quarterly, 79*(4), 853–866.

Kurpius, D. (2004). Television civic journalism and the portrayal of class. In D. Heider (Ed.), *Class and news* (pp. 325–337). Lanham, MD: Rowman & Littlefield.

Kurpius, D. D., & Mendelson, A. (2002). A case study of deliberative democracy on television: Civic dialogue on C-SPAN call-in shows. *Journalism and Mass Communication Quarterly, 79*(3), 587–601.

Leal, S. (2009). Community radio broadcasting in Brazil: Action rationales and public space. *Radio Journal: International Studies in Broadcast and Audio Media, 7*(2), 155–170.

Malone, M. (2010a, September 20). Multiple platforms key to NBC's local strategy. *Broadcasting and Cable, 140*(35), 22.

Malone, M. (2010b, September 27). Raycom repurposing with a purpose. *Broadcasting and Cable, 140*(36), 32.

Malone, M. (2010c, October 11). Stations aim "4" very early risers: Forget the 4:30 news—Some outlets find viewers at 4 a.m. *Broadcasting and Cable, 140*(38), 18.

McKay, B. (2009). Using community radio in Ghana to facilitate community participation in natural resource management. *Ecquid Novi: African Journalism Studies, 30*(1), 73–93.

McManus, J. H. (1994). *Market-driven journalism: Let the citizen beware.* Thousand Oaks, CA: Sage.

Meadows, M., Forde, S., Ewart, J., & Foxwell, K. (2009). Making good sense: Transformative processes in community journalism. *Journalism, 10*(2), 155–170.

Megwa, E. R. (2007). Bridging the digital divide: Community radio's potential for extending information and communication technology benefits to poor rural communities in South Africa. *Howard Journal of Communications, 18*(4), 335–352.

Mhlanga, B. (2009). The community in community radio: A case study of XK FM, interrogating issues of community participation, governance, and control. *Ecquid Novi: African Journalism Studies, 30*(1), 58–72.

Miller, J. D., Augenbraun, E., Schulhof, J., & Kimmel, L. G. (2006). Adult science learning from local television newscasts. *Science Communication, 28*(2), 216–242.

Morabito, A. (2010). Rise of TV 2.0 follows consumer behavior. *Broadcasting and Cable, 140*(41), 10.

Moyo, D. (2010). Reincarnating clandestine radio in post-independent Zimbabwe. *Radio Journal: International Studies in Broadcast and Audio Media, 8*(1), 23–36.

Niekamp, R. (2009). Community correspondent: One broadcaster's attempt at citizen journalism. *Southwestern Mass Communication Journal, 24*(2), 45–53.

Ojebode, A. (2008). Low patronage of development radio programmes in rural Nigeria: How to get beyond the rhetoric of participation. *Journal of Multicultural Discourses, 3*(2), 135–145.

Ojebode, A., & Akingbulu, A. (2009). Community radio advocacy in democratic Nigeria: Lessons for theory and practice. *Ecquid Novi: African Journalism Studies, 30*(2), 204–218.

Papper, R. (2006). *The future of news: A study by the Radio-Television News Directors Foundation.* Retrieved April 28, 2011, from http://www.rtdna.org/pages/media_items/future-of-news-survey-2006493.php?id=493

Prathap, D. P., & Ponnusamy, K. A. (2009). A comparison of mass media channels in terms of knowledge retention. *International Journal of Instructional Media, 36*(1), 73–79.

Rosengard, D. (2004). Preface. In C. A. Tuggle, F. Carr, & S. Huffman (Eds.), *Broadcast news handbook: Writing, reporting and producing in a converging media world* (2nd ed., pp. vii-ix). Boston: McGraw-Hill.

State of the News Media. (2010). *The Pew Research Center Project for Excellence in Journalism.* Retrieved February 16, 2011, from http://www.stateofthemedia.org/2010/index.php

Sussman, G., & Estes, J. R. (2005). KBOO community radio: Organizing Portland's disorderly possibilities. *Journal of Radio Studies, 12*(2), 223-239.

Tanner, A. (2004). Communicating health information and making the news: Health reporters reveal the PR tactics that work. *Public Relations Quarterly, 49*(1), 24–27.

Tanner, A. H., Friedman, D. B., Barr, D., & Koskan, A. (2008). Preparing for disaster: An examination of public health emergency information on local TV Web sites. *Electronic News*, 2(4), 218–234.

Winslow, G. (2010). For hi-def news, it's payoff time: Operational savings are encouraging more newsroom HD upgrades. *Broadcasting and Cable*, *140*(42), 14–15.

The Developing World ●

Considering Community Radio in Africa

Guy Berger

Community journalism varies around the globe, and it varies substantially across sub-Saharan Africa. For a start, community media in Africa tend to be primarily radio rather than newspapers, which are more common in the U.S. But there's also a distinction from southern to western Africa as to whether that sector includes the gamut of ownership forms, which can range from media owned by local business people to media owned by the state, not-for-profit community consortia, religious institutions, or large for-profit entities. In western Africa, especially Francophone countries, commercial and state-owned radio is often dubbed "community media"; however, in southern Africa, the sense is that *community* should mean the media is owned and controlled by civil society rather than by businesses or by the state.

Research is needed to establish how ownership impacts function. For example, South African community radio broadcasters are allowed to run advertising, but not make private profits, yet some don't differ much from their privately owned commercial counterparts. The issue relates back to the regulatory regime, and to conditions that may or may not be attached to licensees. Comparative research would be valuable there.

Much community media in Africa have business models that are often partly dependent on state or donor funding. On its own, such resourcing does not sustain a venture, but it helps with equipment acquisition and with incentives for volunteers (e.g., providing donor-funded training courses). Relationships with the resource suppliers also need scrutinizing, not least when there is government subsidy— as is common in Francophone countries, and even in South Africa. Where large commercial media set up "community" media enterprises (e.g., the Caxton newspaper group in South Africa), it is also worth studying to what extent corporate involvement in community media is compatible with the ethos of media plurality, participation, and diversity.

There's also the question of whether African community media (however defined) actually produce community journalism. That means whether community stations are required to run news bulletins as part of their licensing, but also whether they have alternative formats that nevertheless cover community news. Most community stations do serve important democratic and developmental roles (for example, through talk radio), but there's usually little reportage. That in turn relates to the tight economics of Africa's small-scale radio and print outfits. In South Africa, rank-and-file people in community radio are invariably unpaid (and short-term) volunteers who are otherwise unemployed. One trend to monitor is that such staffers, once trained, often move into the mainstream, meaning the community sector serves to supply the mainstream media with human resources. Further, as Huesca (1995) has found in Latin America, the amount of time people have for voluntary participation in community media is not something to be taken for granted.

On the other hand, anecdotal evidence suggests that those who best promote community radio as a vibrant public sphere are not the general volunteers. They are, for the most part, teachers, workers for non-governmental organizations, priests, and other public-service professionals who give their time on top of other responsibilities or as an acknowledged part of their jobs. Researchers should examine the volunteer model of community media and the ideals upon which it is based, particularly in the economic contexts in many African countries.

The significance of information and communication technologies in Africa's community media merits investigation as well. In southern Africa, community radio is deemed to serve the unique function of providing individuals with direct access to a media platform. In contrast, mainstream media, whether state owned or business owned, are assumed to treat communities as passive consumers. But cell phones increasingly enable people to express themselves in mainstream media, thereby reducing the distinctiveness of community media's access by the public. In that context, researchers could explore relationships between state-owned broadcasters and community radio, and the possibility of mutually reinforcing partnerships that might generate variants of public-service communications on either side of the relationship. Convergence within community media is also a major area of research interest; for example, it is a focus of a project supported by the Knight Foundation called Iindaba Ziyafika ("The News Is Coming") at *Grocott's Mail* in South Africa (http://thenewsiscoming.ru.ac.za/, www.grocotts.co.za).

Finally, there can be productive focus on audience research related to African community media. There is great potential for market-style research for purposes of "selling" audiences to advertisers or donors, as well as research into cost-effective toolkits for such research that can be administered by community media themselves. Qualitative- and localized-audience research is also valuable. Linked to all of that is the question of the impact community media have on local development and democracy. Pioneering work in that area has been done by Birgitte Jallov (2004), but a lot more needs to be done.

❖ REFERENCES

Huesca, R. (1995). A procedural view of participatory communication: Lessons from Bolivian tin miners' radio. *Media, Culture and Society, 17*(1), 101–119.
Jallov, B. (2004). Community radio for empowerment and impact. *Journal of Development Communication, 15*(2), 1–11.

❖ FURTHER READING

Huesca, R. (1996). Participation for development in radio: An ethnography of the *Reporteros populares* of Bolivia. *Gazette: International Journal for Mass Communication Studies, 57*(1), 29–52.
Huesca, R., & Dervin, B. (1994). Theory and practice in Latin American alternative communication research. *Journal of Communication, 44*(4), 53–73.
Jallov, B. (n.d.). *Stories of community radio in East Africa: Powerful change.* Retrieved September 26, 2009, from http://www.communicationfor socialchange.org/photogallery.php?id=395
Jallov, B. (2005). *Assessing community change: development of a "bare foot" impact assessment methodology.* Retrieved September 26, 2009, from the Communication Initiative Network website: http://www.comminit.com/ pdf/ImpactAssessment-FinalRadioJournalVersion.pdf

Guy Berger *is a professor at the School of Journalism & Media Studies at Rhodes University in South Africa. He has worked in the press and television and has a Ph.D. from Rhodes. He was deputy chair of the South Africa National Editors Forum 2003–2004 and remains an active member. Berger also writes "Converse" —a fortnightly column for* Mail & Guardian Online.

10

Community Journalism in an Online World

Hans K. Meyer and George L. Daniels

Research about community journalism in the online environment often forces scholars to shift perspective away from defining *community* in geographic terms alone. Community instead becomes more about shared interests than shared locations, as the Internet has greater power to bring geographically dispersed people together than any other medium (Rafaeli, Raban, & Kalman, 2005). Much of the research of online community to date has focused on what brings people together online, rather than whether the connections they form have power in the "real" world (the notion that online communication is not "real" is a quaint and perhaps even archaic suggestion now that online communication is ubiquitous in modern society). Beyond the well-evidenced contention that such virtual collectives are complex and vibrant are questions more germane to journalism scholars: do those communities produce or have their own "journalism," and can virtual communities bring people in geographic areas together in the same ways community newspapers and radio stations do? There are very fuzzy boundaries between *community journalism online* (that is, traditional community journalism being published online) and *journalism in the online community* (journalism produced by/for online communities).

This examination of online community research, coupled with the few studies that have examined how community journalism practices on the Web have affected established communities, suggests that the goals of those who bring online communities together through information sharing are similar to the goals of those who do so for geographic communities. In fact, the online environment may be a viable realm in which professional journalists can create and build connections to the communities in which they live.

❖ ONLINE COMMUNITY

When it comes to research about journalism that reflects "community connectedness," the literature appears to focus more on online communities than on geographic ones. The evolution of online "virtual communities" goes back several decades; Rheingold (2000) first chronicled his exploration of the Whole Earth 'Lectronic Link, or WELL, in 1992, years after the network was launched in the mid 1980s. In the preface to his 2000 update, he acknowledged how much virtual community had grown in just a few years: "Now, the entire world seems to be undergoing an Internet-enabled transformation. This new edition has afforded me the opportunity to try to cover some of the enormous new territory that has opened up over the past seven years" (p. xi).

The advances Rheingold chronicled in 2000 predicted what have become some of the most ubiquitous online communities in the early 21st century. At this writing, social networking websites such as Facebook, Myspace, and LinkedIn, as well as microblogging sites such as Twitter, Plurk, and Flickr, make it easy for people to create and engage in communities that exist almost entirely online.

Online communities thrive on all manner of information (Joyce & Kraut, 2006; Rafaeli et al., 2005). Early conduits for online communities, such as CompuServe and Prodigy, were not just Internet service providers; they also provided information streams, education tools, and socialization functions (James & Wotring, 1995).

Information sharing, by itself, is a form of socialization; people who posted comments to the online forums provided by those early services said they were satisfied to just answer questions online, while others said they found quality, accuracy, and detail in posts from people who were probably experts in the field. Those conversations helped early online bulletin boards to serve as a "surrogate for interpersonal communication" because they relied on many of the "same conventions, habits and demands as face-to-face communication" (James & Wotring, 1995). In online discussion communities where users generate most of the information, information quality is vital to predicting whether people will remain involved (Ridings & Gefen, 2004). To find quality, people turn to information they can trust, and they find it from people with whom they have relationships, including relationships that exist entirely through online communication. By sharing information, users are providing something of value to others and are extending themselves into social life (Bakardjieva, 2003). That forms the foundation of virtual social networks.

Ridings and Gefen (2004) underscored their finding regarding the need for quality information with the need for friendship and social support. Together, those motivations made up more than one third of the reasons people participated in virtual communities, according to that study. "Even in such an information-centered medium, friendship is a crucial bond, keeping patrons in communities."

Those friendships do not exist only in large virtual communities, such as those established early on by the WELL, CompuServe, and Prodigy. One of the most examined online platforms is the blog, a form of online publishing that includes a broad array of content, from the personal musings of individuals to serious discussions among groups of people interested in specific topics. Rutigliano (2007) differentiated types of blogs based on the degrees of control blog creators exercised over content posted to their blogs. "Controlled" blogs, Rutigliano argued, utilize a centralized format, whereas "open" blogs have administrators and/or an advisory board, but a small degree of obvious direction or intervention with regard to content. Between the two are "hybrid" blogs, which combine small, centralized staffs and decentralization strategy. Using a case study approach, Rutigliano studied an example of each of the different types of community blogs and analyzed the type, subject, and source of the posts over a one-month period. That study helped to define categories for expanded research about community blogs.

Rutigliano later joined three colleagues in a larger study of blogging communities bound by political ideology (Reese, Rutigliano, Hyun, & Jeong, 2007). The team analyzed the linking patterns in three "conservative" and three "liberal" blog sites for a one-week period in February 2005. The links were analyzed for types of websites and content being linked to, tone of hyperlink language, and geographic locations of site managers. Among the team's findings was that the "blogosphere" heavily relies on making links to content published on professional news sites and produced by journalists associated with professional media organizations (p. 257).

Those scholars concluded that the blogosphere does, in fact, weave together citizen and professional voices in a way that extends the so-called "public sphere." That concept of public sphere (attributed most often to critical theorist Jürgen Habermas, 1962/1984) has been a launching point for other online community journalism research projects. For example, Hutchins (2007) used a single case study of the *Tasmanian Times*, a news website in one Australian state, in which the editor used the concept of the public sphere in describing the Web-based venture. The study noted that the *Tasmanian Times* was on a "fault line of contemporary news media and journalism culture where quality reporting and discussion of politics, civic issues and current affairs was on one side while tabloidization, celebrity, scandal and infotainment were on the other" (p. 211). From a research perspective, that particular case study exemplifies the benefit of going in depth to study a single journalistic website that incorporates the community as a necessary component but does not use categorizing terms such as *community journalism* or *civic/public journalism* or even *citizen journalism*.

Also useful is a similar study by Haas (2005) of two blogging sites, Indymedia.com and Slashdot.com, in an examination of whether blogs represent an opportunity for public journalism. Haas acknowledged the public potential of the blogosphere, but questioned whether blogs represent a challenge to traditional journalism:

> While weblogs are produced by and for the public, they are decidedly not "of" the public. Not only do few weblog writers engage in any independent news reporting, most weblog writers

cover the same topics as mainstream news media and, perhaps more significantly, rely on them for information on those topics. (pp. 393–394)

Although Haas's research provided a brief review of two websites, it was more a commentary about blogging as a place for discourse than an in-depth study of the cases. Such a commentary-focused approach to the research of community journalism online has been echoed by several other studies. For example, Klinenberg (2005) used data from a multiyear ethnographic study of the news organization *MetroNews* to examine convergence and the "new media market." A single community was the focus of the research, and it highlighted more how reporters were operating internally than it did the involvement of those in the community. In another study, Tumber (2001) described in detail the arguments of such key figures in the public-journalism movement as Jay Rosen and Dave "Buzz" Merritt, but did not provide much empirical evidence to support his arguments for how the Internet may be displacing traditional journalism in providing information and interpretation for the citizenry.

Lowman (2008) took a case study approach in reporting on a community journalism project undertaken by one of her classes at the University of North Dakota, in which the students developed multimedia content and blog entries for the *Grand Forks Herald* in the fall of 2007. The outcome included recommendations for how weekly newspapers could use the online medium to augment their weekly print offerings by utilizing the additional capacity and immediacy of the Web (Lowman, 2008).

As a whole, the examples mentioned above suggest that case study and content analysis are the most common methods used to study community journalism, while the conceptual approach often cited (at least in the research focused on blogging) is Habermas's "public sphere." Although there have been numerous studies of blogging, particularly since 2004, few have made specific contributions to explicitly defining the role of community journalism in the online world.

Those studies also did not specifically address whether online community can have any impact beyond the Internet. Uslaner (2004), for one, was skeptical that the Internet can reach its community building potential:

Most people don't go on-line looking to build a sense of community—or to destroy it. Yes, there are plenty of opportunities to deceive on the Web. . . . And yes, there are more opportunities on the Web to give to charities, to find volunteering opportunities, and to give solace to others. But that isn't the whole Internet either. The World Wide Web is very much like the World. It makes things better in some ways and worse in others. But it is not transforming. If you want to make a revolution, you have to go offline. (p. 239)

On the other hand, Shah, McLeod, and Yoon (2001) suggested that virtual communities can generate social capital. They found that use of the Internet for information exchange had stronger community building effects for young adults than for older adults, and might even help users bridge generation gaps (Shah, McLeod, & Yoon, 2001). Beaudoin and Thorson (2004) demonstrated that media use in general can lead to greater levels of social trust, especially in rural communities. That study did not specifically mention the Internet, but Thorson and Duffy (2006) suggested that Internet information sharing offers more choices and divergent voices that allow audiences to connect better. Meyer, Marchionni, and Thorson (2010) used that model to suggest that audiences connect better and may in the end trust voices that are similar to theirs. In other words, journalists can build online bonds with their audience to strengthen their news organization's overall connection to the geographic community.

❖ COMMUNITY-BUILDING JOURNALISM

Studies conducted on the development and exchange of social capital through online interaction demonstrate how community journalism and online community formation often have the same goals. Online communities, like most journalistic enterprises, seek to inform and educate. They are more effective when community members actively take part in the enterprise (Rafaeli, Ravid, & Soroka, 2004). Continued online-community participation often leads to engagement, in which people do more to help others than to gain anything for themselves (Rodgers & Chen, 2005). Those communities end up creating a public sphere, but journalism can takes community creation a step further.

Kovach and Rosenstiel (2001) claimed that one of the goals of journalism is to provide citizens with the information they need to be free and self-governing. Gillmor (2004) said journalism fills that role better as it provides a conversation rather than a lecture:

> The lines will blur between producers and consumers, changing the role of both in ways we're only beginning to grasp now. The communication network itself will be a medium for everyone's voice, not just the few who can afford to buy multimillion-dollar printing presses, launch satellites, or win the government's permission to squat on the public's airwaves. This evolution—from journalism as lecture to journalism as a conversation or seminar—will force the various communities of interest to adapt. Everyone, from journalists to the people we cover to our sources and the former audience, must change their ways. The alternative is just more of the same. (p. xiii)

One way in which journalism will change is that professionals will not solely be in charge of the gates of information (Bruns, 2005). That is already happening. Deuze (2003) categorized online journalism through the following dimensions: focus on content or connection and degree of editorial control. Sites most successful in adapting to the changing communication landscape were those that balanced control and connection equally in a way he called "dialogic" (Deuze, 2003). In online journalism practice, Tremayne (2007) saw editors' roles "skew[ing] heavily toward teaching and coaching" rather than assigning reporters to coverage areas.

Ceding some control to the audience, however, is not necessarily a new idea. At the turn of the 21st century, Lasica (1999), who wrote the "World of New Media" column for *American Journalism Review*, predicted that by the end of the first decade of the new century, online journalism would be in the hands of more and more regular folks, many of whom might not even think of themselves as journalists. In its purest sense, the kind of journalism Lasica predicted is what we now call citizen journalism.

Some have linked citizen journalism to civic journalism, the late-20th-century movement in which some news media actively involved community members in the news process and the media in turn participated in efforts to address community issues. Civic journalism (also called public journalism) was meant to enhance the role of professional news outlets as conduits for communication about important issues. Citizen journalism is more often about bypassing professional journalists. Consider one of the earliest citizen journalism efforts, *OhmyNews*, launched in 1999 by Oh Yeon-Ho. Oh said he started *OhmyNews* because he was frustrated with the "one-way journalism of the 20th century and the haughty attitude common in the Korean media" (Oh, 2004). Four years later, the site had more than 32,000 citizen reporters. "The citizens of the Republic of Korea had long been preparing for a grand revolution in the culture of news production and consumption," he wrote. "All I did was raise the flag."

The *OhmyNews* model inspired other sites to bring communities together, but many times it was legacy media organizations that started them. One of the earliest such efforts began when *The Californian*, a 70,000-circulation daily newspaper in Bakersfield, California, started *The Northwest Voice* in May 2004 to reach an underserved part of its readership area. Mary Lou Fulton, the site's publisher, said the idea was to open up the gates and let the readers in. "We are a better community newspaper for having thousands of readers who serve as the eyes and ears for the Voice, rather than having everything filtered through the views of a small group of reporters and editors," she said (Glaser, 2004). After the success of *The Northwest Voice*, *The Californian* added a *Southwest Voice* site and weekly tabloid in 2006. The paper combined both sites into *The Bakersfield Voice* in 2008, and it was still online as of April 2011.

As with most phenomena in online communication, it is difficult to pin down exactly how many legacy news outlets have started citizen journalism projects, although there are lists that help identify some of those efforts. Dube's (2010) citizen media wiki lists 23 citizen media initiatives published by major news organizations. They include major public and citizen journalism ventures, such as CBS's cbseyemobile.com (which was in beta testing as this was written), ABC News' i-Caught, and the BBC's iCan. The highest-profile venture is CNN's iReport, which Jennifer Martin, CNN's director of PR, said gives the network the opportunity to publish information about breaking news events well before its reporters and photographers arrive on the scene:

What iReport has done for us, is that it has provided an added dimension to our newsgathering. We're not doing less reporting because of iReport, but it is enriching the stories that we are doing. . . . Take [the April 2007 shooting massacre at] Virginia Tech, for example. That was a horrific breaking news tragedy, and that cell-phone video of shots being fired, that was an iReport. Those [types of videos] provided an extra dimension, but it's not like we didn't send journalists there because we had that. (Washkuch, 2008, p. 10)

CNN's iReport, which started in August 2006, now receives more than 10,000 submissions a month, and CNN recently spent $750,000 to purchase the iReport domain name to allow users to upload their stories and videos directly to the site and have them instantly appear (Learmonth, 2008). In fact, iReport gives users more flexibility and exposure. It displays all submitted stories and videos, not just those handpicked by editors to appear on CNN broadcasts (CNN .com, n.d.).

The question with legacy media–supported citizen journalism ventures is often how much community building is really occurring. Interactivity, and not merely providing one-way conduits so that anybody can publish, is the key to online community. Lacy, Riffe, Thorson, and Duffy (2009) analyzed 64 citizen journalism sites across the U.S. and found that although more than 60% actively sought stories from volunteers, few of the sites— whether news site or blog—provided much interactivity, and opportunities for participation were limited. That is also true of sites from major networks, which enhance their audience's ability to send comments to journalists who rarely respond. CNN, for example, trumpets the exclusive Johnny-on-the-spot content iReport provides, but the majority of online content is ignored, especially when iReport becomes the source for pop culture rumors such as erroneous reports that tween heartthrob Justin Bieber had died (Anderson, 2010). According to the 2010 State of the News Media report, only 35% of national journalists and 36% of local journalists had a positive view of citizens' posting news content on news organizations' websites (Pew Project for Excellence in Journalism, 2010). That disdain was sometimes reflected in how the submissions appeared online, because they were often either hastily edited or not edited at all; deep staffing cuts in legacy news organizations during the recession of 2008–2010 meant even fewer professional journalists were editing submissions from their audiences.

Even if the efforts are superficial or commercially motivated, recent research suggests publishing citizen journalism can better connect news organizations to their readers. An online experiment using iReport as a framework demonstrated that journalist-written stories are still the most credible, but audience-written stories are closing the gap (Meyer, 2009). Participants also connected better with audience-written stories, and gave nearly identical credibility rankings to the organizations that published audience- and staff-written stories. Real community connections can be forged through citizen journalism, that study suggests, but news organizations have to commit to them fully, in the same way they committed to offline civic and community building initiatives.

Studying the online publishing efforts of legacy news media poses a number of challenges for researchers, particularly the fact that online efforts cannot be adequately analyzed on their own. The development of online media has been more about complementing than competing. Unlike radio, which was seen as separate from newspapers, and television, which was seen as a competitor of both radio and print media, the websites of established media can expand their reach. Consider: when readers refer to the websites of their hometown newspapers, they consider those websites extensions of the newspapers themselves. That has been the case almost from the beginning. Stempel, Hargrove, and Bernt (2000) found that a newspaper's website did not cannibalize readership from its print product, and Hargrove (2007) confirmed that finding years later, as in that later study a newspaper's website not only didn't diminish readership within its community, but actually helped to expand its potential audience outside its geographic location.

That expansion of coverage holds intriguing promise for community journalism. Not only does effective use of the Internet allow a news organization to better engage its core geographic audience through comments, user-generated content, and breaking news alerts, but it also allows the organization to better define the community as a whole. For example, the editors and reporters of the *Collegiate Times*, the student newspaper at Virginia Tech, were interviewed dozens of times in the aftermath of the tragedy regarding how they gathered and transmitted information to their communities (Furnas, 2009). One of the key findings of a Dart Center for Journalism and Trauma study was a focus on how that community enabled the staff of the student newspaper to get through the week:

It's all about the readers. It sounds like a simple notion, but when big news breaks, sometimes journalists worry more about headlines and deadlines than readers. It's important that the focus of the staff's efforts remains on the community in all aspects of production, from newsgathering and online updates to photography and page design. (Furnas, 2009)

The opportunities that online community journalism present make it much more difficult to understand why news organizations as a whole initially approached the Internet with such trepidation (Gilbert, 2000). A focus on the purposes of journalism, whether defined in civic or democratic terms, will guide news organizations to use different media to their fullest potential. The Internet can be a powerful tool for facilitating community. A smart news organization can and will find ways to translate that to the real world. Researchers must do a better job examining when and where the intersection between virtual and real-world community takes place.

❖ LINKING THE ONLINE WORLD WITH THE OFFLINE WORLD

The logical next step in online community journalism research is identifying cases in which journalists have successfully used the Web to build community. But researchers can't stop there. Their study of those cases should lead not just to best practices of online community building, but also to evidence on which to base theories about how communities are built online and how journalists can facilitate them. For journalism as a whole, that requires an examination of the different delivery methods now available, because each one allows the news media to identify and serve distinct communities. For example, when a television station or newspaper places its contact information online, does that not change the scope of the "community" it serves? Can the community really be geographically based when anyone, anywhere, can post on the forums, watch the videos, or engage reporters in email discussions? Does the content lose its "unique flair" of being tied to a particular place on the map, or is it that sense of place that appeals to readers and contributors from far away? And, most important, does online journalism continue to be "relentlessly local" when the content can come from people who have no ties to the local community where the station or newspaper is based?

Much of the impact journalism can have in building community revolves around two aspects Deuze (2003) used in his definition of what makes online journalism different. He typified online journalism efforts based on the degree to which the news organization focused on content or connection, and how much control over the final product the organization exerted. His definition encourages online community journalism researchers to dig deeper and focus on much more nuanced aspects of online journalism. There has been some useful research in that vein. Niekamp (2007) explored journalism as a conversation by studying 226 blogs of 60 television stations in the 50 largest media markets in the U.S. He found the blogs did little to foster a "conversation" between the community viewer and the station, as only 31% of the blogs included ways for viewers or readers to comment on blog entries. Meanwhile, Tanner, Friedman, Barr, and Koskan (2008) analyzed nearly 300 news stories on local television websites. More than half of the stories focused on natural disasters, most frequently addressing the topic of emergency preparedness in the community (p. 229). Schaudt and Carpenter (2009) considered how "convergence" affected the definition of community. Their content analysis of the stories on 15 community websites suggested proximity was the most frequent news value present (they found it to be a factor in 76% of stories); "conflict" was the second most frequent news value, and "prominence" was the least frequent news value (p. 22). All of those studies provide insights into how journalists may or may not be altering their routines and news values in providing community news in the online age.

Two case studies the authors of this chapter participated in suggest other possible approaches to online community journalism research. The first (Daniels, 2010) focused on the multimedia news delivery strategy of one community newspaper, *The Tuscaloosa News* of Alabama, which at this writing was owned by the New York Times Company. After getting out of the over-the-air television business in 2007 by selling its television group, the New York Times Company developed the capability to do online video journalism in its newspaper newsrooms (Smolkin, 2007). At its Tuscaloosa paper, that meant the installation of a studio for regular video recordings that could be posted online. In 2008, those offerings (similar to those of a broadband channel) included three regularly scheduled video offerings: *Slowe Cooking*, a cooking show featuring the paper's food editor, Betty Slowe; *Town Hall*, an interview show hosted by the newspaper's associate editor; and *The Cecil Hurt*

Show, a weekly interview show featuring the eponymous sports editor and another editor discussing University of Alabama football. The analysis provided some insight into how online media could be used to produce personality-driven community journalism, how videos produced by newspaper journalists do not always adopt the conventions of television news, and how robust online offerings can expand community journalism beyond narratives and mini-documentaries. In sum, the newspaper-produced video programs represented a somewhat new type of content for community news organizations.

The second case study examined the process behind creating a citizen journalism website in a rich media environment. Bentley and his colleagues (2007) critically examined the thinking behind MyMissourian.com, a website for residents of Columbia, Missouri. Although the site's original intention was to provide a place for discussion of what editors thought was the most important news of the day, such as politics before the 2004 presidential election, the audience decided to use the site more to connect with each other and to publicize stories that did not get much attention in the community's traditional media outlets. Community groups without a logical forum, such as deer hunters, used the site to connect with one another and forge their own community connections. MyMissourian produced a weekly print edition that highlighted what were considered the best submissions from the website; a follow-up phone survey of residents suggested that building a sense of community was one of the main reasons people read the print edition (Bentley, Hamman, Ibold, Littau, & Meyer, 2005).

Those cases studies suggest that established news media certainly can branch out from their geographic communities and find ways to expand their content beyond the reach of their printed products or broadcast transmitters. More research, however, should focus on how news organizations are applying the community journalism model online, and those studies must go beyond case study approaches that focus on specific communities.

❖ METHODOLOGICAL CHALLENGES

To date, the methods used to study community in electronic media have been rather limited. Perhaps that is due to the decreased feasibility of utilizing methods besides online surveys, content analysis, or case studies. Best and Harrison (2009) wrote that the technologies involved in generating scientific samples of general populations online are still in their infancy and may never be fully developed. Online studies require attention to detail, even if strict sampling procedures cannot be observed. Johnson and Kaye (2002, 2004, 2010) have consistently used online samples to study blog readers and politically interested Web users. That can be effective when the study's focus is on a specific group that is known to almost universally have Web access. An online study might not be suitable to get broad representation; for example, the latest research suggests that more than 20% of U.S. residents do not have Internet access (Pew Internet and American Life Project, 2010). Obviously, any study conducted via the Internet can provide only data about Internet users; beyond that, a seemingly infinite number of confounding variables can negatively affect an online study's reliability.

However, a multimodal approach can be effective, particularly if the study is limited to geographic regions. The best Web studies identify the population to sample offline before reaching out to them online (Best & Harrison, 2009). For the Web, that can mean specifically targeting the visitors to a particular site or group of sites. It can also mean coupling Web surveys with mail and telephone efforts, which can make it more reasonable to generalize findings to the whole population. Smyth, Dillman, Christian, and O'Neill (2010) found that Web-only surveys excluded important population segments in studies of specific small towns and communities; however, online sampling rates, when coupled with a mailed invitation, produced results similar to those from mail-only surveys.

One area in which online data collection can expand the range of participants and stimuli is experimental research. Online experiments designed to isolate the effects of a limited number of controlled variables can effectively suggest and test theories as applied to community journalism. Wise, Hamman, and Thorson (2006), for example, examined the role social presence plays in the intent to join and participate in an online community.

No matter the research method, the key to an online study, as it is for any worthwhile research project, is knowing and understanding the goals of the study (Best & Harrison, 2009):

> In particular, researchers need to be especially careful in specifying and considering the relationship between the target population

of their study and the available sampling methods. Though Internet data collection offers great promise, it also has limitations that can make an otherwise useful data collection method inappropriate for some studies. (p. 430)

As researchers approach the questions of how journalism serves communities on the Internet and what physical-world efforts, if any, that information sharing can have, it is more vital than ever to establish the goals of a particular study. It also becomes more and more necessary each day for community news organizations to understand how people use the Internet and how it affects their information needs and goals. As news organizations, even community ones, shift more and more of their product to the Web, they will need to explore whether their audiences react differently to online information. Do they find Web stories more or less credible? Are they better able to connect with the community news organization and their peers online or off? Can the easy access to information online and the easy ability to share create the kinds of public spheres Habermas envisioned? Or does the Internet need journalists—who are trained to vet information, present the most important information first, and educate community members on their role in a democracy—now more than ever? Online community journalism research does not need studies that take those questions lightly, or studies that attempt to answer them with unsuitable methods. Even though probability samples are difficult to obtain online, researchers should not assume that non-probability samples, such as snowball samples or convenience samples, are good enough for anything but exploratory case studies. Such studies are important, but what we need now is more follow-through on the suggestions that come at the end of those case studies—the ideas for future research we can so easily think of, but not so easily execute.

❖ REFERENCES

Anderson, C. (2010). *Justin Bieber: Not dead.* Retrieved February 14, 2011, from MTV Newsroom website: http://newsroom.mtv.com/2010/01/05/justin-bieber-dead/

Bakardjieva, M. (2003). Virtual togetherness: An everyday-life perspective. *Media, Culture and Society, 25,* 291–313.

Beaudoin, C., & Thorson, E. (2004). Social capital in rural and urban communities: Testing differences in media effects and models. *Journalism and Mass Communication Quarterly, 81*(2), 378–399.

Bentley, C., Hamman, B., Ibold, H., Littau, J., & Meyer, H. K. (2005). *Sense of community as a driver for citizen journalism*. San Francisco: Association for Education in Journalism and Mass Communication.

Bentley, C., Hamman, B., Littau, J., Meyer, H. K., Watson, B., & Welsh, B. (2007). Citizen journalism: A case study. In M. Tremayne (Ed.), *Blogging, citizenship, and the future of media* (pp. 239–259). New York: Routledge.

Best, S. J., & Harrison, C. H. (2009). Internet survey methods. In L. Bickman & D. J. Rog (Eds.), *The Sage handbook of applied social research methods* (2nd ed., pp. 413–434). Thousand Oaks, CA: Sage.

Bruns, A. (2005). *Gatewatching: Collaborative online news production*. New York: Peter Lang.

CNN.com. (n.d.). *About CNN iReport*. Retrieved May 2, 2011, from http://ireport.cnn.com/about.jspa

Daniels, G. (2010, August). *Video expectations for non-television producers of community news: Two newspapers' online video strategies*. Paper presented at the annual convention of the Association for Education in Journalism and Mass Communication, Denver, CO.

Deuze, M. (2003). The Web and its journalisms: Considering the consequences of different types of newsmedia online. *New Media and Society, 5*(2), 203–230.

Dube, J. (2010). *Citizen media initiatives list*. Retrieved May 1, 2011, from CyberJournalist.net: http://www.cyberjournalist.net/news/002226.php

Furnas, K. (2009). *Virginia Tech: Tips from a newsroom adviser*. Retrieved February 14, 2011, from Dart Center for Journalism and Trauma website: http://dartcenter.org/content/virginia-tech-tips-from-newsroom-adviser

Gilbert, C. (2000). Newspapers and the Internet. *Nieman Reports, 56*(2), 35.

Gillmor, D. (2004). *We the media: Grassroots journalism by the people, for the people*. Sebastopol, CA: O'Reilly Media.

Glaser, M. (2004). *The new voices: Hyperlocal citizen media sites want you (to write)!* Retrieved May 1, 2011, from USC Annenberg, Online Journalism Review website: http://www.ojr.org/ojr/glaser/1098833871.php

Haas, T. (2005). From public journalism to the public's journalism? Rhetoric and reality in the discourse on weblogs. *Journalism Studies, 6*(3), 387–396.

Habermas, J. (1984). *The theory of communicative action* (T. McCarthy, Trans.). Boston: Beacon Press. (Original work published 1962)

Hargrove, T. (2007). Use of blogs as a source of news presents little threat to mainline news media. *Newspaper Research Journal, 28*(1), 99.

Hutchins, B. (2007). Public culture, independent online news and the *Tasmanian Times*. *Journalism, 8*(2), 205–225.

James, M. L., & Wotring, C. E. (1995). An exploratory study of the perceived benefits of electronic bulletin board use and their impact. *Journal of Broadcasting and Electronic Media, 39*(1), 30–51.

Johnson, T. J., & Kaye, B. K. (2002). Webelievability: A path model examining how convenience and reliance predict online credibility. *Journalism and Mass Communication Quarterly, 79*(3), 619–642.

Johnson, T. J., & Kaye, B. (2004). Wag the blog: How reliance on traditional media and the Internet influence credibility perceptions of weblogs among blog users. *Journalism and Mass Communication Quarterly, 81*(3), 622–642.

Johnson, T., & Kaye, B. (2010). Choosing is believing? How Web gratifications and reliance affect Internet credibility among politically interested users. *Atlantic Journal of Communication, 18*(1), 1–21.

Joyce, E., & Kraut, R. E. (2006). Predicting continued participation in newsgroups. *Journal of Computer-Mediated Communication, 11*(3), 723–747.

Klinenberg, E. (2005). Convergence: New production in a digital age. *Annals of American Academy of Political and Social Science, 597,* 48–64.

Kovach, B., & Rosenstiel, T. (2001). *The elements of journalism.* New York: Three Rivers Press.

Lacy, S. R., Riffe, D., Thorson, E., & Duffy, M. (2009). Examining the features, policies, and resources of citizen journalism: Citizen news sites and blogs. *Web Journal of Mass Communication Research, 15.* Retrieved February 14, 2011, from http://wjmcr.org/vol15

Lasica, J. D. (1999, July/August). Citizens as budding writers and editors. *American Journalism Review.* Retrieved April 30, 2011, from http://www.ajr.org/Article.asp?id=424

Learmonth, M. (2008, February 11). *CNN launching iReport.com as YouTube for news.* Retrieved May 1, 2011, from Business Insider website: http://www.businessinsider.com/2008/2/cnn-launching-ireport-com-as-youtube-for-news

Lowman, J. (2008). Seeking the essence: Community journalism meets the digital age. *Grassroots Editor, 49*(4), 4–8.

Meyer, H. K. (2009). *The user-generated dilemma: Can the ways in which media organizations publish audience contributions affect the way the audience feels about the site and their intention to contribute?* Doctoral dissertation, University of Missouri, Columbia. Retrieved April 30, 2011, from https://mospace.umsystem.edu/xmlui/handle/10355/9671

Meyer, H. K., Marchionni, D., & Thorson, E. (2010). The journalist behind the news: Credibility of straight, collaborative, opinionated, and blogged "news." *American Behavioral Scientist, 54*(2), 100.

Niekamp, R. (2007). Opportunity lost: Blogs on local TV station Web sites. *Electronic News, 1*(3), 149–164.

Oh, Y. (2004). *New book: "OhmyNews story."* Retrieved May 1, 2011, from http://english.ohmynews.com/articleview/article_view.asp?menu=c10400&no=181975&rel_no=1

Pew Internet and American Life Project. (2010). *Demographics of Internet Users, May 2010.* Retrieved April 30, 2011, from http://pewinternet.org/Static-Pages/Trend-Data/Whos-Online.aspx

Pew Project for Excellence in Journalism. (2010). *The state of the news media: An annual report on American journalism.* Retrieved May 1, 2011, from http://stateofthemedia.org/2010/

Rafaeli, S., Raban, D., & Kalman, Y. (2005). Social cognition online. In Y. Amichai-Hamburger (Ed.), *The social net: Understanding human behavior in cyberspace* (pp. 57–90). Oxford, UK: Oxford University Press.

Rafaeli, S., Ravid, G., & Soroka, V. (2004, January). *De-lurking in virtual communities: A social communication network approach to measuring the effects of social and cultural capital.* Paper presented at the 37th Annual Hawaii International Conference on System Sciences, Big Island, HI.

Reese, S., Rutigliano, L., Hyun, K., & Jeong, J. (2007). Mapping the blogosphere: Professional and citizen-based media in the global news arena. *Journalism, 8*(3), 235–261.

Rheingold, H. (2000). *The virtual community: Homesteading on the electronic frontier.* Cambridge, MA: MIT Press.

Ridings, C. M., & Gefen, D. (2004). Virtual community attraction: Why people hang out online. *Journal of Computer-Mediated Communication, 10*(1). Retrieved May 1, 2011, from http://jcmc.indiana.edu/vol10/issue1/ridings_gefen.html

Rodgers, S., & Chen, Q. (2005). Internet community group participation: Psychosocial benefits for women with breast cancer. *Journal of Computer-Mediated Communication, 10*(4). Retrieved May 1, 2011, from http://jcmc.indiana.edu/vol10/issue4/rodgers.html

Rutigliano, L. (2007). Emergent communication networks as civic journalism. In M. Tremayne (Ed.), *Blogging, citizenship, and the future of media* (pp. 225–238). New York: Routledge.

Schaudt, S., & Carpenter, S. (2009). The news that's fit to click: An analysis of online news values and preferences present in the most-viewed stories on azcentral.com. *Southwestern Mass Communication Journal, 24*(2), 17–26.

Shah, D. V., McLeod, J. M., & Yoon, S. (2001). Communication, context, and community: An exploration of print, broadcast, and Internet influences. *Communication Research, 28*(4), 464–506.

Smolkin, R. (2007, February/March). Challenging times. *American Journalism Review, 29*(1), 16–27.

Smyth, J. D., Dillman, D. A., Christian, L. M., & O'Neill, A. C. (2010). Using the Internet to survey small towns and communities: Limitations and possibilities in the early 21st century. *American Behavioral Scientist, 53*(9), 1423–1448.

Stempel, G., III, Hargrove, T., & Bernt, J. P. (2000). Relation of growth and use of the Internet to changes in media use from 1995–1999. *Journalism and Mass Communication Quarterly, 77*(1), 71–79.

Tanner, A. H., Friedman, D. B., Barr, D., & Koskan, A. (2008). Preparing for disaster: An examination of public health emergency information on local TV Web sites. *Electronic News, 2*(4), 218–234.

Thorson, E., & Duffy, M. (2006). *A needs-based theory of the revolution in news use and its implications for the newspaper business.* Unpublished manuscript.

Tremayne, M. (2007). Harnessing the active audience: Synthesizing blog research and lessons for the future of media. In M. Tremayne (Ed.), *Blogging, citizenship, and the future of media* (pp. 261–272). New York: Routledge.

Tumber, H. (2001). Democracy in the information age: The role of the fourth estate in cyberspace. *Information, Communication and Society, 4*(1), 95–112.

Uslaner, E. M. (2004). Trust, civic engagement, and the Internet. *Political Communication, 21*, 223–242.

Washkuch, F. (2008, April 28). Analysis—News sites gain from citizen journalism. *PRWeek US,* p. 10.

Wise, K., Hamman, B., & Thorson, K. (2006). Moderation, response rate, and message interactivity: Features of online communities and their effects on intent to participate. *Journal of Computer-Mediated Communication, 12*(1), 24.

Citizens, Journalists, and User-Generated Content ●

Nicholas W. Jankowski

Long before Web 2.0, user-generated content constituted the core component and main principle of community media. From the underground press and guerilla television of the 1960s, through the birth of public-access television stations in New York and eventually across the United States in the 1970s (Engelman, 1996), through the European-wide experimentation with variations of community radio and television in the 1980s (Jankowski, 1982, 1988; Jankowski, Prehn, & Stappers, 1992), to the recent emergence of Ourmedia as a world-wide phenomenon with strong roots in Latin America and Africa (Kidd, Rodriguez, & Stein, 2009), the notion of lay citizens constructing their own interpretation of events, sharing and debating such inter-pretations with others, and using resulting insight to inform political and cultural engagement has been central to community media, and reflects the contemporary notion of user-generated content.

Researchers have been following and monitoring alternative vari-ants of media and of journalism since those first initiatives, sometimes at a distance and through the scientific facade of objectivity, sometimes very close at hand and with a strongly stated position of support. Most of those studies were situated in pre-Web environments and dressed in the theoretical and methodological attire of an earlier era. Concepts such as emancipatory media, participation, and the "public sphere" often guided the studies (e.g., Brown, 2005; Day, 2008; Downing, 2000). Research designs ranged from small ethnographic case studies to large surveys based on random samples drawn from community-wide populations—scientific structures within which to examine questions of theoretical and societal concern: Did such community or alternative media "matter"? Did citizens in some magical and mysterious manner gain "voice" and become not merely consumers of the media but pro-ducers of local versions of newspapers, radio, and television? And if they did become media producers, did it make any difference in terms of societal engagement and, ultimately, societal change?

Those questions have been on the agenda of community-media researchers for decades, albeit in different forms with different degrees of theoretical refinement and methodological focus. Many of those researchers have, along the way, suggested frameworks for further study, refined research questions, and provided overarching research agendas. Most of those agendas, including my own contributions to such direction (Jankowski, 2002, 2006; Jankowski, Van Selm, & Hollander, 2001), have missed the mark when it comes to community media in a Web-based environment, and particularly since the rapid spread of what are known as "social media" in a Web 2.0 world (e.g., blogs, wikis, social networking sites, file sharing sites). The possibilities for user-generated content have never been greater, and the relation of such content to the profession and practices of journalism has never been as salient as in the Web 2.0 world.

Without striving to sketch a new and improved, all-encompassing research agenda, let me suggest the above saliency with one concrete illustration: the OhmyNews initiative in Korea, essentially a website where citizens and journalists fuse their respective concerns and expertise into a single endeavor—providing news, analysis, and direction for social action on topics of relevance for the Korean citizens engaged in the initiative (Joyce, 2007). There are other such collaborative initiatives between journalists and citizens around the world, and much study is needed to understand how and under what conditions such collaboration between the journalist and the citizen may flourish.

Young researchers concerned about community media will find the area of tension and collaboration between citizens and journalists rich in potential, both for theoretical understanding and for transformation of practice. How insightful it will be when a new generation of scholars addresses the concerns of this niche area of media studies.

❖ REFERENCES

Brown, D. R. (2005). *Ethnic minorities, electronic media and the public sphere: A comparative study.* Cresskill, NJ: Hampton Press.

Day, R. (2008). *Community radio in Ireland: Building community, participation and multi-flow communication.* Cresskill, NJ: Hampton Press.

Downing, J. (Ed.). (2000). *Radical media: Rebellious communication and social movements.* Thousand Oaks, CA: Sage.

Engelman, R. (1996). *Public radio and television in American: A political history.* Thousand Oaks, CA: Sage.

Jankowski, N. W. (1982). Community television: A tool for community action? *Communication, 7*(1), 33–58.

Jankowski, N. W. (1988). *Community television in Amsterdam: Access to, participation in and use of the "Lokale Omroep Bijlmermeer."* Unpublished doctoral dissertation, University of Amsterdam.

Jankowski, N. W. (2002). Epilogue: Theoretical perspectives and arenas for community media research. In N. W. Jankowski & O. Prehn (Eds.), *Community media in the information age: Perspectives and prospects* (pp. 359–374). Cresskill, NJ: Hampton Press.

Jankowski, N. W. (2006). Creating community with media: History, theories and scientific investigations. In L. Lievrouw & S. Livingstone (Eds.), *Handbook of new media: Social shaping and consequences of ICTs* (pp. 55–74). London: Sage.

Jankowski, N. W., Prehn, O., & Stappers, J. (Eds.). (1992). *The people's voice. Local radio and television in Europe.* London: John Libbey Media.

Jankowski, N. W., Van Selm, M., & Hollander, E. (2001). On crafting a study of community networks: Considerations and reflections. In L. Keeble & B. Loader (Eds.), *Community informatics: Community development through the use of information and communication technology* (pp. 101–117). London: Routledge.

Joyce, M. (2007). *The citizen journalism Web site "OhmyNews" and the 2002 South Korean Presidential Election.* Internet and Democracy Case Study Series. Retrieved April 30, 2011, from http://cyber.law.harvard.edu/sites/cyber .law.harvard.edu/files/Joyce_South_Korea_2007.pdf

Kidd, D., Rodriguez, C., & Stein, L. (Eds.). (2009). *Making our media: Global initiatives toward a democratic public sphere.* Cresskill, NJ: Hampton Press.

Nicholas W. Jankowski *is a visiting fellow at the Virtual Knowledge Studio for the Humanities & Social Sciences (VKS), a collaborative research and educational project based in the Netherlands. In 2004 he was visiting fellow at the Oxford Internet Institute, University of Oxford. He has been involved in the study of new media and research methodology since the mid 1970s and is coeditor of* New Media and Society.

11

Magazines and Community

Cary Roberts Frith

Many successful consumer magazines, across many content categories, help audience members with similar interests connect with one another and imagine themselves as members of communities of interest. For example, whitewater enthusiasts can read *Paddler* magazine not just to learn new techniques and find rivers to explore, but also to read about their fellow canoeists, kayakers, and rafters and receive mobilizing information about various events where they can gather in person. Cancer survivors can read *Heal* magazine for inspiration and support from those who endured similar experiences fighting the disease. Region-specific publications can bring together like-minded people across broader geographic areas: *Texas Monthly*, for example, allows Texans to consider issues facing their state, discover interesting places and people, and fuel their Lone Star pride, and *Down East* magazine does the same for people who live in or have an interest in Maine (including year-round residents, owners of camps and summer homes, and people who just like to vacation there).

Magazines have, in many ways, been conduits of virtual community since the middle of the 20th century and into the Internet age. Although there are some general-interest magazines that target large, diverse audiences, most magazines cater to well-defined audiences, and many magazines go so far as to serve virtual communities. Countless magazines provide targeted content to audiences defined by geography, ethnicity, shared characteristics, common interests, or some combination of those traits, which are also boundaries that define communities. Editors and writers for such magazines spend most of their professional lives getting to know the communities they serve and ensuring their content addresses readers' ever-changing ideals and information needs. New media such as online discussion boards, blogs, and social networking tools are providing magazine journalists with more ways than ever to make direct connections with readers and tailor content to their niche audiences.

Kitch (2005) argued that the content of even large-circulation, general-interest magazines helped to define the "imagined community of the nation" in the U.S. in the early 20th century. Kitch noted how the once-popular U.S. magazine *Life* filled that role: the magazine's editors wrote that their magazine "imparted a feeling that a vast nation could be brought together as a community" (Kitch, 2005, p. 9). As the magazine industry expanded, many publications headed down a path of increasing specialization. Starting in the 1950s and 1960s, many special-interest publications were launched to zero in on narrow, well-defined audiences. In *Magazine-Made America: The Cultural Transformation of the Postwar Periodical*, Abrahamson (1996) traced how and why the magazine industry shifted from general-interest publications "with their emphasis on large-scale conformity" to special-interest publications "with their emphasis on individual fulfillment and fragmented communities of interest" (p. 25). With increasing amounts of disposable income and leisure time, magazine readers' diverse interests ran the gamut from golf to gourmet cooking. Abrahamson highlighted the role that such interests, and their attendant magazines, played in binding readers together in new forms of communities:

> For many enthusiasts, it is even possible that the activities themselves served as substitutes for a more conventional sense of community, replacements for the lost small-town sociality so central to

the enduring American myth. In this context, the special-interest magazines may have served as not only the small town's newspaper, but as both an essential element in the coherence and an important validator of these communities' very existence. (p. 50)

Echoing Abrahamson, Demers (2007) credited the community building role for magazines' ongoing success: "From a structural perspective, the most notable characteristic of magazines is specialization. The history of magazines, in fact, is one of specialization. Magazines create and maintain communities of interest, and that's way they've been able to survive" (p. 128).

A driving force behind magazines' role in creating and reinforcing community cohesion is the interdependent relationship between editors and readers. Writing about niche magazines, Johnson and Prijatel (2007) noted, "Magazine editors see their readers as part of a community; readers of a successful publication have a sense of ownership of *their* magazine" (p. 7). In a cultural history of Canada's most popular women's magazine, *Chatelaine*, Korinek (2000) asserted, "The writers and editors encouraged, educated, and entertained readers, but, most important, they responded to their demands. These readers were not passive consumers whose interaction with the magazine was limited to writing their yearly subscription cheque" (p. 8). Casting that relationship in terms of journalistic distance—"the ideational and figurative distance between the producer and consumer of media form," Abrahamson (2007) pointed out that magazine editors and readers often share no journalistic distance because they are members of the same "direct community of interest" (p. 69).

This chapter discusses the scholarship on alternative and consumer magazines and their role in fostering community. (For a discussion of the literature on alternative versus consumer magazines, see Reader and Moist, 2008). That is an emerging area of research, which should be encouraging to scholars interested in both magazines and community—considerable opportunity exists for groundbreaking research along those lines. Although that is largely uncharted territory for research, some studies have provided a foundation for the study of magazines as examples of community journalism. Those varied works reflect the diversity of magazine genres themselves and cross theoretical and methodological boundaries, as well as academic disciplines.

❖ AUDIENCE CONTRIBUTIONS TO MAGAZINES

One way in which magazines can foster community is by including audience members in the journalistic process. That is of course possible in most media—Schudson (1992) noted the collectivizing potential of media, and stated that a key characteristic of the mass media is that their "production becomes increasingly embedded in a network of interaction, negotiation, and feedback over time," becoming "more collective than was earlier the case" (p. 49). Kitch (2005) asserted that magazines are the "most dialogic" of all media (p. 9). Aronson (2002) addressed the dialogic nature of magazines specifically:

> In functional terms, the "dialogism" inherent in the American magazine configured a kind of forum. Its miscellaneous form embraced multiple voices, and its participatory format entertained the ongoing exchange of views. . . . As communities of readers and writers together wrote, revoked, reinforced, and renovated contents, they collectively negotiated and authorized—and the magazines disseminated—new discourse for public use. (p. 11)

In a 2006 case study, Webb linked magazines' dialogic nature to Anderson's (1991) concept of imagined community, which argues that mass media can influence and foster national identity. Webb studied two magazines produced by Wisconsin-based Reiman Publications, which publishes various magazines targeted to rural women in the United States. Webb observed how the predominantly reader-generated content in *Taste of Home* and *Country Woman* helped to "bind readers into a community by voicing shared values and a shared self-image" (p. 866). Her qualitative analysis revealed that

> Reiman editors have been adept at creating community through narrative structures and rhetorical strategies. Their reader-centered model invites the reader in, asks the reader to contribute, reports on reader interests, appears to foster reader agency, and relies on reader submissions for 80 percent of content. The critical aspect of this model is that it appeals to a subscriber to join a community that shares values and beliefs and that places the past and the future within the context of family and religion. (p. 875)

Webb's findings showed how editors in one publishing house used reader contributions to reinforce a sense of community. Adding to the literature is a comparative study of two alternative magazines that considered the differences between Anderson's "imagined community" and the concept of "virtual community." Reader and Moist (2008) argued that virtual community is "essentially a collective phenomenon," whereas imagined community is an "individual-level phenomenon" (p. 824). They used critical cultural analysis to examine letters to the editor in alternative magazines that serve very different audiences: the *Small Farmer's Journal* and *Shambhala Sun*. Their goal was a more nuanced understanding of how individual readers establish, sustain, and modify the community via letters to the editor (LTEs) submitted to and published in the magazines. They found that

> writers use the LTEs to position themselves within the context of the community as much as they use them to position their community within broader society. LTEs are a means by which community members maintain and express their individuality within the collective. (p. 834)

In short, the authors provided evidence that published audience feedback in magazines helps to build—not simply reflect—community values via those magazines.

Webb (2006) and Reader and Moist (2008) have provided a theoretically sound foundation for future studies of audience involvement in the community building process of print and online magazines. Their findings also documented a clear difference in reader agency between consumer and alternative magazines that deserves further exploration.

❖ MAGAZINES SERVING COMMUNITIES OF PLACE

Some magazines identify as their communities people who live in or have special interest in specific geographic areas. Regional and city magazines have a long history of covering communities that are within geographic boundaries. Johnson and Prijatel (2007) cited the 1888 introduction of *Paradise of the Pacific*, the precursor to *Honolulu*, as the beginning of the modern genre of city magazines. Other notable titles quickly followed, including *Sunset*, a regional magazine for the western states and territories of the U.S., in 1898; *Philadelphia* in 1909; and the venerable *New Yorker* in 1925. As post–World War II demographic shifts expanded urban and suburban populations and advertisers sought to reach the increasing numbers of educated, affluent residents, a rapid growth in city and regional titles occurred in the 1960s, when more than 60 such publications launched in the U.S. (Riley & Selnow, 1991).

Not surprisingly, the genre of city/regional magazines drew the attention of journalism scholars. Fletcher (1977) surveyed local and regional magazine publishers and editors to identify the genre's attributes. He found that fundamental aspects of such magazines' success are that they establish a strong local identity, provide readers with a sense of their community, and fill voids left by other local media, especially newspapers. Hynds (1979), Hayes (1981), Fletcher and VandenBergh (1982), and Riley (1982) continued that line of research. Their findings echoed the importance of readers' appetite for local content and need to feel part of their communities. Emphasizing those qualities, Fletcher and VandenBergh (1982) quoted Rick Graetz of *Montana Magazine*: "Because they cover subjects of local interest . . . people get the feeling that the particular publication is their own. In Montana, *Montana Magazine* is considered 'Your Montana'" (p. 314). The studies suggested that the editors of those magazines were very much in tune with their imagined communities and felt a cultural connection to their readers.

During the civic journalism movement of the 1990s, Hynds (1995) surveyed city magazine editors to determine if they were helping their communities to identify, define, and deal with local issues. His results showed a commitment to public service and coverage of knotty issues such as transportation, government reform, planning/zoning, human rights, and hunger. Many respondents pointed to the high volume of letters to the editor they received after covering such topics as proof of their ability to mobilize community members to join the debate on important issues. Hynds also addressed important distinctions between city magazines and their competing newspapers:

> More than half of the city magazine editors see providing an alternative voice to that of the local newspaper as important. Most could serve effectively as alternative voices because they have differing philosophies from the newspapers, they have potential for in-depth reporting, and their generally affluent audiences could make a difference in the community. (1995, p. 98)

Casting a more critical gaze on the content of three well-established regional magazines (*Midwestern Living, Southern Living,* and *Sunset*), Fry (1995) was less laudatory and documented the genre's tendency to reinforce regional stereotypes and exclude non-white, less affluent residents in their coverage. Fry cautioned, "Representational patterns and the ideal readership of all three magazines recall and reinforce power relations that are foundational to U.S. regional identity" (p. 187). Scholars should not overlook that important point.

There is a need for much more research of regional and city magazines. Additional content studies are needed to expand that line of inquiry regarding the relationship between the communities portrayed in such magazines and the realities of the regions they cover. The majority of studies of city and regional magazines have emphasized the producers' point of view, while it appears none have addressed the magazines' effects on readers, providing a conspicuous hole in the literature.

❖ COMMUNITIES OF IDENTITY

Although geographic boundaries have long defined *community* in journalism practice, group identity has emerged as a less obvious but equally important boundary. As Hoggett (1997) explained,

> In interest or "elective" communities people share a common characteristic other than place. They are linked together by factors such as religious belief, sexual orientation, occupation or ethnic origin. In this way we may talk about the "gay community," the "Catholic community," or the "Chinese community" (p. 7)

Demographic traits—such as gender, ethnicity, and sexual preference—are core components of group identity. People who share such traits often look to identity-focused magazines to stay informed about and in touch with one another; for example, many magazines are overtly gendered (think *Cosmopolitan* and *Gentleman's Quarterly*). In recent decades, mass communication scholars have studied the role various identity-focused magazines, such as women's publications (Aronson, 2002; Bailey, 2003; Korinek, 2000), black and Latina publications (Kitch, 2005; Martinez, 2004; Rowley & Kurpius, 2003), and gay and lesbian publications (Streitmatter, 1995), have played in representing and reflecting (or not) their intended communities. Such publications have been particularly ripe for critical cultural analysis. For more than 30 years, feminist scholars such as Friedan (1963) and Wolf (2002) have censured popular women's consumer magazines for their stereotypical portrayals of women as either wives and mothers who take care of the home or as sex objects and stick-thin models who sell products for advertisers. More recently, third-wave feminists have begun to look at more nuanced critical readings of those texts in an effort to explain women's continued appetite for such stereotypical content. In the preface to a history of early American women's magazines and their readers, Aronson (2002) presented a possible explanation based in part on a desire to belong to some kind of community:

> The pleasures of self-expression, particularly in the defiance of silencing elsewhere, the boost in belonging to a community of equals, the satisfaction of feeling central as well as part of something with influence and cultural impact—these factors, present from the start, may remain behind the phenomenal levels of reader involvement characteristic of women's magazines to this day. (p. 12)

One of Aronson's chapters dealt directly with the role of identity and community through a case study of editor-in-chief Sarah Hale and her *(American) Ladies' Magazine*, published from 1828 to 1836. Hale solicited contributions from her readers and published ongoing dialogues with them on the magazine's letters page. Aronson (2002) celebrated that exchange within the pages of the first women's magazine to last more than five years, and noted, "By expressing a democratic preference for lateral collaboration among women over hierarchical obedience to men, she [Hale] positions and empowers the magazines' readers to act as the authors of their own public identities and power" (p. 105). Aronson praised women's magazines for empowering and uniting women in such fashion:

> The interactivity and audience agency compelled by the early American women's magazine capitalized on the democratic association Tocqueville predicted for newspapers while forestalling the onset of mass society he feared. By encouraging women's

public expression and collective participation, publicizing it, and legitimating the entire process in both gendered and political terms, magazines did even more than enable women to constitute themselves as a public. (p. 21)

Korinek (2000) also pointed to reader participation as a key element of community formation in her extensive cultural history of Canada's most popular women's magazine, *Chatelaine*, during the 1950s and 1960s: "The participatory nature of the magazine, the topics addressed, and the importance placed on reader input and suggestion . . . resulted in the development of a national community of readers, writers, and editors" (p. 8). Such themes were also considered as part of a broader rhetorical analysis of *Bitch*, a modern alternative magazine for feminists; in that study, Bailey (2003) examined the multiple voices or "multivocality" represented in the magazine's content. Bailey concluded, "*Bitch* does not simply reflect a pre-existing feminist community or identity. It also offers a particular constitution of that community and identity, one that revolves around reading pop culture in a highly stylized way" (p. 7).

Beyond gender, a key component of identity is race and ethnicity. Magazines targeted to specific racial or ethnic groups have long been a noteworthy segment of the community publishing industry. Titles for African Americans paved the way, starting with *Mirror of Liberty* launched in 1838 and continuing with the long-standing success of *Ebony* since 1945 and *Essence* since 1968. Titles targeted to Hispanics have expanded rapidly since the 1990s, with more than 60 now being published in the United States (Johnson & Prijatel, 2007). The largest-circulation Hispanic magazine in the U.S. is *Latina*, launched in 1996. Despite the growth in the ethnic-magazine industry and the established body of literature focused on ethnic newspapers, Johnson and Prijatel (2007) have noted an overall lack of scholarship on ethnic magazines, which, again, provides an opportunity for scholars looking for new research directions.

There are some must-read studies along those lines, however. In her book about how magazines help to create cultural narratives that shape collective memory, Kitch (2007) examined the historical content of *American Legacy* and *Ebony*. She argued that they engaged in "counter-memory" by documenting past events while at the same time challenging popular memories about them: "This is a process not merely of rebuilding, but also of reassembling those 'pieces' of history in new ways that serve present needs and that enable current readers to use them to form a living sense of cultural and racial identity" (p. 107). A content analysis of *Black Enterprise*, a magazine for the business community, revealed that its emphasis on financially successful African Americans helped to shape a more positive identity for readers (Rowley & Kurpius, 2003). That study argued that *Black Enterprise* achieved its "goal of lifting up the Black community by showing readers what life could be like if they just acquired the right skills and worked hard" (p. 250). Similarly, Martinez (2004) found that *Latina* reinforced its female readers' pan-ethnic identity and evoked a sense of family in its pages. Combining interviews with the editorial staff and textual analysis of articles, she provided a detailed account of the magazine's role in reflecting and constructing culture: "Acknowledging the diversity of Latina experiences, attitudes, and ideologies has been central to the identity-building project of *Latina* since the early stages in the creation of the magazine" (p. 170).

Another understudied segment is the genre of magazines serving gay, lesbian, bisexual, and transgendered communities. Streitmatter (1995) traced the history and examined the content of three pioneering and widely distributed gay and lesbian magazines founded in the 1950s. He argued that *One, Mattachine Review*, and *The Ladder* gave voice to previously unheard points of view and created a sense of collective identity that had not existed in print. He credited them with "helping to build a national lesbian and gay community" and helping readers to "identify their common goals and aspirations" (p. 443).

Although those historical and qualitative analyses help to shed light on how magazine content can shape and reflect such communities of identity, much more research is needed in that important segment of the magazine industry. Although content studies are useful for mapping cultural territory, they cannot explain the effects of production and consumption of such magazines. There is a need for more robust study of such magazines that textual analysis alone cannot provide, although efforts in that regard have been attempted, such as those by Martinez (2004), who included interviews with *Latina* editors along with the analysis of the texts, and Korinek (2000), who combined textual analysis with in-depth interviews of producers and archival material from the publisher. Those more comprehensive analyses can serve as models for future research in that area.

❖ MAGAZINES AND COMMUNITIES OF INTEREST

There is another form of community that magazines serve: communities of interest. As Abrahamson (1996) documented, the magazine industry has grown since the 1950s and 1960s by targeting content to ever-narrower market niches defined by psychographic characteristics such as attitudes, lifestyles, and cultural values. A quick glance at new magazine launches in 2009 reveals titles for such esoteric interests as beading and jewelry making, fantasy films, and journaling (Husni, 2009). Expanding the concept of communities of interest beyond demographic to psychographic traits, several scholars have considered how magazines serve readers who share common passions and pursuits. That work has been done by cultural studies researchers from a variety of disciplines, including mass communication, physical education, and music, who have examined the role of alternative and consumer magazine content in shaping, reflecting, and reinforcing culture and power relationships among community members. Such studies have focused on *Wired* magazine's "netizens" (Frau-Meigs, 2000), female skateboarders (Wheaton & Beal, 2003), musicians (Théberge, 1991), and fans of heavy metal music (Brown, 2007).

Frau-Meigs (2000) examined how print content in *Wired* magazine and content on its companion website, HotWired, celebrated the notion of virtual community and technology-driven identity construction as the content producers and readers were actually creating them individually and collectively. Frau-Meigs contrasted the magazine's virtual community to traditional proximate community:

In *Wired*, members selected themselves according to their capacity to communicate, to manipulate images and to process computerized texts. In real life, it was a network of private individuals, linked primarily by their professional competence. The network ideology, as constructed by the magazine, itself a reflection of a large social context, is therefore not directly equivalent to the classic civil community—defined as a combined structure of public and private associations of individuals in which group interests prevail over individual interests. (p. 235)

Through an examination of advertisements and editorial content in six Canadian and U.S. consumer magazines produced for musicians,

Théberge (1991) documented the formation of dual reader groups—a community of shared interest in creating music and a market for consumption of instruments and technical equipment. He wrote, "It is interesting to explore the manner in which the musicians' magazines themselves work to simultaneously construct their readers as both a kind of musical 'community' and a market" (p. 285). In a similar vein, Brown (2007) analyzed three British heavy-metal magazines targeted to young fans of the genre. He found that the content conveyed "a sense of what it is to be a global member of metal-oriented youth culture" and served as "conduits for the markets and commerce that sustain the niche categories around which contemporary metal music is packaged as a commodified experience" (p. 643). Brown argued, "If there is a consumer lifestyle being carried in the magazines it is one concerned with informing and supporting readers in their active pursuit of music consumption through buying albums, attending concerts and contributions to the letters page" (p. 651). The study of audience feedback has already been mentioned in the studies by Webb (2006) and Reader and Moist (2008), but it should be noted here that both of those studies also focused on communities of interest: Webb's study focused on magazines aimed at the rural lifestyle in the U.S., and Reader and Moist focused on two different magazines, one devoted to small-scale sustainable farming and another to the practice of Western "engaged Buddhism." As with previously mentioned lines of research, however, most of the studies related to niche-interest magazines is focused on content rather than audience members' personal opinions, and research into how people select and utilize such magazines is not only a wide-open area for new research, but also clearly needed.

❖ CONCLUSION

The various streams of research reviewed in this chapter seem to coalesce into a shared belief that magazines can play a role in creating and reflecting community. Most of the studies mentioned here looked to the texts themselves for evidence, employing content analysis, historical research, or qualitative methods of textual analysis. A few viewed the texts through a cultural or feminist theoretical lens. Several scholars relied on input from content producers, but the actual voices of readers (via direct communication with researchers) were silent in all but one study. More commonly, readers' points of view were divined from their published letters to the editor and other content contributions. Future research of the role of magazines in community journalism needs to allow readers to speak for themselves, and directly to researchers, to better understand readers' interactions with their preferred magazines. Another promising direction for scholarly inquiry is analysis of readers' participation in building community in print magazines' companion Web spaces, as well as in online-only magazine sites.

Because magazines have long served well-defined communities of readers, they offer opportunities to study historical and contemporary community in action, and as such provide an important if often overlooked segment of the overall study of community journalism.

❖ REFERENCES

Abrahamson, D. (1996). *Magazine-made America: The cultural transformation of the postwar periodical.* Cresskill, NY: Hampton Press.

Abrahamson, D. (2007). Magazine exceptionalism: The concept, the criteria, the challenge. *Journalism Studies, 8*(4), 667–670.

Anderson, B. (1991). *Imagined communities: Reflections on the origins and spread of nationalism.* London: Verso.

Aronson, A. B. (2002). *Taking liberties: Early American women's magazines and their readers.* Westport, CN: Praeger.

Bailey, C. (2003). Bitching and talking/gazing back: Feminism as critical reading. *Women and Language, 26*(2), 1–8.

Brown, A. R. (2007). "Everything else louder than everything else:" The contemporary metal music magazine and its cultural appeal. *Journalism Studies, 8*(4), 642–655.

Demers, D. (2007). *History and future of mass media: An integrated perspective.* Cresskill, NJ: Hampton Press.

Fletcher, A. D. (1977). City magazines find a niche in the media marketplace. *Journalism Quarterly, 54*(4), 740–749.

Fletcher, A. D., & VandenBergh, B. G. (1982). Numbers grow, problems remain for city magazines. *Journalism Quarterly, 59*(2), 313–317.

Frau-Meigs, D. (2000). A cultural project based on multiple temporary consensus: Identity and community in *Wired. New Media and Society, 2,* 227–244.

Friedan, B. (1963). *The feminine mystique.* New York: Bantam Doubleday Dell.

Fry, K. (1995). Regional consumer magazines and the ideal white reader: Constructing and retaining geography as text. In D. Abrahamson (Ed.), *The American magazine: Research perspectives and prospects* (pp. 186–204). Ames: Iowa State University Press.

Hayes, J. P. (1981). City/regional magazines: A survey/census. *Journalism Quarterly, 58*(2), 294–296.

Hoggett, P. (1997). Contested communities. In P. Hoggett (Ed.), *Contested communities. Experiences, struggles, policies* (pp. 3–16). Bristol, UK: Policy Press.

Husni, S. (2009). *What's new*. Retrieved March 25, 2009, from www .mrmagazine.com

Hynds, E. C. (1979). City magazines, newspapers serve in different ways. *Journalism Quarterly, 56*(3), 619–622.

Hynds, E. C. (1995). City magazines have diverse roles. *Mass Comm Review, 22*(1–2), 90–101.

Johnson, S., & Prijatel, P. (2007). *The magazine from cover to cover*. New York: Oxford University Press.

Kitch, C. (2005). *Pages from the past: History and memory in American magazines*. Chapel Hill: University of North Carolina Press.

Korinek, V. J. (2000). *Roughing it in the suburbs: Reading* Chatelaine *magazine in the fifties and sixties*. Toronto: University of Toronto Press.

Martinez, K. Z. (2004). *Latina* magazine and the invocation of a panethnic family: Latino identity as it is informed by celebrities and *papis chulos*. *The Communication Review, 7*, 155–174.

Reader, B., & Moist, K. (2008). Letters as indicators of community values: Two case studies of alternative magazines. *Journalism and Mass Communication Quarterly, 85*(4), 823–840.

Riley, S. G. (1982). Specialized magazines of the South. *Journalism Quarterly, 59*(1), 447–455.

Riley, S. G., & Selnow, G. W. (1991). *Regional interest magazines of the United States*. Westport, CT: Greenwood.

Rowley, K. M., & Kurpius, D. D. (2003). Separate and still unequal: A comparative study of Blacks in business magazines. *The Howard Journal of Communications, 14*, 245–255.

Schudson, M. (1992). The new validation of popular culture: Sense and sentimentality in academia. In R. K. Avery & D. Eason (Eds.), *Critical perspectives on media and society* (pp. 48–68). London: Guilford Press.

Streitmatter, R. (1995). Creating a venue for the "love that dare not speak its name": Origins of the gay and lesbian press. *Journalism and Mass Communication Quarterly, 72*(2), 436–447.

Théberge, P. (1991). Musicians' magazines in the 1980s: The creation of a community and a consumer market. *Cultural Studies, 5*(3), 270–293.

Webb, S. M. (2006). The narrative of core traditional values in Reiman magazines. *Journalism and Mass Communication Quarterly, 83*(4), 865–882.

Wheaton, B., & Beal, B. (2003). "Keeping it real": Subcultural media and the discourses of authenticity in alternative sport. *International Review for the Sociology of Sport, 38*(2), 155–176.

Wolf, N. (2002). *The beauty myth: How images of beauty are used against women*. New York: Harper Perennial.

Making the Mundane Matter ●

Carolyn Kitch

In local newspapers, as Bill Reader explains in the first chapter of this book, it is "the trivial and the routine that provide observable clues of community connections." Such mundane content attracts little attention from mainstream journalism scholarship, which traditionally has been concerned with major news media and with dramatic news events.

Writing about the work of journalism historians, Catherine Covert (1981) once suggested that we might have a different understanding of the past if we focused not on wars and revolutions but on the ordinary aspects of daily life, if we saw journalism as an agent of continuity rather than change, and if we regarded that continuity as valuable (rather than "static"). The same case surely can be made for journalism of the present. Yet in the three decades since Covert offered that advice, few scholars have followed it.

One reason may be our ongoing belief, mirroring that of the journalism profession itself, that "hard" news ("breaking" announcements of social disruption) is more worthy of our attention than "soft" news (reminders of commonality and connection). The hard/soft dichotomy accounts, in part, for researchers' lack of attention to non-daily newspapers. It also fuels the academic view that magazines are not so much journalism as "popular culture." The latter semantic distinction, which contains the interesting implication that journalism is something that exists apart from "people," is generally a dismissal of commercially successful journalism. Yet the term also has an anthropological meaning, one that offers promise for serious critical engagement with these media forms.

Researchers who study magazines and researchers who study local newspapers make many of the same arguments, but these parallel streams of inquiry rarely meet. In fact, the two types of media are similar in several ways. While city and regional publications invite the most obvious comparison, even national magazines—from *Guitar World* to *Dog World*—represent communities that are lived as well as imagined. Like weekly newspapers, magazines provide content that is recurring and predictable; their editorial voice is conversational, with readers' views and experiences regularly included; their audiences embrace a self-defined social identity based on shared beliefs and interests (as do their editors, whose in-group status increases rather than compromises their editorial authority); their readers pass them around, cut things out of them, and save them.

Community newspapers provide a record of the mundane, the stuff of life that is not conventionally newsworthy but that matters locally, on a regular basis. Perhaps it is this keepsake function that accounts for their relative health in 2009 while readers have abandoned subscriptions to *The New York Times* and fidelity to the evening television news. The Internet and TiVo may have made time irrelevant in media consumption, but place and materiality remain important for certain kinds of news—news of deaths, marriages, school sports, soldiers' homecomings, local festivals, and memorials. In newspapers, tangible documentation of such milestones literally circulates, casting a net around a group of people united by personal experience and residence.

The survival of community journalism through decades of economic upheaval is proof that there is still a need for "a journalism of place"—and not only in rural areas. Some of the most important current work is being done not by "the country editor" but by local, often ethnic, urban newspapers, especially in de-industrializing cities with rapidly changing demography. At Temple University, the journalism students in our Multimedia Urban Reporting Lab (MURL) report on neighborhoods whose news usually does not make it into *The Philadelphia Inquirer* unless it is negative (that is, "breaking" news). The MURL project is becoming an incubator for journalism research as well as journalism practice. This is community journalism, too. It also is, simply, journalism.

Definitions are at the heart of all the fretting over "the future of news." What *is* useful journalism today? How does it look or sound? Where is it found? Whom should it serve, and how? Why is it needed? Those are cultural as well as institutional questions. To answer them, we need to set aside our old assumptions about what is worth studying and reconsider what else may matter, after all.

❖ REFERENCE

Covert, C. L. (1981). Journalism history and women's experience: A problem in conceptual change. *Journalism History, 8*(1), 2–6.

Carolyn Kitch is a professor in the School of Communications and Theatre at Temple University. Her research focuses on media and memory and on journalism history, with an emphasis on gender issues and the medium of magazines. Among her many publications are the books The Girl on the Magazine Cover: The Origins of Visual Stereotypes in American Mass Media *(University of North Carolina Press, 2001),* Pages From the Past: History and Memory in American Magazines *(University of North Carolina Press, 2005), and* Journalism in a Culture of Grief *(with Janice Hume; Routledge, 2007).*

12

Community Journalism as an International Phenomenon

John A. Hatcher

It likely won't come as a surprise that, in the burgeoning field of international communications, community journalism has been largely excluded from the discussion. Nicholas W. Jankowski, noted scholar of community media, observed that a great deal of work has been devoted to studying the global transformation of the media landscape, but "the evidence presented is restricted to national and international media systems; no attention is paid to regional and local media systems" (Jankowski, 2002, p. 3). This chapter reviews research being done by scholars who are working toward a more global understanding of community journalism, and concludes by suggesting some directions that could be explored to build a more international approach to the study of community journalism.

❖ OVERVIEW OF INTERNATIONAL COMMUNICATIONS

Broadly, international communications could be seen as the desire to explain mass communication in a global context by looking for larger theoretical models that explain media systems at national and international levels. It also includes comparative analysis that is driven by a desire to look for country-level and cultural differences in mass communication (Hallin & Mancini, 2004). As such, it feels almost counterintuitive to attempt to position the inherently "local" concept of community journalism in a discussion of international communications. However, the question to consider is whether what Artz and Kamalipour (2007) referred to as transnational media forces are having the same effect on community media that has been observed in national and regional media.

The study of international communications evolved from what many consider a normative approach with a largely Western bias to current attempts that explore media differences, especially in light of increasing globalization and homogenization (Hallin & Mancini, 2004). Artz and Kamalipour (2007) made the distinction between international and transnational media organizations, explaining that international organizations are media outlets based in one country that reach out to global audiences, and transnational media, in contrast, are organizations that work independent of any particular country and instead serve a global class of citizens. The result, Artz and Kamalipour noted, has been that "the deterritorialization of media production and distribution has ruptured media national characteristics. The transnational media represent the class interests, class perspectives, and class ideology of the transnational capitalist class, albeit smoothly marketed in a diversity of cultural forms" (p. 151).

It seems as if many scholars rarely find anything meritorious as they explore the global media landscape. The oft-cited Hallin and Mancini (2004) described the phenomenon that appears to be most important to community journalism: driven by technology and increased mobility, global media are homogenizing mass communication, erasing cultural differences, and overtaking culture-specific media. The questions being asked in international communications—through survey research, content analysis, and other empirical approaches—is whether cultural differences remain or whether global media are imposing their values on the world in hegemonic fashion.

Yet there is little research as to how that phenomenon is manifest in community journalism around the world, and consideration of that can be done only in a largely speculative way. It doesn't take much to imagine how a hegemonic global media system would threaten the subcultural focus of various community journalism enterprises. However, there is also the possibility that community media could be insulated from such a global wave of homogenization, and may even flourish. As Lyombe Eko (2002) observed in his analysis of media in Africa, the decentralization, openness, redundancy, simplicity, ubiquity, and statelessness of the Internet lends itself "to innovation even in circumstances of hegemony and asymmetrical power relations as in sub-Saharan Africa. Africans have shown they can bridge the digital divide through localization and domestication of the Internet" (p. 25). Much as community media in North America appear to have weathered the economic turmoil of the global recession of 2008–2010, there is the possibility that community media around the world have operated—perhaps even thrived—under the radar of the global media machine. That possibility begs serious inquiry.

❖ DEFINING COMMUNITY JOURNALISM FOR INTERNATIONAL STUDY

An important question to consider relates to the external validity of the work presented so far in this book. It's the old apples-to-apples question: Does this concept called *community journalism*, developed largely by studying "small" news media outlets (mostly in the U.S., Canada, and Australia) explain something similar in all countries and cultures? When we make generalizations about "community journalism," do we risk diluting the very aspect of community journalism that makes it distinct—its cultural relativism? Furthermore, how do differences in cultural settings affect the journalism-community relationship?

The first step toward answering those questions is, once again, developing consistent definitions for the concepts in play, particularly the term *community media*. Almost instinctively, U.S. scholars see community media as meaning newspapers, magazines, radio/television stations, and websites serving specific geographic regions or niche audiences. However, in a global context, the term does not have universal application. In their discussion of community journalism, for example, Moore and Gillis (2005) contrasted community media with community journalism, arguing that the latter defines a "process" of doing journalism that is similar to the advocacy style of journalism espoused by scholars of civic or public journalism such as Jay Rosen. Things get more complicated when the term *community media* is brought in. Jankowski, one of the most cited scholars in electronically mediated community journalism, used "community media" as an all-encompassing term to refer to "a diverse range of mediated forms of communication: print media such as newspapers and magazines, electronic media such as radio and television, and electronic network initiatives that embrace characteristics of both traditional print and electronic media" (2002, p. 6). He pointed to U.S. scholars such as Janowitz (1952) and Stamm (1985) as the foundational works for the study of community press, but focused his own efforts on community radio, television, and other electronic media. Fuller's (2007) definition of community media did not seem as inclusive; she used "community media" to define electronic media that is operated by citizens, has roots in social justice movements of the 1960s in North America, and has begun to take hold in developing nations through the support of non-governmental organizations (NGOs).

If those distinctions between the concepts of community journalism and community media meant only differences in the type of media channel, it would be one thing, but those differences may also speak to differences in the roles those media play in their communities—differences based on those media's organizational structures, community relationships, and what they consider to be news values.

Development journalism is another term that appears often in community journalism research. Usually that concept defines a style of journalism that is sponsored by NGOs and used in developing nations. Although it has been critiqued by some as being largely a propaganda tool for government-driven work, others have found development journalism to embody many of the ideals valued in community journalism while operating in economic systems that simply could not support commercially driven media. For example, Banjade (2006) conducted a qualitative analysis of a community newspaper started by an NGO in Nepal and found that the newspaper was actually much more concerned with presenting what might be described as "hyperlocal journalism," driven by the voices of community members more than by the agendas of policymakers.

❖ COMMUNITY PRESS AROUND THE WORLD

For the most part, research into the community press has been conducted at the country level with almost no attempt to build theory that explains cross-cultural variations in community journalism, let alone to position community journalism in the current global landscape. Much of that research seems to follow the line of research already delineated in earlier chapters of this book, often involving qualitative assessments of independent rural newspapers.

Perhaps some of the earliest attempts at any cross-cultural comparisons were conducted by Crispin C. Maslog, a community journalist turned scholar from the Philippines who eventually went on to earn a Ph.D. from the University of Minnesota and authored numerous books and articles on community journalism in the 1980s and 1990s. Using titles such as *The Dragon Slayers of the Countryside* (1989), Maslog produced qualitative narratives that told the stories of courageous independent community newspapers in the Philippines and Southeast Asia. In one of his key works, *Five Successful Asian Community Newspapers* (1985), a UNESCO-funded study of five newspapers from Bangladesh, India, Indonesia, and the Philippines, Maslog observed how community newspapers there were driven by a common desire to serve the local community and to champion issues important to those regions. His work has since transitioned toward a greater interest in citizen-driven development journalism.

Another pioneering group in exploring the concept of community journalism in a global context is The International Society of Weekly Newspaper Editors (ISWNE), which published its first journal volume, *Grassroots Editor*, in January 1960, with one of its tenets being the forging of an alliance of small-town journalists interested in helping avoid a nuclear holocaust ("A Challenge to Editors," 1960). The name used to describe the community journalist in that journal was the "grassroots editor" (Waring, 1960, p. 5). The grassroots editor lived in a "village, a small city, or a metropolis" and yet shared the common trait of a "nearness to his people" (p. 5). "People," in that sense, was defined by Waring as a well-defined community tied together by geographic boundaries or common cultural bonds, such as ethnicity or religious affiliation. Waring described grassroots editors as having a close relationship with their communities' leaders, with the newspapers acting as social centers and communication tools for civic leaders. Still, Waring emphasized the importance of journalistic independence—a value he argued must be upheld even at the risk of community backlash. Even in 1960, Waring worried that grassroots journalism would be silenced by the growth of corporate-owned media. Independence may have been admired, but Howard Rusk Long (1977) later noted that only a small group of journalists could be said to truly champion its cause.

A perusal of the *Grassroots Editor*'s indices from 1960 to 1970 shows that it provided a central location from which to read examples of great community journalism, from editors such as civil rights advocate Hazel Brannon Smith of the Lexington, Missouri, *Advertiser*, and Henry Beetle Hough, editor of Martha's Vineyard's *Vineyard Gazette*. It was also a place where the challenges of community journalism in different countries were explored. With titles such as "Mexico's Crusading Weekly Newspapers," "The Press and Its Problems in Tanganyika," and "Latin America's Fading Hometown Weeklies," the journal explored issues facing journalists in specific countries, but also included writing about more general topics such as ethical standards, community involvement, and how to deal with community backlash on controversial issues. The journal remains a place where both scholars and practitioners can read about commonalities and differences of the community press around the globe. Today, ISWNE has members throughout not only the U.S., but also Canada and Great Britain (at this writing, the president of ISWNE is a weekly newspaper editor in northwestern England).

From an international perspective, there exist many studies focusing on community journalism, but those studies are limited to country-level explorations often done within those nations (and as such are essentially domestic studies). For example, a team of scholars at Rhodes University conducted a detailed case study of six independently owned community newspapers in South Africa (Milne, Rau, Du Toit, & Mdlongwa, 2006). They found that those newspapers shared common values, such as a desire not just to produce a local news product but also to be active members of their communities, to provide a voice for the voiceless, to serve a role in their democracy, and to bridge cultural divides. The team also found that those news organizations faced similar challenges, including the difficulties of independent ownership and the hardship of selling advertising space to companies hesitant to invest with organizations that were small or owned by marginalized groups. They also found that community newspapers shared a hesitancy to report on contentious issues in their communities, preferring to see their role as community builders.

Australian scholar Kathryn Bowd (2003) has done similar work in her home country, comparing community journalism (or "country journalism") to both metropolitan journalism and development journalism. Bowd has suggested that the emphasis on "local" and the community relationship may mean that community journalism has more in common with what she calls non-Western forms of journalism than with conventional journalism. Bowd (2006) went a step further in explicating community journalism at an international level with a comparison of community journalism in Singapore and in Australia. She noted that in spite of different perceptions of community in those two cultural settings, the journalists shared an emphasis on local news—an emphasis which, she argued, may insulate journalism from the force of globalization.

❖ THE "COMMUNITY MEDIA" DISTINCTION

In part driven by the support and efforts of NGOs such as Internews Network (Fairbairn, 2009) as well as European scholars concerned about the loss of national identity as the European Union grows, there is a much richer body of research exploring international ideas related to electronically driven versions of community media—perhaps none more important than Jankowski's work. In a collected volume exploring community media in the current era, Jankowski (2003) and other scholars defined community media on an international level, presented case studies of community media in different cultural settings, and set the agenda for future research.

Jankowski defined the characteristics of community media as (a) empowerment of the politically disenfranchised, (b) shared, local ownership, (c) local content, (d) nonprofessional and volunteer ownership, (e) electronic distribution, (f) geographic distribution, and (g) noncommercial finance structure, although they might also include sponsorship, advertising, and so forth. That definition offers one of the key distinctions between the traditional, commercially driven community press of the United States and the social movement style of journalism that seems to dominate radio and television.

In the introduction to a recent edited volume that includes case studies of community media internationally, Fuller (2007) drew on a similar set of criteria to define community media, and went further to define community media in opposition to commercially driven models of media. Fuller did not draw on traditional community journalism research, focusing instead on a style of alternative media that is citizen driven and focuses on providing a means by which marginalized groups can participate in community discourse and create their own community identity.

In many developing nations that have diverse language groups and lower literacy rates, it is radio that may do the work of defining community. In South Africa, for example, it's been said that there are more radios than there are mattresses. In her detailed analysis of the now-famous Bush Radio in Cape Town, scholar Tanja Bosch (2005) explored how a station designed to serve the impoverished Cape Flats community has evolved to build a larger community through a process she described as "rhizomatic." Countless fibrous networks, no one stronger than another, reach out and build community networks that bridge communities in a process akin to the "bridging capital" concept explicated by scholars such as Robert Putnam. Bush Radio has provided a voice for the residents of Cape Flats, but also has expanded the discussion and perhaps the community to include other residents of Cape Town. Community radio has served a similar function in other developing nations. As Bosch noted, the roots of community radio may go back decades, such as to the 1940s and 1950s in Central America when Bolivian miners used community radio as a mobilizing tool (O'Connor, 1990).

It's one thing to understand some of the common traits of community media, but Jankowski's desire has been to build a stronger theoretical understanding. He proposed that most of the research examining community media to date falls into four general themes: (a) democratic processes, (b) cultural identity, (c) the concept of "community," and (d) an "action perspective to communication" (Jankowski, 2003, p. 11). He encouraged scholars of community media to consider theoretical models that explain community media within the contexts of organizational structures, the media produced, the users of those media, and the environments or settings in which media operate (Jankowski, 2003).

❖ SETTING THE STAGE FOR FUTURE RESEARCH IN
COMMUNITY JOURNALISM

For the study of community journalism as an international phenomenon, it's important to understand that the relationship between a community and a journalist occurs within the context of a larger cultural
backdrop. For a long time, many scholars have studied the various
phenomena that hold cultures together: Durkheim (1915/1965) saw
society as constructed through shared cultural meaning, and Parsons
(1951) used those ideas to build a functionalist model that saw society
as a self-regulating system that maintains its own order, stability, and
equilibrium. Weber (1958) suggested culture is created through an
understanding of what's valued in a society.

What follows are some of the logical directions that cross-cultural
comparisons of community journalism could take based on existing
work in both international communications and comparative analysis
being conducted in various social science disciplines.

The political scientist Ronald Inglehart (1997) has created
the now-famous World Values Survey, which attempts to gauge
social and cultural distinctions, based on surveying the residents of
78 countries. Inglehart believed that those results, when aggregated
at the country level, reveal strong, predictable relationships among
economic development, cultural change, and political change (1997).
Inglehart's survey, first conducted in 1990 and at this writing
now in its fourth wave, approaches culture from a sociopolitical
angle: "Cultural elements tend to go together in coherent patterns"
(Inglehart, 1997, p. 69). The World Values Survey has been used as
the foundation for countless studies of religion, values, beliefs, and
political institutions. There are endless opportunities to explore
cross-cultural aspects of community journalism based on that exhaus-
tive data set. For example, it's accepted that community journalism is shaped by the nature of the community in which it functions
(Tichenor, Donohue, & Olien, 1980), but perhaps that relationship
explains what happens in a media system in only one cultural situation. The opportunity to test that theory in a comparative fashion
based on differences in cultural settings—as measured by the World
Values Survey—might proffer insight into the culturally specific factors that mediate the community journalism dynamic.

In the global marketplace, it's become understood that business practices deemed acceptable in one country could be viewed as outlandish in another country. Dutch writer Geert Hofstede's (1980) research stands as the foundational work in the field of cultural mapping. He began with surveys of IBM employees in 40 countries in the 1960s and 1970s and has since expanded his work to consider 74 countries. Hofstede suggested that there are four dimensions of culture: individualism-collectivism, power distance, masculinity-femininity, and uncertainty avoidance. That kind of comparative work should entice community journalism scholars to explore larger theoretical questions based on the media's cultural context and to begin to create cultural maps of community journalism.

Hofstede's mapping of value dimensions is very popular in social science research, but his scales are somewhat limited in their application, especially for scholars hoping to use more rigorous quantitative comparisons of culture. More recently, cross-cultural psychologist Shalom Schwartz (2004) has produced theory-driven work that "maps" the cultural nuances of countries that represent 75% of the world's population. Each culture is evaluated based on seven cultural-level values: egalitarianism, harmony, embeddedness, intellectual autonomy, affective autonomy, mastery, and hierarchy. Schwartz's work shows that individuals in different countries have distinctly different visions of society—and therefore of community—that offer important cautions to those who would ascribe universal definitions. They also offer an enticing opportunity to study the relationships between community and journalism at a cultural level. The implications of how those differences might affect conceptions of community and the journalists' role in a community are profound.

Another way to study community journalism as an international phenomenon is by examining its role within different political contexts. The great debate in political science is what matters more, institutions or culture? As scholar William Riker (1980) noted,

> it is of course true that this easy predictability is an illusion—but it is an illusion by which many scholars are hoodwinked because in quiet times the institutions are constant and only tastes are in dispute, while in turbulent times the institutions are in flux and only human greed seems constant. One fundamental and unresolved

problem of social science is to penetrate the illusion and to learn to take both values and institutions into account. (p. 432)

Putnam (2000) further argued that comparative work, to be effective, must understand the history, narrative, and context of a culture to avoid making broad generalizations. However, to have broader application, theory also must do more than explain one case. Nevertheless, institutions do matter in that they create the rules that constitute political behavior, as suggested by Carey (2000), who noted that institutions can be studied in two different ways: either by their historical origins or by the effects of different kinds of institutions.

Scholars in comparative political analysis spend a great deal of time looking for differences in political and civic life based on different aspects of political life. Economists and sociologists compare countries using different factors, such as health, wealth, and education levels. And, of course, community journalism cannot help but be influenced by the press freedoms journalists enjoy, which vary widely by nation, and even fluctuate within nations as political climates change. Some of those differences have been used to explore media differences across cultures, but generally in terms of the performance of large, national news media. The potential to apply those same concepts to a cross-cultural discussion of community journalism is wide open.

❖ CONCLUSION

As this chapter suggests, there are more questions than answers for scholars interested in exploring the concept of community journalism at the international level. Does the concept of community journalism vary from culture to culture? Does it even exist in some cultures? What impact is globalization having on community journalism? Does the homogenization of mass media that is seen in mainstream media portend similar results for community journalism?

Decades of research in international mass communication have all but ignored community journalism. That is not just a shame, but it is misleading and may deprive us of seeing truly important aspects of community journalism. Concepts of community must be embedded in culture, so how can those concepts be adequately explained if we are not comparing journalism within a culture to journalism practiced outside of that culture? The task for scholars of community journalism is spelled out clearly by Jankowski (2003), who said he hopes

> that all community media researchers will take seriously their mandate as social scientists to contribute to our collective theoretical understanding of small-scale media. This mandate entails, in my estimation, more than mere alliance with a theoretical perspective; it also necessitates refinement of concepts and generation of models relating these concepts. (p. 12)

Examples of grassroots and community media can be found in many countries and cultures around the world. In developing nations in Africa, community journalism plays the role of assisting in the diffusion of health care information and in the reporting of news in countries ravaged by war, usually in situations where journalists often face great impediments to press freedoms (Dadge, 2006). In the eastern-European nations, the community press is exploring new terrain as it tries to help formerly communist countries transition toward democratic governance and discussions of national identity in the face of a homogenizing "European" identity (European Journalism Centre, n.d.). In China, where in recent years news media have seen lessened governmental restrictions, a fascinating transition may be occurring away from a highly regulated, national media toward a more locally autonomous system with less government control and a new possibility for community media. Those examples, among many, show the challenge of applying universal truths about community journalism to all cultures. Variations in language, faith, values, freedoms, wealth, ideology, and the other attributes of culture offer enticing opportunities to explore the relationship that exists between journalists and their communities, and show why research of such relationships cannot be limited to (let alone based on) one narrow, cultural viewpoint of what community journalism is. Community journalism scholars must expand their view or risk being excluded from the discussion.

❖ REFERENCES

Artz, L., & Kamalipour, Y. (2007). *The media globe: Trends in international communication.* New York: Rowman & Littlefield.

Banjade, A. (2006). *Gaunle Deurali*: Barefoot community journalism in Western Nepal. *Global Media Journal, 5*(8). Retrieved May 1, 2011, from http://lass.calumet.purdue.edu/cca/gmj/sp06/gmj-sp06-banjade.htm

Bowd, K. (2006). Intersections of community and journalism in Singapore and Australia. *Asia Pacific Media Educator, 17*, 56–70.

Bosch, T. (2005). Community radio in post-apartheid South Africa: The case of Bush Radio in Cape Town. *Transformations, 10.* Retrieved May 3, 2011, from http://www.transformationsjournal.org/journal/issue_10/article_05.shtml

Bowd, K. (2003). How different is "different"? Australian country newspapers and development journalism. *Asia Pacific Media Educator, 14*, 117–130.

Carey, J. M. (2000). Parchment, equilibria, and institutions. *Comparative Political Studies, 33*(6–7), 735–761.

A challenge to editors. (1960). *Grassroots Editor, 1*, 2–3.

Dadge, D. (2006). *Africa overview.* Retrieved April 4, 2008, from International Press Institute website: http://www.freemedia.at/cms/ipi/freedom_detail.html?ctxid=CH0056&docid=CMS1176887458165

Durkheim, E. (1965). *The elementary forms of religious life.* New York: Free Press. (Original work published 1915)

Eko , L. (2002). Africa: Life in the margins of globalization. In N. Jankowski & O. Prehn (Eds.), *Community media in the information age: Perspectives and prospects.* Cresskill, NJ: Hampton Press.

European Journalism Centre. (n.d.). *Media landscape.* Retrieved April 4, 2008, from http://www.ejc.net/media_landscape/

Fairbairn, J. (2009). *Community media sustainability guide: The business of changing lives.* Retrieved May 3, 2011, from Internews Network website: http://www.internews.org/pubs/pdfs/internewscommunitymediaguide2009.pdf

Fuller, L. (2007). Introduction. In L. Fuller (Ed.), *Community media: International perspectives.* New York: Palgrave Macmillan.

Hallin, D. C., & Mancini, P. (2004). *Comparing media systems.* Cambridge, UK: Cambridge University Press.

Hofstede, G. (1980). Motivation, leadership, and organization: Do American theories apply abroad? *Organizational Dynamics, 9*, 42–63.

Inglehart, R. (1997). *Modernization and postmodernization: Cultural, economic, and political change in 43 societies.* Princeton, NJ: Princeton University Press.

Jankowski, N. (2002). The conceptual contours of community media. In N. Jankowski & O. Prehn (Eds.), *Community media in the information age: Perspectives and prospects.* Cresskill, NJ: Hampton Press.

Jankowksi, N. (2003). Community media research: A quest for theoretically-grounded models. *The Public, 1*(10), 5–14.

Janowitz, M. (1952). *The community press in an urban setting.* Glencoe, IL: Free Press.

Long, H. R. (1977). *Main Street militants: An anthology from Grassroots Editor.* Carbondale: Southern Illinois University Press.

Maslog, C. C. (1985). *Five successful Asian community newspapers.* Singapore: Asian Mass Communication Research and Information Center.

Maslog, C. C. (1989). *The dragon slayers of the countryside.* Manila, Philippines: PPI.

Milne, C., Rau, A., Du Toit, P., & Mdlongwa, F. (2006). *Key editorial and business strategies: A case study of six independent community newspapers.* Cape Town, South Africa: Media Digital.

Moore, R. C., & Gillis, T. L. (2005). Transforming communities: Community journalism in Africa. *Transformations, 10.* Retrieved July 15, 2009, from http://www.transformationsjournal.org/journal/issue_10/editorial.shtml

O'Connor, A. (1990). The miners' radio stations in Bolivia: A culture of resistance. *Journal of Communication, 40*(1), 102–110.

Parsons, T. (1951). *The social system.* New York: Free Press.

Putnam, R. (2000). *Bowling alone: The collapse and revival of American community.* New York: Simon & Schuster.

Riker, W. (1980). Implications from the disequilibrium of majority rule for the study of institutions. *American Political Science Review, 74,* 432–446.

Schwartz, S. H. (2004). Mapping and interpreting cultural differences around the world. In H. Vinken, J. Soeters, & P. Ester (Eds.), *Comparing cultures: Dimensions of culture in a comparative perspective* (pp. 43–73). Leiden, Netherlands: Brill.

Stamm, K. (1985). *Newspaper use and community ties. Toward a dynamic theory.* Norwood, NJ: Ablex.

Tichenor, P. J., Donohue, G. A., & Olien, C. N. (1980). *Community conflict and the press.* Beverly Hills, CA: Sage.

Waring, H. (1960). What is a grassroots editor? *Grassroots Editor, 1,* 5.

Weber, M. (1958). *The Protestant ethic and the spirit of capitalism.* New York: Charles Scribner's Sons.

Studying the Global Community
of Community Journalists ●

Chad Stebbins

In 2008, the International Society of Weekly Newspaper Editors lost a member in Nebraska who couldn't afford to continue paying the $50 annual dues. The publisher/editor/ad manager of the 1,000-circulation weekly suggested that ISWNE was not providing enough material about "the money side" of running a community newspaper. He explained:

> While I found the editorial content helpful, I would have preferred to read more articles on what newspapers my size are doing to survive, maybe with some specific ideas or programs. I realize you're more geared toward editors, but in my situation it all fits together in the same puzzle.

He was right. Although ISWNE's mission is to encourage and promote wise and independent editorial comment, news content, and leadership in community newspapers throughout the world, we cannot forget that some of our members also are responsible for keeping their newspapers in business. We therefore dedicated the Spring 2009 issue of *Grassroots Editor*, ISWNE's quarterly journal, to examining how twelve struggling weeklies in rural parts of the United States and Canada were coping with the economic crisis of the late 2000s. To some extent, their rural isolation shielded them from several of the problems the mainstream press had been experiencing. As one editor so aptly put it, "While the rest of the nation is in a recession, we've been in a recession for the last 50 years, so it won't affect us as much."

Such weeklies, however, face their own set of challenges—declining population bases, a shortage of retail businesses in agrarian communities, staffing issues, and attempting to sell advertising and subscriptions on fledgling websites. A few of those papers have the smallest circulations in their states, yet they persevere even as large-city dailies shrink or even fold. The financial strategies of such weeklies deserve further study by the growing cadre of academicians who now specialize in community journalism.

U.S. journalism scholars also tend to ignore the vibrant community newspapers published by our neighbors to the north, in Canada, and across the Atlantic in the United Kingdom, where many ISWNE members work to provide quality journalism to rural communities. Consider this: Despite having a population only one tenth that of the United States, Canada boasts more than 700 weekly and twice-weekly newspapers (ComBase, 2010a). Interestingly, more than 80% utilize the tabloid format. Most weekly newspapers are printed on high-quality presses, due to the significant investment in improved printing facilities made by corporate ownership a few years ago (ComBase, 2010b). At the same time, about a quarter of Canada's community papers were still independently owned at this writing (Newspapers Canada, 2010).

Studies of the Canadian community-media scene could pay big dividends for researchers. Why, for example, do 83% of adults in Saskatchewan regularly read a community newspaper? Nationwide in Canada, 74% of adults read a community paper. Exclusive community newspaper readers also tend to be light TV watchers (the average watches television three hours or less per week). Comparative studies along the U.S.-Canadian border may help scholars in both countries better understand the commonalities and differences between those countries, and inspire similar studies in other border regions of the world.

But there is much more cross-cultural information to be gleaned from the community press by researchers than merely a comparison of statistics. Comparing social values as expressed via community media also is a worthwhile venture. Take as an example the following case. In 2009, a weekly editor in New Brunswick asked the ISWNE hotline service whether he should publish a letter to the editor bashing an area high school for holding an anti-harassment, anti-homophobia event. The letter writer condemned the school's staff and students for their public display of support for the gay and lesbian community. Of the 55 ISWNE members who responded, an overwhelming majority (mostly from the U.S.) agreed the letter should be published. The handful of Canadians who weighed in, however, were largely opposed to printing it. One wrote, "The letter writer's beliefs are his right, but he does not have the right to use the paper as a platform to promote intolerance against gay people." Others cited Canada's hate-crimes legislation as a reason to toss the letter in the recycling bin. The Canadian editor did end up publishing the letter, explaining that "it is, ultimately, fair comment on a public event and we just don't feel comfortable stifling this writer's opinion when it isn't libelous, profane or an attempt to incite violence." Still, his Canadian peers disagreed, one even saying, "I just don't know why we justify hate as free speech."

Such comparisons of professional concerns and values among community newspaper editors in neighboring countries are worthy of further study, particularly given the important cultural roles community newspapers continue to have in many parts of the world.

❖ REFERENCES

ComBase. (2010a). *ComBase launches 2008–2009 study results.* Retrieved May 3, 2011, from http://www.combase.ca/news/149/combase-launches-2008-2009-study-results

ComBase. (2010b). *Community newspaper readership remains strong across the country.* Retrieved May 3, 2011, from http://www.combase.ca/wp-content/uploads/2007/12/ComBase-2008-2009_ALL-MARKETS-PROVINCES.pdf

Newspapers Canada. (2010). *Ownership: Community newspapers.* Retrieved May 3, 2011, from http://www.newspaperscanada.ca/about-newspapers/ownership/ownership-community-newspapers

Chad Stebbins is a professor of journalism and director of international studies at Missouri Southern State University, and also is executive director of the International Society of Weekly Newspaper Editors. He is editor of Grassroots Editor, *a quarterly journal published by ISWNE. A scholar in community journalism, Stebbins is the author of* All the News Is Fit to Print: Profile of a Country Editor, *published by the University of Missouri Press in 1998.*

Appendix: Resources for Community Journalism Scholars

The two overarching goals of this book project have been to collect into distinct chapters the foundational works upon which the concept of community journalism has been built, and we also point to gaps in the literature that might provide new research paths for scholars who want to blaze new trails in the field. We do this at a time when scholarly interest in community journalism is being recognized as a formal subdiscipline. Beyond groups such as the National Newspaper Association in the U.S., the International Society of Weekly Newspaper Editors, the Community Broadcasting Association of Australia, and numerous professional organizations around the world, several academic initiatives have been launched in recent decades to support outreach and research efforts focused on community journalism. Of course, regional or niche professional organizations are often excellent points of contact for community journalism researchers—for example, state/provincial press associations often have many members who are community journalists, as do national journalism organizations around the world, particularly in nations that have strong traditions of community journalism. Also, organizations devoted to ethnicity, such as the Native American Journalists Association, or organizations devoted to particular topic areas, such as the North American Agricultural Journalists or the Louisiana Sports Writers Association, often have members who are very familiar with community journalism as practice.

But this book is devoted to theoretical research, not practice, and so we wanted to provide some starting points for community journalism researchers to find like-minded scholars and germane programs that can help them locate and connect with, well, the community of community journalism scholars.

The list below is hardly comprehensive. The editors of this book frequently are delighted and surprised to learn of other organizations that are doing work related to community journalism. The list also is not nearly as global as we would like. With that in mind, we welcome recommendations for adding to this rudimentary catalog. Please send suggestions either to Bill Reader at reader@ohio.edu or to John Hatcher at jhatcher@d.umn.edu.

The list below includes only Internet URLs for contact information, and the URLs were accurate at the time this Appendix was finalized in early 2011. We hope that they are still accurate as you read this, and we also hope that the organizations themselves are thriving and continuing their important good work.

HUCK BOYD CENTER FOR COMMUNITY MEDIA

At Kansas State University, the Huck Boyd National Center for Community Media was founded in 1990 to focus on issues facing news media serving small-town America. It is one of the first and most important academic centers devoted to the issue of community journalism. It works with the National Newspaper Association to sponsor the annual Newspapers and Community Building Symposium. (Longtime director Gloria Freeland, assistant professor in the A. Q. Miller School of Journalism and Mass Communications, is largely responsible for the Huck Boyd Center's importance in our discipline, and the editors of this volume are most appreciative for her essay in Chapter 2.)

For more information: http://huckboyd.jmc.ksu.edu/

CAROLINA COMMUNITY MEDIA PROJECT

In 2001, the School of Journalism and Mass Communication at the University of North Carolina launched the Carolina Community Media Project, which is focused on helping that state's community media through research, teaching, and outreach. Through the center, community journalists across North Carolina receive training and consulting, as well as access to some very talented journalism students; the center also is a regular participant in programming of the North Carolina Press Association. Founding director Jock Lauterer has been at the forefront of the contemporary "community journalism movement" in higher education; the editors are honored and humbled to have been able to coax our old friend to write the foreword to this book.

For more information: http://www.jomc.unc.edu/special-programs-content-items/carolina-community-media-project

TEXAS CENTER FOR COMMUNITY JOURNALISM

Launched in 2009, the Texas Center for Community Journalism at Texas Christian University represents one of the more recent state-focused academic centers in the subdiscipline. Its mission is primarily to serve the community journalism industry in Texas with training, consulting, and research. Founding director Tommy Thomason left his post as founding director of TCU's Schieffer School of Journalism to launch the center.

For more information: http://www.tccj.tcu.edu

COMJ MASTER'S DEGREE PROGRAM, UNIVERSITY OF ALABAMA

A partnership between the University of Alabama and the storied *Anniston Star* community newspaper, with funding from the John S. and James L. Knight Foundation, created a master's degree program centered on using the *Star* as a "teaching newspaper," similar to teaching hospitals for medical students. The one-year program involves two semesters of coursework at the university and three months of professional experience at the newspaper. Two of the contributors to this book, George Daniels and Wilson Lowrey, are on the faculty at Alabama and are directly involved in the ComJ program.

For more information: http://www.comj.ua.edu/

THE INSTITUTE FOR RURAL JOURNALISM AND COMMUNITY ISSUES

Based at the University of Kentucky, the Institute for Rural Journalism and Community Issues is devoted to the challenges and work of journalists across rural America. The institute has academic partners at nearly two dozen universities across the United States. The founding director of IRJCI, Al Cross, and the website he oversees, are excellent resources for information about rural community journalism, and Al is a good colleague and friend to many of the contributors to this book. The chair of the IRJCI academic partners is Elizabeth Hansen at Eastern Kentucky University, and she also is a good person to talk to about rural community journalism research.

For more information: http://www.ruraljournalism.org/

COMMUNITY JOURNALISM INTEREST GROUP

The Community Journalism Interest Group is a subdivision of the Association for Education in Journalism and Mass Communication. Founded in 2004, COMJIG brings together scholars and professionals who have an interest in both teaching and research related to community journalism. Both editors and many contributors to this book project, from chapter authors to essayists to reviewers, have been and remain active in COMJIG.

For more information: http://comjig.blogspot.com

THE CENTER FOR COMMUNITY JOURNALISM AND DEVELOPMENT

The Center for Community Journalism and Development, founded in 2001, is focused on improving journalism to help communities in developing nations, with particular emphasis on Southeast Asia. It was formed by journalists and community development workers and provides professional development training and support.

For more information: http://www.ccjd.org/index.php

MURL PROJECT AT TEMPLE UNIVERSITY

Many universities have community journalism projects, some very well funded and organized, others short-lived bursts of effort thrown together and run mostly with passion and personal commitment. The Multimedia Urban Reporting Lab at Temple University's School of Communications and Theater is an example of both. It is a robust journalism-practice effort based in Temple's Center City campus (near City Hall). The project publishes *Philadelphia Neighborhoods* (philadelphianeighborhoods.com), a source of news and information focusing on a variety of Philadelphia neighborhoods, particularly those that do not see much coverage in the city's mainstream news media. The MURL has partnerships with a number of local media outlets to provide news and information about those neighborhoods.

For more information: http://www.temple.edu/sct/journalism/about/murl.html

CHICAGOTALKS

Chicagotalks, originally called Creating Community Connections, was launched in 2006 at Columbia College Chicago by journalism faculty members Barbara Iverson and Suzanne McBride. The site provides a rich array of community-focused news from a variety of communities—neighborhoods, ethnic communities, communities of interest, and so on. As they explain it on their website, "Our stories come from all corners of the city; our reporters are young journalists learning to cover their communities and community people with a story to tell."

For more information: http://www.chicagotalks.org/

KNIGHT COMMUNITY NEWS NETWORK AT J-LAB: THE INSTITUTE FOR INTERACTIVE JOURNALISM

The KCNN (and the J-Lab itself, now based at American University), is a multifaceted effort to research and provide guidance for citizen-focused media projects, almost always with a keen eye on innovative community journalism efforts. Related to the KCNN is J-Lab's New Voices project, which provided several years of grant funding for dozens of new-media initiatives, most of them directly related to community journalism. For researchers, the KCNN's reports, guide sheets, and experts provide excellent starting points for thinking about community journalism in the digital age, as well as links to any number of specific community journalism efforts that may be ripe for more focused research projects.

For more information: http://www.kcnn.org/

IN MEMORIAM: CENTER FOR COMMUNITY JOURNALISM

Based at SUNY Oswego, the Center for Community Journalism for more than a decade provided professional support and training for community journalists, primarily in its home state of New York. The project was the brainchild of then-professor Mary Glick, now at the American Press Institute, who worked closely with members of the New York Press Association, including newspaper publisher, the late Vicki Simons, to launch the program. John Hatcher, one of the editors of this book, was the first education director of the center; the subsequent director, Eileen Gilligan, contributed Chapter 3 to this text. Sadly, the pioneering project appears to have been a victim of the Great Recession: as of this writing, it had ceased operations due to dire financial constraints in public higher education. We list the CCJ here in recognition of its contributions to our collective efforts, as an appreciation for its early work in this field, and with the hope that it may some day be revived and continue its good work.

Index

About the Authors

George L. Daniels is an associate professor of journalism at the University of Alabama in Tuscaloosa. Daniels spent eight years in television newsrooms working as a producer at stations in Richmond, Virginia; Cincinnati, Ohio; and Atlanta, Georgia. Daniels then moved from the newsroom to the classroom. He received his doctorate from the University of Georgia's Grady College of Journalism and Mass Communication. At the University of Alabama, he taught courses at "the teaching newspaper," *The Anniston Star*, via the Knight Community Journalism Fellows program. His research has appeared in *Journalism and Mass Communication Quarterly, Journalism and Mass Communication Educator, Electronic News,* and *The Journal of Radio Studies.*

Cary Roberts Frith joined the faculty of Ohio University's E. W. Scripps School of Journalism in 2004 after spending two years as a Park Fellow at the University of North Carolina at Chapel Hill. Previously, she had worked in the magazine industry, including serving as associate publisher and managing editor of Resources for Educators, a division of Wolters Kluwer. She was also editor of *CompuServe Magazine*'s business section and a reporter for Crain Communications' *Business Insurance.* She teaches courses in the magazine sequence and serves as faculty adviser of *Southeast Ohio* magazine, a student-produced regional magazine serving 20 rural counties in Appalachian Ohio.

Eileen Gilligan is a professor in the Department of Communication Studies at the State University of New York at Oswego, where her teaching areas include investigative reporting, editing, and communication theory. Her research areas include community journalism, the behavior of journalists, and cognitive processing of media. She is the former director of the Center for Community Journalism at SUNY Oswego. Gilligan is a former statehouse reporter for the *Wilmington News Journal* in Delaware. She has a Ph.D. in journalism and mass communication from the University of Wisconsin–Madison. She writes a monthly column for a regional magazine and has published in the *Newspaper Research Journal, The Journalist,* and *The Journal of Broadcasting and Electronic Media.*

John A. Hatcher is a professor of journalism in the Department of Writing Studies at the University of Minnesota Duluth. His research focuses on community journalism and the sociology of news. His current work examines these concepts through a comparative analysis of community journalism in Norway, South Africa, and the United States. He holds a Ph.D. and master's degree from Syracuse University's Newhouse School of Public Communications. He is the former education director at the Center for Community Journalism at SUNY Oswego and worked for years as a community newspaper editor and columnist at the *Daily Messenger* in upstate New York.

Janice Hume is a professor of journalism in the Grady College of Journalism and Mass Communication at the University of Georgia. She teaches magazine writing, magazine management, and media history, including graduate-level historical research methods. Her research concerns journalism history as it relates to public memory and the social construction of death. She is author of *Obituaries in American Culture* (University Press of Mississippi, 2000) and coauthor of *Journalism in a Culture of Grief* (Routledge, 2008), as well as numerous journal articles. She is a former lifestyle editor at *The Mobile Register* in Alabama and holds a Ph.D. from the University of Missouri.

Wilson Lowrey is an associate professor of journalism at the University of Alabama, where he coordinates the department's master's program in community journalism. He holds a Ph.D. and master's degree from the University of Georgia. Lowrey's scholarship focuses on the sociology of the news, and he has published research in a number of academic journals, including *Journalism and Mass Communication Quarterly, Journalism, Journalism Studies, Mass Communication and Society,* and *Political Communication.* He is also coeditor of *Changing the News*, published by Routledge in 2011. Lowrey worked in newspapers throughout most of the 1990s, including two years with *The Athens Banner-Herald* and five years with *The Atlanta Journal-Constitution*, both in Georgia.

Diana Knott Martinelli spent nearly 15 years working in public relations, including positions in local broadcasting, regional health care, and government organizations, before earning her Ph.D. in mass communication at the University of North Carolina at Chapel Hill. As the Widmeyer Professor in Public Relations at West Virginia University, she teaches advanced public relations and graduate research courses and spends time at Widmeyer Communications each summer. Her research has been presented and published nationally and internationally, and she has authored a number of book chapters by invitation. She regularly gives media relations seminars to local business and community leaders.

Hans K. Meyer teaches online journalism as an assistant professor at Ohio University. His research focuses on the effects of user-generated content, such as citizen journalism and comments, on legacy media. He worked for nearly a decade in community newspapers as a reporter and editor before getting his Ph.D. at the University of Missouri.

Bill Reader is an associate professor in the E. W. Scripps School of Journalism at Ohio University, where he teaches courses in community journalism, news editing, and media ethics. He earned his master's degree in media studies from Pennsylvania State University while simultaneously working as an award-winning opinion page editor of the *Centre Daily Times* newspaper in State College, Pennsylvania. His research of community journalism has focused on ethics and audience feedback, and his research has been published in *Newspaper Research Journal, Journal of Mass Media Ethics, Journalism: Theory, Criticism and Practice, Journal of Broadcasting and Electronic Media*, and *Journalism and Mass Communication*. He is on the editorial board of *NRJ* and was guest editor of a special issue of the journal, "The Future of Community Newspapers," published in winter 2011. He is coauthor, with Steven K. Knowlton of Dublin City University in Ireland, of *Moral Reasoning for Journalists* (Praeger, 2008).

Jack Rosenberry is an associate professor of communication at St. John Fisher College in Rochester, New York. Before joining the academy, he spent 25 years as a community journalist, working as a reporter and editor for small-town newspapers and as editor of a zoned community news section for a metro daily. His research is focused on Web-based community journalism, and he has published articles related to that topic in *Newspaper Research Journal* and *Journalism and Mass Communication Quarterly*. He is coeditor, with Burton St. John, III, of *Public Journalism 2.0: The Promise and Reality of a Citizen Engaged Press* (Routledge, 2010).

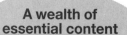
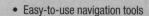